Approaching the Presence

A Year for Living Faithfully

By
David Jordan

with
Diane Jordan

Pure Heart Press
Main Street Rag Publishing Company
Charlotte, North Carolina

Copyright © 2012 David Jordan

Cover Photo Art by Jim Tucker

Cover Design by Anne M. Hicks

Original Cover Photograph by David Jordan of Mt. McKinley in Denali, Alaska, August, 2012

Contributing Author's Bio:
Diane Jordan, David's mother, has been a homemaker, pastor's wife, and teacher, and has enjoyed a wide variety of roles in church and community life over the years. She has won several hymn writing competitions and loves music, volunteering, and her six grandchildren. She is retired and lives in Brentwood, Tennessee.

Library of Congress Control Number: 2012918876

ISBN: 978-1-59948-403-7

Produced in the United States of America

Pure Heart Press/
Main Street Rag Publishing Company
PO Box 690100
Charlotte, NC 28227-7001
www.MainStreetRag.com

Dedication

Dr. Adiel Moncrief (Monty) Jordan
(May 30, 1933 – September 29, 2011)

*We dedicate this book to him
with the deepest love,
highest respect
and greatest gratitude.
A devoted husband,
loving father and grandfather,
committed pastor, loyal friend,
staunch defender of religious liberty,
and a generous, conscientious human being.
We are proud and thankful to have been
a part of his beautiful life.*

SPECIAL THANKS

I am so thankful for the countless people who contributed to this book. At the forefront of this "great cloud of witnesses" is my mother, Diane Jordan, whose love, support, and contributions have been vital and numerous. Your selfless love and unshakable care for Dad during his long illness is inspiring. And what a joy it has been to work on *Approaching the Presence* with you!

To my wife, Beth, and my children, Christopher, Catherine and Olivia, I am truly blessed and incredibly thankful. Your support, patience, and love keep me going. I am amazed at the richness I feel in my life thanks to each of you. I love you more than you can imagine.

To my good friends and fellow travelers in faith at Providence Baptist Church in Charlotte, I offer my most heartfelt gratitude. For almost ten years, I've had the privilege of participating with you in this great congregation. I consider myself unspeakably fortunate to be part of your lives and have you in mine. Many of the devotions, essays, ideas, and Bible studies shared here began and grew with you. Your questions, responses, participation, and enthusiasm, pushed me to work harder and research better, to dig deeper and think more broadly. Thank you for your love, continued interest, patience, and humor. It's been a great ten years!

To my sister, Joy Jordan-Lake, your persistence and love of the craft of writing continues to motivate my own journey. Thank you for your love and support—and keep up the great work!

To Jim Tucker, my friend and colleague at Providence. As with *Subversive Words*, your advice and encouragement were invaluable. From web site work to cover photo enhancement and recommendations, your kindness and staunch support are deeply appreciated!

And last but not least, just as it was in our previous literary journey together, it has been a pleasure and a joy to partner with my loyal, long-suffering, and wise editor, Anne Hicks. Your patience, hard work, gentle advice, and valuable insight push me to offer my best while affirming and supporting my work. A tough balance but one you provide gracefully and professionally. Thank you, Anne!

Sincerely and fondly,
David Jordan
Fall, 2012

Foreword
A Spiritual Travelogue

Some years ago, my mother and father began compiling a notebook full of useful sayings and quotes around various biblical and spiritual themes. As a pastor husband-and-wife team, they planned to use these writings for retreats and teaching opportunities. Mom carefully organized all the growing material under the title: "Approaching the Presence."

Not long after Dad's death in September of 2011, Mom and I discussed incorporating that material, along with the words from some of her hymns and songs, into a book of devotionals I was already in the process of writing.

As a result, our combined work efforts have grown into this book, *Approaching the Presence: A Year for Living Faithfully*. And, though we only refer to Dad specifically a couple of times, his kind and humble way, sense of humor, love of people, devotion to God, spiritual insight, concern for racial reconciliation, and commitment to justice are all reflected here.

With Bible in hand and an open mind, we hope you are ready to take this journey with us, one that will stimulate your imagination, challenge your intellect, and deepen your faith. From familiar biblical stories and characters, to historical figures and places, to our own personal stories, we seek to provide a guide for daily spiritual living. We hope you enjoy and benefit from what we offer.

One of our readers referred to *Approaching the Presence* as a "spiritual travelogue." That is, there are numerous references to or illustrations of places, people, and experiences from all over the world. And there is a progression to the year we hope you find meaningful.

We begin with some basic spiritual grounding. Then, as the year progresses, we have attempted to move more deeply into passages, sometimes longer but still ones we think you'll find familiar. As you move through the year, may your biblical understanding expand and your spiritual growth be enhanced. Bless you and enjoy!

David and Diane

Contents

Introduction ix

January: Beginning 1
   The First Week: Let There Be Light 2
   The Second Week: Know Who You Are 9
   The Third Week: Jesus and a Healthy Lifestyle 15
   The Fourth Week: How to Live a Better Life 21

February: Preparing 27
   The First Week: Disciples or Apostles 28
   The Second Week: Open Heart, Open Mind 33
   The Third Week: Out of Nothing, Venice! 41
   The Fourth Week: A Limited Vision 49

March: Waging Peace 57
   The First Week: Malta and Hospitality 58
   The Second Week: Forgiveness and Transformation 64
   The Third Week: The Holy Grail and Compassion 72
   The Fourth Week: Lessons in Humility 79

April: Resurrection 85
   The First Week: Honest Appraisals 86
   The Second Week: Redeeming Lost Causes 93
   The Third Week: Corinth and Options for Renewal 100
   The Fourth Week: Jesus and Claiming Your Potential 107

May: Beauty 113
   The First Week: Working with Beauty 114
   The Second Week: Remembering Who You Are 121
   The Third Week: A Call to Illumination 128
   The Fourth Week: Who Gets the Glory? 134

June: Passion 141
   The First Week: Fire and Approach of the Presence 142
   The Second Week: The Quest for Justice 150
   The Third Week: Aliens and Jesus 157
   The Fourth Week: Speaking the Truth Then and Now 165

July: Insight 171
   The First Week: Ancient Connections 172
   The Second Week: The Necessity of Wisdom 181

 The Third Week: Recycled Stardust and Us 189
 The Fourth Week: Imaginative Responses to Life 196
 The Fifth Week: The Dead Sea and Stagnation............................201

August: Imagination 207
 The First Week: Rome and Living Testimonies 208
 The Second Week: Spiritual Love and Physical Life..................214
 The Third Week: The Complexity of Simplicity 220
 The Fourth Week: Zacchaeus and Tough Love 227
 The Fifth Week: Remembering the Future 234

September: Wisdom 241
 The First Week: Philip, A Eunuch, and Choices..........................242
 The Second Week: Philip, A Eunuch, and Change 249
 The Third Week: The World Is Round 256
 The Fourth Week:The World Is Flat 262

October: Staying Power 269
 The First Week: Retreat is Not Defeat..270
 The Second Week: On Dying and Living.....................................277
 The Third Week: Bad Things Do Happen 284
 The Fourth Week: Go and Do; Sit and Listen 290
 The Fifth Week: Vesuvius and the End of the World................298

November: Gratitude and Giving...305
 The First Week: Unheralded Devotion 306
 The Second Week: A Man's Ambition..312
 The Third Week: We're All in this Together................................320
 The Fourth Week: A Woman's Thanksgiving..............................326

December: Advent..333
 The First Week: Hope...334
 The Second Week: Love...342
 The Third Week: Joy 349
 The Fourth Week: Peace 356
 The Fifth Week: Faith 363

Bibliography..373

INTRODUCTION
Uncontainable Enthusiasm

"I, Tertius, the writer of this letter, greet you in the Lord" (Romans 16:22).

Have you ever been so excited about something you just *had* to tell someone? Here, we have a beautiful example of exactly this dynamic: a Christian life so overjoyed by God's presence and the powerful ties of community he cannot remain silent. He breaks the rules of literary propriety and virtually jumps off the page in his desire to meaningfully connect with his friends in Rome.

A favorite Bible Study question of mine is "Who *wrote* Romans?"

As the scripture above makes clear, it was Tertius, not Paul. Paul, as was custom in those days, spoke the words as Tertius, the scribe—the well-educated pen behind the text—recorded them in the clear, organized form we have today. The thoughts and words are Paul's; the careful grammar and order can be attributed to Tertius.

But interjected is this strange and captivating line: "I, Tertius, who write this letter, greet you in the Lord." My New Revised Standard Version of the Bible translates this sentence with a period. But, since the Greek language of the day didn't use punctuation marks, we can only guess as to the tone Tertius intended when he wrote those glad words of greeting. If I translated this text today, my rendition would be more emphatic: "I Tertius, the writer of this letter, greet you in the Lord!"

It may well be that, while writing, Tertius' eyes twinkled with a thankful smile, for he was thinking of a congregation of friends, brothers and sisters in Christ. How did he know them? How much time did they spend together? What did they have in common? Perhaps they learned together, asked questions together, ate together; maybe they comforted each other, laughed, sang, and cried together. We have no idea. But, from this bizarre insertion—this carefree breaking of the rules of literary circumspection and scribal ethics, this beautiful, unbounded, heartfelt example of uncontainable enthusiasm for partners in the gospel on the other side of the Roman Empire—here blossoms a blessed example of what the Spirit of God birthed in the hearts and minds of men and women whose lives had been changed.

The word *enthusiasm* serves as an appropriate noun to associate with what we hear from Tertius: *en-theos-ism*. The word literally means: "God within." It describes a person so filled with good that the uncontainable, joyful energy comes bursting out. I have a sense of Tertius' urgency and joy, of thoughts I want to share and relationships I want to celebrate. Like Tertius, I count you, my readers, as brothers and sisters in this world. With great gladness, I share my feelings of sacred connections with you in our common journey of faith.

This book is set up so that each month represents a different focus and is divided into weeks. First, we discuss that week's topic, followed by a prayer for the week, then we move to further discussion for each day and "reflections" that provide you with helpful suggestions as you move through your day, week, and month.

As you move through this, may you, like Tertius, be so filled with God's palpable goodness that you cannot contain yourself; you simply have to greet somebody in the name of the Lord—even as you grow deeper in your faith and gain a better perspective in life.

JANUARY
Beginning

January was a month represented by the Roman god Janus. He was two faced, literally, with one facing forward, the other facing backward. His figure stood for what we still expect today: evaluate the past; anticipate the future.

The following devotionals, essays, and considerations for January will attempt to do this. Our scriptures for the month reflect spiritual calling, inventory, and anticipation. We will attempt to remind ourselves what it is that God creates, intends, and expects.

The First Week:
Let There Be Light

In the beginning when God created the heavens and the earth, the earth was without form, and darkness was over the face of the deep. Then the spirit (the wind, the breath)[1] of God blew over the face of the waters, and God said: "Let there be light!" And there was light (Genesis 1:1).

New Year's resolutions don't work. Talk to most anyone you know, and they will tell you of early January's lofty plans and great expectations. Then, before long, there are rationalized distractions, legitimized excuses, expected decline, anticipated failure, and, finally, guilt.

The tendency for most of us is to want to improve. We become aware of shortcomings or recognize weaknesses. We see in the mirror sagging waistlines and ill-fitting clothes. We know something needs to be done at some point, and we want to make some changes. But we can also admit, trying to use January 1 as the kickoff to some magic change in our behavior might not be the healthiest strategy. By many accounts, it doesn't work and might do more harm than good.

Instead, let us acknowledge what the Bible has known all along. The earliest light of God's creation offers particular insights into the truth of reality, how life works and who we are, really. And from these biblical standards, this bedrock of biblical beginnings, we can offer ourselves realistic ways of bringing about positive, authentic change—without the ineffective, guilt-inducing New Year's resolutions.

As we embark on our journey in the New Year, we begin, appropriately, with the very first verse of the Bible. And with the beginning, there is something interesting about the way the Bible describes what occurs. There is no cosmic battle or magic wand being waved. Instead, notice that God *speaks*

---

[1] The Hebrew word *ruach* has all three meanings: breath, wind, and spirit. This is just like *pneuma* in Greek and is utilized in similar word plays.

creation into being: "...and God said: 'Let there be light!' And there was light" (Genesis 1:1).

It is the voice of God proclaiming the "word" of God.[2] And it is this word, this truth that activates all that is and that is to be. God calls forth light as the actualizing power for the rest of creation. But also notice as you continue to read the rest of the first chapter of Genesis that God creates physical light—the sun, the moon, and the stars—on *day four* of the story segments. And yet, in this first verse, God speaks forth light on *day one.*

The portrayal need not be a literal understanding of six days and step-by-step analysis of biological creation. Rather, it is better and more profoundly heard as a powerful and insightful rendition of Spiritual Truth. And this *truth* is conveyed in poetic, figurative language that speaks eternally to the nature of God's Providence: not only is life good and worthy of blessing (as we are told at the end of the chapter); there also exists a spiritual light above and beyond physical light that represents the true conductor of reality.

Physical light generates the energy of photosynthesis and the conditions essential for physical life as we know it. But the first chapter of Genesis lets us in on the truth behind and beyond what we can see. There is a spiritual realm—the Being of light, existence, and power—that emanates from God's presence and speech and generates a light different and more real, more primal, and more essential. Like the breath of God that calms the waters and centers creation, the calling forth of light pronounces a thundering reminder of who is in control and for what purpose.

May you remember this deep wisdom from beyond time and the very beginning of creation as you begin your year. Now commences a new and good cycle of life lying before you. You may still choose to set goals for the New Year and work on

---

[2] In John 1:1, the writer uses this same idea of God's "word" in his opening to the fourth Gospel: "In the beginning was the Word..." This word in Greek, *logos*, translates into far more than a collection of letters communicating an idea. The combination connects the hearer and reader to the creation event, as well as to the multiple meanings of the Greek *logos*: logic, wisdom, rationality, purpose, divine intent, and the sacred intimately woven into the human. This linguistic combination provides the perfect platform for John's proclamation of God's work in Jesus.

resolutions that might or might not succeed. But your good news remains: regardless of your success or failure in maintaining a positive trajectory for your goals, there is something far bigger and more brilliant beyond what you have set before you.

> "For all that has been, thanks. For all that shall be, yes!"
> — Dag Hammarskjold

Live this week with a bold and redemptive vision: in spite of distractions or focus, disappointment or thrill, noise or silence, chaos or order, confusion or resolution, life is still good. God is still in control. God's light is life-giving, and along with God's resounding voice in the first moment of creation, you, too, are now enabled to call forth that blessed light in yourself and others.

> Thank you, O God, for this New Year. What a gift we share in your remarkable creation. And what grand opportunities lay before us. As we begin this new time, give us vision for what can be, discipline for what needs to be, wisdom for what ought to be, and courage for what must be. Amen.

REFLECTIONS FOR THE WEEK

MONDAY

So God created humankind in his image, in the image of God he created them; male and female God created them. God blessed them... (Genesis 1:27-28a).

It is probable these scriptures we call *Torah*[3]—the first five books of the Bible—were composed during a traumatic time in the history of the Jewish people known as the Babylonian Captivity, or Babylonian Exile (587-539 B.C.). Read Psalm 137 to get a feel for the angst and anger these people felt amidst such tremendous loss. The temple had been desecrated then destroyed, Jerusalem lay in ruins, and the leading citizens, if not killed outright, had been abducted and sent to live in a foreign land.

In spite of swirling emotions, incredible loss, and the desire for revenge, these people composed this remarkable biblical insight. It bears no mark of vengeance but, rather, declares that all, even mortal enemies, are created in God's image.

Take time today to remind yourself that you are created in God's image. You are the walking, talking, and very real incarnation of God's presence among all those with whom you interact. What might you do differently today, given this biblical reminder? There will be many whose lives you can touch in meaningful ways simply by being you and, therefore, the image of God for those around you. This is an amazing thing. May you move through this day with great reverence and new understanding.

> "Deep within us all, there is an amazing inner sanctuary of the soul, a holy place, a Divine Center, a speaking voice to which we may continuously return. Eternity is at our hearts..."
> — Thomas Kelly

---

[3] *Torah*, in Hebrew, is best translated as "teaching" since it contains within these five books much law. But the majority of what comes to us from these books is in the form of story. Read Genesis, and you will find virtually no law and all story and teaching.

TUESDAY

Have you not known? Have you not heard? Has it not been told you from the beginning? Have you not understood from the foundations of the earth? It is God who sits above the circle of the earth, and its inhabitants are like grasshoppers; who stretches out the heavens like a curtain, and spreads them like a tent to live in..." (Isaiah 40:21-22).

Yesterday, we reminded ourselves we were made in God's image and looked at others as partners in that image. Today, we focus on humility and seek understanding through our common humanness. God is God; we are not. We have the great privilege to serve and represent God in our lives. But Isaiah brings us back to earth, back to ourselves living in these very fragile, human bodies. We tend to be selfish and our attitudes are less mature and insights less wise than we would like to admit. Today, work for humility; remember how alike we all are.

> "Only those who come to God with a sincere and humble heart will find him."
> — Randall O'Brien

WEDNESDAY

Where can I go from your spirit? Or where can I go from your presence? If I ascend to heaven, you are there; if I make my bed in Sheol, you are there (Psalm 139:7-8).

Find a quiet spot and focus on the landscape outside. What do you see? Is it bleak? Is there any color? Look for details of God's handiwork. Notice how, in all of nature, God's work abounds. Recognize God's creative hand in bringing these things into being.

The words of this Psalm and ones following also come from scripture likely composed during the trauma of exile in Babylon (*see Monday's devotion*). The devastation of invasion, then captivity, in a foreign land wreaked havoc on the people of Judah. Yet, they still found around them the all-encompassing presence of God.

Today and for the rest of the week, may your perspective be this: no matter what happens or how difficult circumstances get, you are never alone. What you face is never insurmountable. May you live with renewed confidence and reinvigorated hope.

> "People are not prisoners of fate, but only prisoners of their own minds."
> — Franklin Delano Roosevelt

THURSDAY

If I take to wings of the morning and settle at the farthest limits of the sea, even there your hand shall lead me, and your right hand shall hold me fast (Psalm 139:9-10).

Be still. Breathe in through your nose deeply, slowly. Notice your breath. In the silence, feel the breath filling your lungs, giving you life. With each breath, feel the presence beyond yourself, that which makes you more than skin and bone, sinew and muscle. The breath that fills you, the Bible shares, is like the spirit that makes you more than your physical self. God is with you, in you, around you—and will never let you go. Embrace this truth today.

> "Our prayer life suffers so much because our hearts are not silent."
> — Mother Teresa

FRIDAY

If I say, "Surely the darkness shall cover me, and the light around me become night, even the darkness is not dark to you; the night is as bright as the day, for darkness is as light to you" (Psalm 139:11-12).

There are always times when we are less than we wish to be. Circumstances alter, actions create alienation, loneliness intrudes. This psalmist unveils a clear awareness of the resulting feelings: absence of light, absence of presence, darkness. But remember

God's first words of creation and the divine call to be: "Let there be light, and there was light." Your circumstances do not control God's created order. God's light permeates even the darkest corners of our human frailties and vulnerabilities. Today, allow this truth to enlighten your way; walk in God's grace and truth.

> "The basic response of the soul to the Light is internal adoration and joy, thanksgiving and worship, self-surrender and listening. The secret places of the heart cease to be our noisy workshop. They become a holy sanctuary of adoration..."
> — Thomas Kelly

SATURDAY

So God blessed the seventh day and hallowed it, because on it God rested from all the work that he had done in creation (Genesis 2:3).

Biblically, the Sabbath was Saturday,[4] but this day is often consumed with activities nowadays. If you're like our family, you have extracurricular activities, household chores, and a multitude of distractions to keep you busy. Sadly, Sunday, the Christian Sabbath, is not much better: church activities, shopping, games on TV, studies to complete. There are so many things we allow to distract us from the gentle, refreshing task of rest and renewal.

Make this Saturday your Sabbath. Rest, relax, regain your composure and perspective. Look on God's creation and allow yourself to say: "It is good. It is very good. Thanks be to God."

> "Jesus' good news about the kingdom can be an effective guide for our lives only if we share his view of the world in which we live ... that this is a God-bathed and God-permeated world..."
> — Dallas Willard

---

[4] Reflected in the Spanish word for Saturday: *sabado*; and Italian: *sabato*, both meaning "Sabbath." The Christian recognition of Sunday as Sabbath reflects the celebration of Jesus' resurrection on the first day of the week, which, for Jesus and the Jews of his day, was Sunday.

THE SECOND WEEK:
Know Who You Are

"Who are you? Let us have an answer for those who sent us. What do you say about yourself?" He said, "I am the voice of one crying out in the wilderness, 'Make straight the way of the Lord'" (John 1:22-23).

In the Gospel of John, we are introduced to John the Baptist with this passage. Just preceding it comes this series of questions inquiring about his identity:

"Are you a prophet?"

"No."

"Are you Elijah?"

"No."

"Who are you then?"

"I am a voice crying in the wilderness, make straight the paths for the Lord..."

One of the great fathers of analytical psychology, the Swiss psychiatrist Carl Jung, said: "The world will ask you who you are. And if you do not know, the world will tell you."

All the time, we are confronted with images and voices attempting to define us, tell us who we're supposed to be, what we're supposed to do, urging us to acquire what we don't need.

John the Baptist makes three declarations of who he is not. Some wanted to make him into their hero; perhaps they wanted John to embody their visions of what might be. But three times, John stated without hesitation whom he was not.

He knows this because he knows something more important: he understands who he *is*. He understands his role in life is not to be famous or rich; he is not to be the center of attention or the one everybody hopes for. John the Baptist realizes his role is not to call attention *to* himself but *beyond* himself. Likely through the kinds of personal trials and errors each of us experiences, he has learned and grown and finally discovered his role for

God's purposes in his life. As he lives out his purpose, his self-discovery creates purposeful opportunities *for* and *with* others.

By understanding what he was and what he was supposed to be doing with what God had given him, John was able to recognize the distractions and delusions that often sidetrack even the best of us. Stressful situations arise, our lives become complicated, others attempt to impose irrelevant agendas opposed to or in contradiction of what God hopes and dreams for us.

As Jung recognized in the first half of the twentieth century, others will always try to persuade us. Countless forces desire our generous contributions to causes they passionately espouse. They vie for our attention. But our role in life has less to do with what is outside or what others tell us, and everything to do with what is inside—what God inspires, offers, contributes, and provides. With grateful hearts, discerning minds, and insightful spirits, we are to respond accordingly. May it be so for all of us this week.

> Give us wisdom, O God. Allow us to filter out the noise and listen carefully to your gentle guidance. Let us deepen our understanding of who we are in your grace and goodness and strengthen our resolve to say no to distractions and those that lead us along paths of envy and insufficiency. Instead, let us say yes to your ways that lead to life—those ways of being ourselves in the best and most holy understanding of who we are and whose we are. Amen.

REFLECTIONS FOR THE WEEK

MONDAY

Who are you? Let us have an answer for those who sent us (John 1:22a).

From the earliest days of history, people have posed this question. Though we're often too busy to dwell on it, it still creeps into our consciousness. The question may arise when a job becomes mundane, a task no longer stimulates us, or conditions create malaise. Sometimes, we ask: "Who am I really?" Or co-workers or bewildered family notice our change in attitude and question, "Who are you today?"

At the heart of this scripture lies a deeply philosophical and meaningful proposition: "Who has God created you to be?"

How do you answer? Today, take a moment to consider what you are passionate about. I once had a colleague in ministry who asked: "What is it that makes your heart sing?" What gifts has God given you to be used for the benefit of the world?

What would you have said to those posing this question to John? Give this serious thought as you move through your daily routine. Know that, as you do so, you walk on sacred ground.

> "Open yourself like a question mark to God. Listen for anything shaped for you that seems to come from God's liberating Presence."
> — Tilden Edwards

TUESDAY

What do you say about yourself? (John 1:22b)

Consider how John came to his self-understanding, in part by recognizing what he did well. What you say about yourself and how you understand yourself are really two different things. The first sounds like a job interview: "I like to think of myself as a great team player..." How we understand ourselves begins to plow further the ground of the sacred. What has God created us for? Biblically, we have clear answers:

> *In everything, do to others as you would have them do to you; for this is the law and the prophets* (Matthew 7:12).

> *God has told you, O mortal, what is good and what does the Lord require of you but to do justice, to love kindness, and to walk humbly with your God* (Micah 6:8).

Both passages get to the heart of the matter: at the core of who we are is how we treat others and how we view ourselves within God's created order. We treat others with kindness, doing justice and walking humbly with God, because these are the very things we want and need from others. As we learned from Genesis, we are created in the image of God. Remembering to be true to that is critical to understanding justice and kindness. Humility follows because we are the created, not the creator.

Today, demonstrate in tangible ways your commitment to who you are—by how you treat others.

> "Do or do not. There is no try."
> — Yoda, The Empire Strikes Back

WEDNESDAY

He said, "I am the voice of one crying out in the wilderness..." (John 1:23a).

The wilderness where John preached was barren, a desert near the Dead Sea.[5] People came because John captivated them with his eloquence and convicted them with his passion. There is much to be passionate about—hunger, peace, poverty, homelessness, quality education for all. If you are involved in a church, there are likely volunteer opportunities. There are many in

---

[5] Little grows here, yet the starkness is beautiful—the multi-colored hues of the sands, the water against the blue sky and surrounded desert. This unique body of water contains minerals in quantities surpassing any other on earth.

your community who might be interested in working with you or who could point you in the right direction. Consider what you do well—someone desperately waits for your passion.

Today, open yourself as God's instrument of peace, hope, and love. Envision how and what that looks like. Then consider the path it takes as a possible message from God's heart.

> "We are to move from a faith that redeems to a faith that risks. Faith is a risky business. It is raw trust in God's power to see us through."
> — Lloyd Ogilvie

THURSDAY

"Make straight the way of the Lord" (John 1:23b).

In the days of Isaiah, the great kings of Egypt, Assyria, Babylon, and Persia traveled wildernesses to visit distant lands. At times, these landscapes were virtually impassible. To facilitate the king's access, teams of engineers and workers "prepared the way." Mountains were "made low" and valleys "lifted up" so "highways could be made" for the king's passage.

Today, prepare an opportunity for a visit with the sacred. Reflect upon how you might allow God to use you to "make straight the way of the Lord."

> "...if we're sensitive and listening, there come clear insights of things to be done ... These insights are precious and to be heeded if we are to live in response to that which we feel in prayer."
> — Douglas V. Steere

FRIDAY

Every valley shall be lifted up, and every mountain and hill be made low; the uneven ground shall become level and the rough places a plain (Isaiah 40:4).

Notice that John's quote from Isaiah prepares for a visit from the king. What in your life today needs smoothing out? Reflect on this, and take some time to make right what is necessary.

Consider, too, how God might use you to make the "uneven become level" and "the rough places a plain."

> "...in the creation and the incarnation the great God of the universe intertwined the spiritual and the material, wedded the sacred and the secular, sanctified the common and the ordinary. How astonishing! How wonderful! If we cannot find God in the routine of home and shop, then we will not find him at all."
> — Richard Foster

SATURDAY

Then the glory of the Lord shall be revealed, and all people shall see it together... (Isaiah 40:5).

Enjoy time today in reflection and relaxation. Consider some part of this day to be your Sabbath time. Be still and remain quiet. Reflect on today's verse and what it might mean for your life in these moments. How is the Lord being revealed to you today?

> "The ground for all spiritual disciplines of the body is our intent to keep ourselves available for God ... Any way you turn, God is there knowing you and the situation. You are there available to that Presence, letting it inform, or better, transform, your awareness and action."
> — Tilden Edwards

The Third Week:
Jesus and a Healthy Lifestyle

Just then a lawyer stood up to test Jesus. "Teacher," he said, "what must I do to inherit eternal life?" Jesus said to him, "What is written in the law? What do you read there?" He answered, "You shall love the Lord your God with all your heart, and with all your soul, and with all your strength, and with all your mind; love your neighbor as you love yourself." And Jesus said to him, "You have given the right answer; do this and you will live" (Luke 10:27-28).

It is a long walk home. The road is dusty, the sun blazing. But there are more important matters. Jesus hears the musical call of birds gliding overhead and the captivating rhythm of his sandals flapping against callused feet. His path glows green. Life-giving winter rains have resurrected a land parched from long days of intense Middle-eastern heat. He doesn't think of this as exercise, these long walks he makes over the countryside. This is simply the lifestyle of his time and place.

I imagine Jesus tending a garden, digging his hands into the rich dirt of the Galilee soil. I see him covered in sawdust from a newly crafted table created for a family down the street. Time for study and prayer was important, I'm sure, but not at the expense of physical labor and recreation. Likely, too, he joined neighborhood friends in fun and competitive games. I see him covered in sweat, physically exhausted, arm around a buddy, smiling with a word of encouragement and a slap on the back: "Good game. Thanks for playing!"

Today, we would call this a "healthy lifestyle"—physical labor, meditation, study, appreciation of beauty, consistent interaction with nature, and friendly competition. Jesus also would have enjoyed a high fiber diet rich in fruits, vegetables, grains, and fish, with very little red meat and virtually no fat or cholesterol.

This is not some fad for losing weight. This is the way Jesus *lived.* In fact, this is the lifestyle the Bible assumes all people of that day lived. But times change. Labor-saving devices and plentiful resources now avail us with far more choices of food, how to spend our time, and modes of transportation than at any other point in history.

These are gifts to appreciate, as long as we don't allow ourselves to be seduced by the avoidance of exercise, the lack of interaction with God's world, and the consumption of less-than-healthy foods.

There is an intimate connection between how we feel physically and how we feel emotionally and spiritually. How we eat, exercise, work, and play has a significant bearing on how, and even *if*, we pray and discipline our spiritual selves. Certainly, our physical well-being, or lack of, profoundly affects our outlook on life and the way we treat one another.

The Bible consistently reminds us that these things all go together: "You shall love the Lord your God with all your heart, and with all your soul, and with all your strength, and with all your mind; love your neighbor as you love yourself."

It takes a whole person utilizing every aspect of ourselves truly to enjoy the kind of existence the Bible advocates and our Lord expects. May our call to healthy faith include attentiveness to lifestyle, attention to wellness, and intentional discipline in every aspect of our walk with God.

TEACH ME, LORD

Lord, I want to pray...	With humility and love
	With pure motives and compassion
	With sensitivity and forgiveness
	With substance and depth.
But Lord, my body is so weak...	My mind is too distracted
	My heart is unforgiving
	My understanding shallow
	And the needs are just too great.
So I wait another day.	Lord, please teach me to pray.

REFLECTIONS FOR THE WEEK

MONDAY

You shall love the Lord your God with all your heart... (Luke 10:27).

I was a Junior in high school when I learned my heart's location. Sure, in biology, I learned the theoretical placement—memorized diagrams and knew where the heart was supposed to fit into the overall design of the human body. But that year, my girlfriend informed me that she thought it would be a good idea for us to "date" other people. I let her know I didn't think this was necessary. I had no desire to date other people.

It wasn't until that night, in a pang of shocked recognition, that I awoke to the horrible fact: *she* wanted to date other people. That's when I discovered the precise location of my heart. In that moment, I thought I was having a heart attack. My heart ached with sadness, loss, and rejection.

I was not the first nor the last. And the Bible knows this—the heart represents more than a pump for the body's blood; it encompasses feelings, emotions, the spiritual interplay of joy and sorrow, connectedness, love, compassion, even apathy and hate. It is within this arena of emotional connectedness we move.

Today, ponder these words: "Love the Lord your God with all your heart..." Consider this as you go through your day. Think about what it means to love God with all your heart.

This evening, get some exercise, relax, think about something pleasant. Allow your heart to warm, physically and emotionally. What are you learning about loving God with your heart?

TUESDAY

Love the Lord your God ... with all your soul... (Luke 10:27).

What is the nature of the soul? Some would say one's soul is really the essence of who we are, the unseen dwelling within the seen, our personalities, the very being that is us when we are alive and the part of us that "crosses over" when we die. The ancient Greeks considered the soul the same as the mind. The word *psychology* reflects this. "Psyche" meant both mind and soul—memory, passion, imagination, recognition, reflection, joy—all these and more were part of some holy and mysterious enterprise explained by combining these concepts to reflect the essence of our innermost being.

What might it mean to love God with your soul? I think this psalmist has a good idea: "Praise the Lord! Sing to the Lord a new song ... praise his name with dancing, making melody to him with tambourine and lyre..." (Psalm 149:1-3).

Can you play a musical instrument? Maybe it's been a while. But try picking it up again and use it to stimulate your soul, to give praise, to feel a sense of rhythm, to make music.

Or, alternatively, do you think you can dance? Try, and not necessarily with someone. Just put on music in the privacy of your home and try moving with the rhythm. As you do, allow your movement to correspond with a thankful heart. Let the gratitude in the depths of your soul speak to you.

> "The pliability of an obedient heart must be complete from the set of our wills right on through to our actions."
> — Catherine Marshall

WEDNESDAY

Love the Lord your God ... with all your strength...
(Luke 10:27).

Later, we will explore the hero, or resistance, stories of Daniel in the Old Testament. Those stories hold interesting and relevant insights into the benefits and biblical expectations of healthy diets and intentionality regarding what we eat and how we live physically. Daily exercise was simply a given in Jesus' world, as was the Mediterranean diet that has since become so sensationalized. Cooking with olive oil, fresh fruit, vegetables, grains, nuts, fish, red wine ... these were and are key ingredients to a diet experts now recognize to be essential to good health.

Today, prepare a healthy, meatless meal; include a salad, at least two other vegetables, preferably uncooked or lightly steamed, and maybe some soup (try going with very little salt). If you do not already have a regular exercise routine (though I hope you do) then take a vigorous walk if it is warm enough. Feel your blood pumping through your body, notice your heart working, be aware of your surroundings, and give thanks. You should feel invigorated—and grateful!

> "The meaning to life is found in three things: good fellowship, good food, and good digestion!"
> — Anonymous

THURSDAY

Love the Lord your God ... with all your mind... (Luke 10:27).

Think good, positive thoughts. Read or listen to something stimulating, something that piques your imagination and adds to your insight. Be aware. What is it that "comes to mind?" What thoughts and images emerge as your heart pumps and your body moves. There are many things we feel we need to think about, but what is it that God desires you to contemplate? Enjoy what comes before you as you take a walk. Allow for gentle, unforced interaction of mind and spirit. Be at peace and know that all is well and all shall *be* well. Allow your mind to guide where your thoughts go. Be glad.

FRIDAY

...love your neighbor as you love yourself (Luke 10:27).

Enjoy a healthy meal with good vegetables and, if possible, some kind of fish, either baked or broiled. Take another walk.

As you move through your neighborhood, give thanks for things that you pass, no matter how small or seemingly insignificant: trees, yards, warm homes, and, especially, neighbors. Pray for specific families in some of the homes you pass—for their well-being and what they will face the next day. Be glad.

SATURDAY

Do this and you will live (Luke 10:28).

Review your week and what you have learned. What do you think Jesus understood about the wisdom of loving God and neighbor in this way? Meditate. Give thanks. Plan on going to church somewhere tomorrow.

The Fourth Week:
How to Live a Better Life

For it was you who formed my inward parts;
You knit me together in my mother's womb.
I praise you, for I am fearfully and wonderfully made.
Wonderful are your works; that I know very well.
My frame was not hidden from you,
When I was being made in secret,
Intricately woven in the depths of the earth,
Your eyes beheld my unformed substance.
In your book were written
All the days that were formed for me,
When none of them as yet existed.
How weighty are your thoughts, O God!
How vast the sum of them!
I try to count them—
They are more than the sand;
I come to the end—I am still with you.
(Psalm 139:13-16)

The great pioneer of psychoanalysis, Sigmund Freud, once called religion an "illusion." Religion, he said, simply fosters an inability to address the actual problems of background and personality development that contribute to psychological difficulties. In many ways, he was right. His culture during the nineteenth century in Vienna, Austria, was steeped in a religion that was pessimistic, cavalier, apathetic, and self-centered. Many of his Austrian clients considered themselves religious. Most were also wealthy, aristocratic, and generally unhappy with their lives (which is why they sought Dr. Freud's services).

So, Freud's appraisal of the religion he encountered each day was largely accurate. The faith his clients exhibited *was* an "illusion"—a sad and insufficient coping device derived more from culture and manipulation than from biblical truth and divine inspiration. This is unhealthy religion.

Unhealthy religion is not necessarily a foreign concept in our own society. A casual scan of religious programming in our media, books, and perspectives about faith reveals a variety of potentially unhealthy ways to view life, faith, and the world.

Yet, just as Freud's perspective on nineteenth century Austrian religion fails to provide an accurate picture of healthy faith, neither does channel surfing through our own cultural messages today. For all the current voices condemning the rising interest in spiritual matters, and for those who persist in calling faith an illusion, let us be more specific about the biblical faith that God intends for us all.

There is a plethora of evidence now suggesting, in fact, that faith can be miraculously healthful. Those who have a sincere belief in a loving God and who attend church regularly literally live better, longer, and more optimistically. This is not an illusion. A number of well-respected studies demonstrate that active involvement in a community of faith fulfills a deep-seated need in us all for love and companionship.[6] The belief in a good and gracious God who loves us and cares for us is not only uplifting spiritually but also calming emotionally and energizing physically. Spiritual growth, Bible study, and the specific charge to live a better, more loving life stimulates us mentally, emotionally, and spiritually in positive ways.

So, the combination of a healthier lifestyle as exemplified by Jesus, and a genuine, hopeful faith in God as taught by Jesus, make for a life that is truly exciting, remarkably fulfilling, and extremely healthy. Want to live a better, longer, and happier life? Go to church. Love God. Care deeply for those around you. Take care of yourself. And have faith!

> Thank you, Lord, for the opportunity to reclaim and to live your gift of health and wholeness. Help us this week to do so! Amen.

---

[6] Dr. Harold Koenig of Duke University Medical Center conducted one of several studies on health, wellness, and church attendance and concluded that the connection is undeniable. The sense of community, well-being, positive self-worth, connectedness, and concern for others all were significant factors in longer, healthier, and more productive lives.

REFLECTIONS FOR THE WEEK

MONDAY

For it was you who formed my inward parts; you knit me together in my mother's womb. I praise you, for I am fearfully and wonderfully made. Wonderful are your works... (Psalm 139:13-14).

On this day, notice God's creation around you. Be aware of the miracle that is your life. Realize how fearfully and wonderfully you have been made. Make time for moderate exercise; be aware of how you feel, your heart beating. Give thanks for your body and God's good handiwork.

> "One of the ways to help us be more aware of God's miraculous gift of life is to draw closer to him in meditative prayer and stillness. Even short periods of quietness before God can produce true health benefits as well as a deeper and more authentic spiritual life..."
> — Richard Foster

TUESDAY

My frame was not hidden from you, when I was being made in secret, intricately woven in the depths of the earth (Psalm 139:15).

Imagine yourself today held in the tender hands of God, known thoroughly, accepted completely. What difference might this understanding make in how you act and interact today? Prepare yourself for a new sense of confidence.

In the Book of Daniel in the Old Testament, the survivors of Nebuchadnezzar's Babylonian invasion are prodded to integrate themselves into the culture of their captors. The temptations loom large—rich food and fine wine straight from the King's table (Daniel 1:1-16). But they resist—partly to temptation but, more broadly and profoundly, they resist the superficiality and self-absorption of the larger, dominant culture.

The young men—specifically Daniel, Shadrach, Meshach, and Abednego—stand firm in their commitment to their own culture and perspective. They resist the pull to be like everyone else. Instead of partaking of the food and wine, they conspire with their overseers who are sympathetic to their plight. The young men choose to eat only fresh vegetables and water.

And here is how the story turns out: "At the end of ten days, it was seen that they were better in appearance and fatter in the flesh than all the youths who ate the king's rich food" (Daniel 1:15). Faith in God, loyalty to a cause, and adherence to a higher standard offer necessary spiritual integrity, deepened mental capacity, and broadened physical vitality.

Tonight, plan and eat a meatless meal: a salad, at least two other vegetables, and maybe soup. Think healthy, eat healthy, be healthy. Take the Bible seriously!

> "Many persons have a wrong idea of what constitutes true happiness. It is not gained through self-gratification, but through fidelity to a worthy purpose."
> — Helen Keller

WEDNESDAY

In your book were written all the days that were formed for me, when none of them as yet existed (Psalm 139:16).

Daniel and his friends could have easily given themselves over to the abundant temptations surrounding them. But these first six chapters of Daniel tell us of commitment to a cause larger than themselves and the recognition that the choices they made had significant consequences. They could have given in, but they remained faithful, demonstrating the benefits of choosing rightly.

The path you walk today is yours alone. The choices you make are free and at your discretion. But you are not alone. You hold in your power the potential to recognize God's presence within your decisions. Your life is infused with and surrounded by the wisdom of God. Claim this gift—and live in its truth. Be aware of life's sacredness and God's presence. Claim these passing moments as good and truly worthy.

> "How small a portion of our life it is that we really enjoy! In youth we are looking forward to things that are to come; in old age we are looking backward to things that are gone past; in adulthood, although we appear indeed to be more occupied in things that are present, yet even that is too often absorbed in vague determination to be vastly happy on some future day we have time."
> — C. C. Colton

THURSDAY

How weighty are your thoughts, O God! How vast the sum of them! (Psalm 139:17).

Along with healthy diets, we are called to consider God's gift to us and maintain healthy bodies through physical exercise. As mentioned earlier, consistent exercise in Jesus' day was simply understood. Walking everywhere, working in the garden, fishing by the sea, planting trees, playing games with friends—these activities would have been a vital part of every day.

It could be cold out, so bundle up, but still take a walk. As you move through your neighborhood, give thanks for things you pass: bare trees and yards, warm homes, neighbors. Pray for families in the homes you pass, for their well-being and what they may face tomorrow. Be glad.

> "To pray is to change. This is great grace. How good of God to provide a path whereby our lives can be taken over by love and joy and peace and patience and kindness and goodness and faithfulness and gentleness and self-control. The movement inward comes first because, without interior transformation, the movement up into God's glory would overwhelm us and the movement out into ministry would destroy us."
> — Richard Foster

FRIDAY

I try to count them—they are more than the sand... (Psalm 139:18a).

In the book *The Secret Garden*, the Scottish word for the rose's state in winter is to "wick." That is, the rose endures winter, neither growing nor blooming, and patiently waits for spring, for what lies ahead.

Today, think of five things you have to be thankful for. Walk in humility and with a vision for the expanse of God's mercy and the greatness of God's world. It is likely still cold, but venture out and see, despite the appearance of winter, how the world quietly prepares for spring. May your perspective be as the rose in the secret garden—patiently waiting with glad expectation.

> "We cannot be born anew if the power of the old is not broken within us; and it is not broken so long as it puts the burden of guilt upon us. Therefore religion, prophetic as well as apostolic, pronounces, above all, forgiveness. Forgiveness means that the old is thrown into the past because the new has come."
> — Paul Tillich

SATURDAY

I come to the end—I am still with you (Psalm 139:18b).

Give thanks. Take time to ponder God's surrounding presence. No matter where you go or what you do, God is with you. Enjoy time with friends or a date with someone special. A positive sense of community is vital to good health—and to appreciating God's presence. Likely, Daniel and his friends would have been less able to resist temptation if they had been alone, without the strength of friendship and community.

Notice today, in your relationships, a sense of holiness and the presence of God within those around you. Plan on going to church tomorrow. If you aren't already, become part of a broader community that offers you fidelity to a purposeful cause.

FEBRUARY
Preparing

The Romans came to view February as a month for purification and the giving of offerings. In a similar way, the Christian tradition moves into February beginning the season of Lent, that part of the Christian year when we remember Jesus' forty days in the wilderness and his preparation for ministry.

With Lent, then, there is an element of purification, of preparation, of offering ourselves in the service of God in imitation of Jesus. Thus, the essays for the start of each week reflect a sense of purification in faith and self understanding in light of daily living as followers of Jesus.

THE FIRST WEEK:
Disciples or Apostles

It is too light a thing that you should be my servant to raise up the tribes of Jacob and to restore the survivors of Israel; I will give you as a light to the nations, that my salvation may reach to the end of the earth (Isaiah 49:6).

Go therefore and make disciples of all nations... (Matthew 28:19a).

This week might be a challenging one. Who knows what lies ahead? But, as a Christian, every week is fertile ground for growing faith. There are a plethora of opportunities to learn, to broaden your perspective, to share God's love. This week, think of yourself in these two biblical terms: *Disciple* and *Apostle*.

Disciple speaks about more than being a follower of Jesus; the definition more accurately means "learner." We make mistakes and share victories. We follow, sometimes well, sometimes poorly. But at all times, we remain learners. In the good and bad, we can take what we experience, process what we now know with what we knew before, and, with humility, deepen our discipleship.

Jesus calls on his followers "to make disciples of all nations" (Matthew 28). His words become an inclusive, leveling call. Through this imperative, we invite others to *join* us in discipleship, to journey with us in learning and faith, and to be equals at the common ground of the cross. We offer this journey with humility and love, and invite others to walk with us into the deeper waters of understanding and compassion.

As you move through this week, consider what it means to be a follower of Jesus, to be a learner on the pathway of faith, and in the ways that lead to life.

> Lord, help me this week to be a better example of your good work. May I be the kind of witness for others that will allow a testimony of hope, faith and love to be spoken without words. Use me in your wisdom for the benefit of others. Amen.

REFLECTIONS FOR THE WEEK

MONDAY

I will give you as a light to the nations, that my salvation may reach to the end of the earth (Isaiah 49:6).

Apostle is more than a person who knew Jesus, or who was with Jesus following his resurrection. Paul called himself an apostle because he knew he had seen the risen Lord and had been called into a particular mission with a particular message. So, like the word disciple, the definition of apostle is instructive. It means "one who is sent with a message." In the Gospel of John, we can say Mary Magdalene was the first apostle since Jesus sends her back to the disciples with the message of new life and new beginning. She was an evangelist (*evangelion* in Greek means "good news") sent as the messenger, an apostle for Jesus.

Today, as followers of Jesus, we rarely hear disciple and apostle used in conjunction with people like you and me trying to live worthy lives. But both of these biblical identifications remain highly relevant for how God views us fulfilling our callings. Regardless of our educational level or natural intelligence, it is clear the Christian faith expects followers of Jesus to continue to learn, to grow, to improve our understanding of what faith is about, and to act accordingly. Just as we learn through our discipleship, we are also called to be apostles—to share the message of good news, offer hope for the future, and continue to participate in the power of God's love and the great gift of Jesus.

Contemplate today how to improve your discipleship, and use that new knowledge to share the good news of Jesus.

TUESDAY

Love your neighbor as you love yourself (Leviticus 19:18).

You are a disciple of Jesus, attempting to broaden your perspective and deepen your understanding. As you continue to learn about life, faith, and what surrounds you, apply that new understanding to how you relate to those around you. The way you interact should be natural and authentic. In you, there should be a genuine sense of self—or we could say self-acceptance and self love ("...love your neighbor *as you love yourself*"). It is not egotistical or self-centered to understand that God first loved you. In your creation, you were "fearfully and wonderfully made" (Psalm 139). Accepting yourself today is the natural celebration of God's good work in your life.

Translate this sacred celebration and self-acceptance outward through acceptance of those around you ("*love your neighbor as you love yourself*"). In doing so, may you stand in awe knowing that—from your life and through your voice and in *your being you*—you carry the message that just might change the course of someone's history. Your discipleship then becomes apostleship.

WEDNESDAY

Go therefore and make disciples of all nations...
(Matthew 28:19a).

The Greeks prospered in southern Italy long before Paul arrived there on his Fourth Missionary Journey. These Greeks had settled the area in and around Naples (Napoli used to mean "new polis" or "new city" in Greek) and had developed a culture similar to the Greek mainland but with a special Italian flair. The people of this beautiful land south of Rome gave bold testimony to their culture and who they were simply by being themselves. The Romans conquered the Greeks militarily, but they were discerning enough to know a good thing. They fully adapted and adopted Greek culture because they saw in it a superior means of government, philosophy, art, architecture, and literature.

Being a disciple and maintaining a commitment to learning, and being an apostle and being willing to share this good message of God's salvation, should have the same result. Our lives will serve as a "light" to those around us. Focus today on doing the right thing, saying the kind thing, going beyond the call of duty for the sake of another with no strings attached. Do your best to learn all you can, give all you can, share all you can, and do so for the glory of God. You need not talk about it. St. Francis of Assisi once said: "Preach the gospel at all times, and, when necessary, use words." Go and do likewise today. You will be an *apostle*.

THURSDAY

I will give you as a light to the nations, that my salvation may reach to the end of the earth (Isaiah 49:6).

Today, consider the nature of God's salvation. What does it mean to be "saved" or to participate in this concept of salvation in connection with God? In earlier years, partly due to the heavy influence of revivals and insistent preachers, too often *salvation* was made to be too *small*.

In my tradition, there was usually a song, rendered emotionally (something like "Just As I Am" sung repeatedly). People came forward to the front of the church to "give their lives to Jesus" and be "saved." There is nothing inherently wrong with this. But, for many of us growing up with this experience, salvation felt like a one-time deal that had to do with a preacher's sermon, a piano or organ, a good bit of emotion, and the sense of escaping the fires of Hell and the grasp of the devil.

That was not what Isaiah had in mind. Isaiah's concept had to do with structures, attitudes, inclusion, and blessing. His words offered a sense of wholeness and relatedness to God and God's purposes for the world and for the broadly scattered people of God all over the earth. This vision is one of universal connection, not "some in" and "some out," but *all in together*. In fact, earlier in Isaiah, in the nineteenth chapter, he paints this dramatic image of a highway connecting Assyria, Israel, and Egypt. These were three bitter enemies and eternal rivals. But, in Isaiah's image of God's salvation, they would speak the same language, worship the same God, have the same goals of peace and prosperity. The vision is nothing the prophet imagines happening by chance, but by a dramatic in-breaking of God's blessedness where erstwhile enemies become passionate friends.

Today, then, as you continue to work with this concept of being a *disciple* and becoming an *apostle* along with God's *salvation*, allow yourself to feel open to the movement of God in your life—and, through your life, into the lives of others. You can trust they will know a good thing when they see it. Be yourself, honor God's presence in your life, let God use you, and leave the grace and blessedness of what happens next up to God.

FRIDAY

Love your neighbor as you love yourself (Leviticus 19:18).

Who is your neighbor? We will explore this question more fully later, but for today, let it challenge you. There will come an opportunity today to do something for someone else. This person is your neighbor. As I share in detail this concept in my book, *Subversive Words: Biblical Counterpoints to Conventional Wisdom*, Jesus is clear on God's real definition of neighbor, and it is not the person living next door. Biblically, it is the person God places in your path: the person in need, the person in line at the store, the person driving in front of you. It might even be your enemy. Your challenge today, this final day of the work week and of the school week, is to be ready, to be on your guard for what God has in store for you today: who will be your neighbor? Who will you make your neighbor? And the final question with your preparation will not be "what impact will you have on them?" Rather it will be: "What valuable impact will they have on you?"

May your day be one filled with fascinating examples of God at work in your life.

SATURDAY

Allow today to be a day of family, friends, contemplation on God's good creation, and a celebration of what you enjoy.

THE SECOND WEEK:
Open Heart, Open Mind

In Caesarea, there was a man named Cornelius, a centurion of the Italian Cohort (Acts 10:1).

Caesarea and Joppa were port cities on the Mediterranean Sea. We will return to Caesarea in a moment, but first a word about Joppa. This was the same seaside town where Jonah set sail in his attempt to flee from God's call to preach to the people of Nineveh. And it was in Joppa, at the house of Simon the Tanner, that Simon Peter had a similar call.

Peter's call came in the form of a dream; we read about it in Acts 10. Peter, like Jonah in the Old Testament, thinks of himself as a loyal Jew, devoted to the Law and certain of God's intentions regarding the covenant with the Jewish people. Yet, for Jonah and Peter, God has other plans.

With Jonah, the episode of the storm and the big fish serves to underline that the dreams of God go beyond our understandings. The Ninevites, hated enemies of Israel and Judah, repent of their sinful ways and are welcomed by God into the family of faith. Jonah is furious. And, at the end of the Old Testament book called by his name, he is chastised by God because he cares more for a withered gourd plant he neither planted nor cultivated than he does for "that great city in which there are more than one hundred and twenty thousand persons who do not know their right hand from their left…" (Jonah 4:11). The story is left hanging as to what Jonah will learn—or if he will—and this should not be lost on us. The lack of a firm conclusion is purposeful. The real question is not what Jonah will choose for his future perspective but what *we* should do with the *Ninevites* of today and how we feel about them.

In the case of Peter, his dream of food items that are declared by God to be clean sends a deeper and, like with Jonah, troubling message to Peter. All that he previously believed is now thrown into flux. Peter had been clear on what it meant to be part of the covenant people. Now he wonders. And just as he is shaking off the sleep from his nap and awakens from his dream, there is a knock on the door.

A small delegation from Caesarea, just up the coast from Joppa, informs Peter of a man, a Roman Centurion, a Gentile, non-Jew, head of a group of soldiers occupying his land. He is named Cornelius. He is the enemy.

But it turns out this soldier is a God-fearing man from the Italian cohort and has generously contributed to Jewish causes in Caesarea. God has also inspired Cornelius through a dream, calling upon him to send for Peter.

Three days later, Peter stands in Cornelius' home. The visit itself was a potential act of sedition in the eyes of other Jews of that day (see Acts 10:28). He proclaims the Gospel, and in this most Roman of Judean cities—this place of occupation, a city divided between Jews and Greeks, Romans and Syrians—the two men, who days before would have been enemies, are now brothers in the Good News of Jesus. On that day, Cornelius and all his household were baptized. How beautiful are the unexpected miracles of new faith in surprising people.

> Lord, when I am blinded by my own agenda, when my prejudices tarnish the beauty of your creation, or when my silence quietly condones injustice, awaken me as you did Peter and Cornelius. Show me the way in your will; give me the courage to stand for your wisdom; and give me the insight to adjust and deepen my convictions. Give me the courage to open my heart; give me the wisdom to open my mind. Amen.

REFLECTIONS FOR THE WEEK

MONDAY

It is too light a thing that you should be my servant to raise up the tribes of Jacob and to restore the survivors of Israel; I will give you as a light to the nations, that my salvation may reach to the end of the earth (Isaiah 49:6).

Sometimes, God teaches us through people different from ourselves. Other times, lessons come through surprising opportunities. In the case of Peter, it was a bizarre dream. In the case of Jonah, it was a crazy calling to people he couldn't stand. For both, the clear parallel is the wideness of God's mercy and the common physical place of departure, the port city of Joppa.

Also, in Peter's dream, there are all kinds of dishes, animals, spices, and strange things Peter knew to be unclean, or non-kosher. In the case of Jonah, God's tool for teaching is a "bush" (4:6). And God reminded him it was a bush "for which you did not labor and which you did not grow" (4:10).

February, though cold at times in North Carolina, can also be a great time for the good, soulful work of preparing a garden for the growing season: readying the soil, composting, buying seeds. If you don't already have a patch of ground to cultivate, February is a great time to put in some raised beds, bring in a load of good dirt, prepare the earth. In the process, imagine what will come as the weather turns warmer. I call this planning ahead for loveliness. And it's good for the soul.

TO PLAN AHEAD FOR LOVELINESS

O what a pleasant recompense,
To cultivate some soulfulness
And plan ahead for loveliness
With sight beyond the present tense.

To see a garden where there's not
And vibrancy of earthen pot
A brilliant colored waving plot

In place of present muddy lot.

Envision blooms soon high astride
A latticed wall securely tied
And flowers shouting out with pride,
Replacing earth tone's wintry side.

I know what pleasure gardens bring,
Because the joy is not just spring;
But souls in early winter sing
Of future plans for gardening.

So nurture now your soulfulness,
And plan ahead for loveliness.

— David Jordan

Give it a try. Imagine a garden somewhere in your yard for the coming spring. Start thinking about what you might need to make it happen. If you already have a garden, consider composting or purchasing soil amendments to prepare the soil for cultivation.

TUESDAY

It is too light a thing that you should be my servant to raise up the tribes of Jacob and to restore the survivors of Israel; I will give you as a light to the nations... (Isaiah 49:6).

Both Peter and Jonah were men of their times. Their perspectives, like many of our own ways of seeing the world, were confined to the culture surrounding them. The idea of God's grace as a part of someone else's life might not be a natural perspective for most of us. Often, we are too busy with our own concerns and agendas. And if the person or people under consideration are the targets of our anger, scorn, or dislike, then our views are skewed further. It took a few nights in the belly of a big fish to get Jonah to see things a little differently. For Peter, it was a series of bizarre dreams and a knock at the door that helped him understand God's grace was bigger than he could imagine. Prejudice remains a convenient distraction for small minds. To

Jonah and Peter, God offered a new vision for understanding of community: *salvation that reaches the ends of the earth.*

Today, be aware of what God may be teaching you about those around you. There are likely some in your life or line of vision who make you uncomfortable. What do you need to learn?

> "Every moment is a fresh moment of the Spirit, unless we chain it to the staleness of a past moment."
> — Tilden Edwards

WEDNESDAY

It is too light a thing that you should be my servant to raise up the tribes of Jacob and to restore the survivors of Israel... (Isaiah 49:6).

Do not let the big fish of Jonah distract you from the real message of this powerful, incredibly subversive part of our Bible.[1] Too many I have taught over the years are concerned with the literalness of the fish and the three days of Jonah's stay there. That misses the ultimate meaning and amazing message of the story as a whole. We must take this story and its message seriously. And we can do so without taking it literally. The point is not the fish. It is the call, or the task, set before Jonah, which to him is utterly unthinkable. His call to go to his bitter enemies is more than he can fathom. The story concludes with God's acceptance of the Ninevites' repentance and rescinding the divine decree of destruction. But Jonah had preached: "Forty days more and Ninevah shall be destroyed" (Jonah 3:4).

With all his heart, Jonah wanted his prophetic utterance to be true. Yet the story is not about destruction, or disobedience, or a man being swallowed but not digested by a big fish. The story, instead, rises to the very vision Isaiah articulates: "It is

---

[1] In my previous book, *Subversive Words: Biblical Counterpoints to Conventional Wisdom*, I devote considerable time to the richness and value of Jonah. When read and heard as intended, it is clear the "fishy" part of the story is about a broader truth: God is in control of and deeply concerned about this world and the people in it, even pagan sailors and the unspeakably cruel and imperialistic Ninevites.

too light a thing" that God's salvation be only for the people of Israel. Rather: "I will give you as a light to the nations, that my salvation may reach to the end of the earth" (Isaiah 49:6). This includes the Ninevites, occupying enemy forces like the Roman soldier Cornelius, and hate groups, even terrorist groups like Al Qaeda. Even them?! Yes, even them.

What new thing must you learn today? What person or group of persons do you need to see in a different light? In what way might God use you, even you, to make a difference in the life and perspective of another?

Today, hear with understanding and respond to God's gentle voice and persistent calling.

> "Today let us remind each other often that the resurrected Jesus no longer needs to be awakened but is a constant companion."
> — Rueben Job

THURSDAY

...I will give you as a light to the nations, that my salvation may reach to the end of the earth (Isaiah 49:6).

Some years ago, my father became the new pastor of First Baptist Church of Jefferson City, Tennessee. The church was in the process of building a new sanctuary to replace the previous one destroyed in a fire. In the process of construction, and as the building was nearing completion, a church member came to my father's study very concerned that a strange-looking man with long hair and a beard was wandering amidst the construction in the sanctuary work area.

My father dutifully headed down to the construction area. Sure enough, there he was, a strong-looking man in very casual clothes—jeans and a loose fitting flannel shirt, long hair and beard. He was not one of the workers, and though my father was still new to the church, this man didn't seem to fit the stereotypical churchgoer at First Baptist.

"Excuse me," my father said. "May I help you?"

"No, that's okay," this guy replied. "I just wanted to see how your stained glass up there turned out."

He pointed up to the large, beautiful window just recently placed into the wall behind the baptistery. It was a picture of Jesus smiling, welcoming and with arms open wide. Dad looked, and there he saw a familiar face.

"See," the man continued, "I was the model for Jesus, and I was curious how it turned out."

When telling us that story, my father said: "And to think, I almost threw Jesus out of the church!"

Sadly, it wouldn't have been the first time, nor will it likely be the last. Therefore, let us do our best to be more discerning, more understanding, and more committed to hearing God's call in our lives to see beyond our circumstances, culture, and current perspective. There is more going on in God's world and with God's hope and dreams than we can imagine.

> "Truly, I tell you, as you did it to one of the least of these, my brothers and sisters, you did it unto me." — Jesus (Matthew 25:40)

FRIDAY

...my salvation may reach to the end of the earth
(Isaiah 49:6).

It is too easy to believe the voices around us. And it is equally easier to believe the voices in our heads. Those voices often intermingle in a confusing echo that fools us into believing they speak the truth and know more than we do. But those voices speak from small places of insecurity harbored since our earliest days. And if we aren't careful, they can be cultivated by events and others to the extent we mistake the lonely, petty rhetoric for reality.

How convenient it is to hear and believe others are less than we, that our ways are best and must be preserved at all cost and for all time. But the wisdom of the Bible is deeper and more profound. Jesus—following in the tradition of Isaiah, who was following in the tradition of the call of Abraham—knew better. We in the human family have far more in common than what separates us. We are more alike than we are different. We have a common origin, and God's hope for us is that we have a common destiny. Ninevites, Romans, Peter, Jonah, Cornelius, you, me—it is too light a thing that you and I be in this only for ourselves. What about being a light unto the nations?

Do one thing today that lightens someone's burden: lift someone's spirit, offer someone hope. In doing so, you might just change the course of history. You never know.

SATURDAY

I will give you as a light to the nations, that my salvation may reach to the end of the earth (Isaiah 49:6).

Rest. Enjoy the day with a good balance of silence. Later, enjoy fellowship with those you love.

THE THIRD WEEK:
Out of Nothing, Venice!

Now faith is the substance of things hoped for, the evidence of things not seen (Hebrews 11:1).

Their world was crashing in around them. The beauty, sophistication, art, and architecture of northern Italy ... crushed, stolen, burned. They ran from the chaos to the only place of refuge they could find: a series of marshy islands just off the coast of Italy in the upper reaches of the Adriatic Sea.

The historian John Julius Norwich once asked: "Who in their senses would build more than a fishing hut on the malarial, malodorous shoals of mud and sandbanks of the Venetian lagoon?" And his own answer: "Those who had no choice."[2]

Their plight resulted from the catastrophe of barbarian invasions initiated by Attila the Hun in the middle of the fifth century A.D. These invasions were followed by Goths in the sixth century. Fleeing as refugees, they carried with them only the bare essentials and hoped merely for survival.

Today, Venice is one of the most beautiful cities in the world. It is the best preserved large city in all of Europe, with no motor traffic, one hundred and fifty canals, four hundred bridges, one hundred and eighteen islands, palaces that border the Grand Canal, musicians on almost every corner, and gondolas that serve as taxis. Venice is a place of particular magic.

The mud, sand, peat, and clay of the islands required solid foundations of oak pilings driven deep into the subsoil. These pilings came from trees as far away as the Alps in the north and Croatia across the Adriatic to the east. Working from the outside in, concentric circles of pilings were driven through the unstable lagoon floor to the bedrock of compacted clay. The number and thickness depended on the weight of the building: La Salute Church, for instance, is supported by over a million pilings.[3]

---

[2] *Insight City Guide: Venice*, from the Discovery Channel, p. 15.

[3] *Insight City Guide: Venice*, p. 18.

How these people saw beyond mere survival is a mystery. Yet, traveling among the alleys and canals of remarkable Venice, one sees the miraculous transformation. Somehow, in the midst of losing everything, these refugees had the "substance of things hoped for and evidence of things not seen" to create a meandering urban garden of architectural beauty for all the world to enjoy.

> Lord, inspire us to do the same. Allow us to take whatever has come our way, the good and the bad, the clear and the confusing, and, with a vision for the future and a faith in your guiding providence, lead us on and beyond any current difficulty. Allow our lives to be that same creative masterpiece that is Venice. Amen.

Reflections for the Week

MONDAY

What does it profit, my brothers and sisters, if someone says they have faith but has not works ... So faith, by itself, if it has no works, is dead (James 2:14-17).

Writer of seventeen novels, John Steinbeck is one of my favorite authors, and, to me, *The Grapes of Wrath* is his greatest and had the most enduring impact. Published in 1939, this novel immediately elicited strong reactions—anger from farm owners, sympathy from the broader public. Deeply troubled by the plight of farm workers near his home in Salinas, California, he gave an extraordinary portrayal of the Joad family and provided a poignant glimpse into the tragic travails of regular people struggling to survive against massive odds. Steinbeck uncovered the dirty secrets of capitalism's dark side—unethical politicians, rough-hewn policemen, exploitive farm owners, and an entire system geared solely toward profit and in opposition to compassion.

Tom Joad, the principle character, victimized but determined not to give in or give up, experiences his own epiphany: "Wherever they's a fight so hungry people can eat, I'll be there ... Wherever they's a cop beatin' up a guy, I'll be there."[4]

Steinbeck was roundly criticized and called all manner of things, including communist, for criticizing the virtues of capitalism. But a U.S. Senate investigation backed his claims and, ultimately, led to changes in conditions and protections of the workers.

Sadly, too often in the history of our country, faith in the system of an unchecked or unregulated industry has allowed a multitude of abuses. Still, similar abuses exist and concerns continue. If you have time, investigate some of the findings related to the meat and poultry industries, both in the ways that animals are treated and humans are exploited.

---

[4] As quoted by Kidder and Oppenheim in *The Intellectual Devotional: American History*, p. 244.

Consider today what God would have you see that might need to be changed and how your faith could generate a new work that will make a difference.

> "Give us the serenity to accept the thing we cannot change, courage to change the things we can, and wisdom to know the difference."
> — Reinhold Niebuhr

TUESDAY

But be doers of the word, and not hearers only, deceiving your selves (James 1:22).

The great Scottish pastor and poet, George MacLeod, shared the following on the dedication of the Abbey on Iona. Hear in his words, the captivating call to be more than mere spectators to life. We are integral participants in the mystery of God's grace and the full embodiment of our faith:

THE ABBEY ON IONA
It is not just the interior of these walls,
It is our own inner beings you have renewed.
We are your temple not made with hands.
We are your body.
If every wall should crumble,
And every church decay, we are your habitation.
Nearer are you than breathing,
Closer than hands and feet.
Ours are the eyes with which you, in the mystery,
Look out in compassion on the world.
So we bless you for this place,
For your directing of us,
Your redeeming of us, and your indwelling.
Take us outside the camp, Lord,
Outside holiness,
Out to where soldiers gamble, and thieves curse,
And nations clash at the cross-roads of the world ...
So shall this building continue to be justified.

In MacLeod's prayer to God, he confesses, and we must hear: "ours are the eyes with which you, in the mystery, look out in compassion on the world... " Look for ways, today, you are called to go "outside the camp." Consider today all that God would have you see.

WEDNESDAY

...We are your temple not made with hands. We are your body. If every wall should crumble, and every church decay, we are your habitation. Nearer are you than breathing... (George MacLeod).

Breathe deeply as you prepare for this new day. Be reminded of the earliest vision of God's creative presence—God's spirit hovering, moving, breathing, blowing across the face of the waters and turning chaos into creation (see Genesis 1:1-3). Whatever kinds of chaos might be a part of your experience this week, know that all is well and all shall be well. Today, be aware that God's presence is with you in every breath you take, in every hand you shake, in every encounter you make. MacLeod's prayer of God's indwelling says it well: "Nearer are you than breathing..." Claim this truth today, and may your confidence grow along with your deepening faith.

> "Our life of contemplation, simply put, is to realize God's constant presence and His tender love for us in the least little things of life."
> — Mother Teresa

THURSDAY

Count it all joy, my brothers and sisters, when you meet various trials, for you know that the testing of your faith produces steadfastness (James 1:2).

Add to your reading list *The Boy who Harnessed the Wind*, by William Kamkwamba. His is an inspiring autobiography of a young man growing up in a struggling village in Africa. He doesn't give up, despite looming obstacles and community derision. One's life takes on new humility, perspective, and appreciation after hearing of William's toils and redemption. Within this story is the faith William has in the value of education and the vision he carries to see beyond his present circumstance. Even when his family is dying of hunger, though there is food available but mismanaged and misappropriated by the government, somehow this young man and those around him endure with dignity.

For William, it is his determination, his vision for a future, and faith in his dream that are most inspiring. Like those who first settled Venice, William and others like him stand as heroic reminders of the power of persistence, vision, and faith. What about you? There might well be obstacles that stand in the way of your goals today or sometime this week. Think carefully about your response. See whatever challenge or trial that arises as an opportunity, a gift for your personal growth and spiritual maturity. Learn and let your faith guide you; in the process, be deepened and "count it all joy." Remember, faith is not a weight to hold us down, but wings to lift us up!

> "Receive today's gift gratefully, unwrapping it tenderly and delving into its depths."
> — Sarah Young

FRIDAY

Count it all joy, my brothers and sisters, when you meet various trials, for you know that the testing of your faith produces steadfastness (James 1:2).

Beware of anyone so filled with certitude they claim to have no doubts. Faith never calls us to squelch curiosity or disregard our questions. In scripture, there is a consistent call to humility. And this is a beautiful thing; humility does not diminish the necessity and beauty of faith. Being humble simply enhances one's view of the universe. We are more able to embrace wonder and stand in awe when our faith is one not of certitude but of graceful acceptance and the desire to learn more.

Peter Berger's book, *In Praise of Doubt*, is particularly helpful on this topic. A Christian sociologist, his work and research over the decades maintains a wise hand on the pulse of our social trends. But, more importantly, he pokes valuable fun at those of us who think we know more than we possibly can. I know some who, I am convinced, think they know more than there is to be known.

The sad state of many faithful people in churches across our nation is the notion that somehow either we, our spiritual leaders, or others in positions of power know enough, and so we can be content.

From Berger's perspective, certitude, complete certainty, and unquestioning fidelity stifles the growth in our understanding of ourselves and the world around us. We need to be the kinds of people God desires. In other words, *faith needs doubt* in order to keep growing. When you are struggling with doubts, you are in the process of deepening a vital aspect of your spiritual self.

A vibrant faith and deepened understanding comes as the result of ongoing inquisitiveness. Experiencing doubt *and* growing in faith should call us all to eager inquiry and investigation into those things we do not understand. We will never have all the answers, but we will at least stimulate a number of new and exciting questions.

Make your journey of faith today one of deep interest in the world and the people around you. God gives us curiosity and discerning minds so we might dig more deeply and learn more thoroughly. Enjoy exploring new ideas and learning something new.

> "Faith is not an alarm system to warn us of burglars in the night, but a light to illumine the darkness."
> — David Jordan

SATURDAY

Count it all joy, my brothers and sisters, when you meet various trials, for you know that the testing of your faith produces steadfastness (James 1:2).

Enjoy this day as your Sabbath. Relax, rest, and find something around you that is beautiful. Allow your mind to move in the direction of wonder and ask yourself what it is that makes what you see lovely. What role does it play in the universe? Why does it exist? Make plans to attend a worship service somewhere tomorrow.

> "Faith is not a fortification against the encroaching sea but buoyancy to roll with the inevitable waves."
> — David Jordan

THE FOURTH WEEK:
A Limited Vision[5]
By Rev. Beth Jackson-Jordan

For now we see in a mirror, dimly, but then we will see face to face. Now I know only in part; then I will know fully, even as I have been fully known. So faith, hope, love abide, these three; but the greatest of these is love
(1 Corinthians 13:12).

The "Creation of Adam," a scene from Michelangelo's fresco on the ceiling of the Sistine Chapel, is perhaps one of the most recognized of all artistic images. Since its completion in 1512, the ceiling has attracted admirers from all over the world who come to gaze at the dramatic depiction of scenes from the Old Testament. In 1951, a cropped enlargement of the bodies of Adam and God with outstretched hands was published and, since then, the image has become popularized, perhaps for the compelling way it conveys humankind's longing for intimate connection with our Creator.

Ironically, Michelangelo was a grudging recruit for this daunting task. He was assigned the project by Pope Julius II (known at the time as "il pape terribile" or the "terrifying" pope), who was hoping to immortalize himself through the rebuilding of St. Peter's Basilica. Michelangelo had many reasons for resisting. He was involved in another project in Florence and had little fondness for Rome. Having earned a reputation as a sculptor and painter, he had little experience with the tedious, difficult technique of frescoing, which involved painting on wet plaster. And Michelangelo was distrustful and intolerant of others. He often worked in solitude and had little enjoyment in life outside of his work. Michelangelo's work on the Sistine Chapel spanned four years and, when he was finally finished, he seemed to view it as a regrettable delay from other projects that had been postponed.[6]

---

[5] This devotional was contributed by my wife, Rev. Beth Jackson-Jordan.

[6] King, Ross. *Michelangelo and the Pope's Ceiling*.

History has long celebrated the breathtaking genius of Michelangelo, whose art engages our senses and emotions so dramatically. Yet the master himself seemed to find little joy in his accomplishments. While so many of us are touched and inspired by his work, he never seemed to find fulfillment in his own creative process. If he had only known how many would be inspired by his work, he might have felt differently.

We may never know the impact of the things God calls us to do. We may underestimate the power of God to work through us to bless others in small or large ways. Today, choose to experience joy and fulfillment while you serve, remembering what we see is not all there is. God's desire is for us to find joy in the journey of faith, even when our work seems inadequate, knowing that some day we will see "face to face."

> Help us this week, O God. Let us trust you to magnify whatever we offer so that it becomes useful, pleasing, and significant. Amen.

REFLECTIONS FOR THE WEEK

MONDAY

For now we see in a mirror, dimly, but then we will see face to face... (1 Corinthians 13:12).

One of Plato's most famous philosophical illustrations for the nature of life utilized a very similar concept to this one in I Corinthians 13 of *seeing in a mirror dimly*. His parable for life was represented by people gathered in a cave and chained as prisoners[7]: a fire burns on the floor in the middle of a cave. The movement of those surrounding the fire casts moving shadows on the rock walls. Around the corner, in another part of the cave, we see the shadows dance against the cave wall, but these distorted and indistinct shadows are all we recognize of reality.

Plato's real point is not to be negative about existence but positive about mystery and the elusiveness of meaning and insight. In his illustration, all we truly know about the real nature and purpose of life is filled with shadow and silence.

Notice the similarities between Plato's parable and Paul's attempt to let us know how much we lack in true insight: "We see through a mirror dimly ... Now I know only in part..." We see and understand nothing more in the present than the equivalent of viewing shadows on the wall of a cave.[8]

Today, focus on humble thoughts. Be aware of how much you *don't* know; acknowledge how little you fully understand. Before the larger reality of God's providence and creation's vastness, allow yourself to be awed; be humble in the sight of the Lord. Breathe deeply and, with quiet recognition, recognize the vast framework of God's sacred history.

---

[7] From Plato's "Allegory of the Cave" found in Book VII of Plato's *The Republic*. He presents the allegory as a part of the dialogue between Socrates and Glaucon.

[8] Paul's use of such language in I Corinthians 13 indicates further his conversance with Greek culture and philosophical teaching. Another clear example comes from Acts with quotes from both a Greek and a Roman in poetry and philosophy (Acts 17:28).

It is good and right to admit our shortcomings, own up to our inadequacies, and recognize our weaknesses. The growth God expects from us will never occur until we begin the process in humility and truth.

> "Time is the mirror in which we see eternity."
> — Paul Tillich

TUESDAY

For now we see in a mirror, dimly, but then we will see face to face. Now I know only in part; then I will know fully, even as I have been fully known... (1 Corinthians 13:12).

Michelangelo, creative genius and Renaissance Man of Italy's golden age of art, created works of beauty that we all share even today. Yet he also struggled with life and relationships.

We know of the trials of Michelangelo's private life from others' accounts; we know of his turmoil, massive expectations, and enormous workloads. We know of his brutal schedules and untold personal pressures, and of his solitary and brooding nature. And we know he didn't share much of his life, but he certainly shared his art.

Through friendship or partnership; children or grandchildren; church, synagogue, or mosque; or work relationships, our lives reach their fullest potential when we share ourselves and God's love to and through us. The greatest of life is this gift God gives to us. And we are expected to share it. When we do, unlike other possessions, it multiplies. This is truly a mystery—one that should be explored for as long as we live and with as many as we can. Today, give your love away.

> "If you want to go fast, go alone; if you want to go far, go together."
> — African Proverb

WEDNESDAY

For now we see in a mirror, dimly, but then we will see face to face... (1 Corinthians 13:12).

John D. Rockefeller was a great businessman. As founder of Standard Oil, his ability to see evolving trends, recognize the growing need for gas and oil, exploit opportunities, and aggressively pursue his goals made him the history's first billionaire and one of the most powerful men in the world by the early twentieth century. Thanks to his wealth and later philanthropy, our nation continues to benefit from his endeavors and benevolent charity.

As with many good things, though, there was a dark side to Rockefeller's fortune. His hard-hitting style, driven competitive nature, unscrupulous business practices, and ongoing worker and environmental exploitation created hardship for many. Of course, cogent arguments can be made regarding the jobs he created even as he dissolved and usurped others. And perhaps, too, one could argue that the good he did with his fortune redeemed the chaos he caused in making it.

Yet Corinthians calls attention to other qualities in our lives that should be taken far more seriously in light of life's potential for harsh competition.

When contemplating business deals, when considering decisions that might effect the lives and well-being of others, when interacting with our fellow human beings at any time and at any level, let us all remember: "For now we see in a mirror dimly, but then we will see face to face." May any dimness of spiritual vision today not adversely impact others or the image of your soul for tomorrow. Live today with others, the world, and the future in mind.

> "Gladly we live in this garden of your creating ... In the garden also: always the thorn. Creation is not enough ... In the garden that is each of us, always the thorn."
> — George Macleod

THURSDAY

...Now I know only in part; then I will know fully, even as I have been fully known (1 Corinthians 13:12).

We do not know what the future holds. We have no crystal ball to tell us what to expect. The Bible is clear about this. In spite of the tendency to believe prophets somehow predicted what and when things would occur, in fact, the opposite is true. Telling the future was forbidden in the Torah. It was considered fortune telling and, therefore, sorcery. The Old Testament prophets weren't telling the future; they *were speaking truth to power.* They interpreted events and attitudes and called others to consider how what they critiqued intersected with what God expected.

The whole point of the prophet's job was to prevent a foreboding future. They called for repentance and change in behavior. When Jonah preached to the Ninevites and predicted destruction, his sermon changed their behavior so that what he envisioned did *not* occur. He affected their minds, behaviors, and lives.

We need those voices speaking truth to power, calling attention to our foolishness, selfishness, inattentiveness. Whether it is the harm we do to one another, the damage we cause to our environment, or the neglect we demonstrate regarding God's dreams for us, all and more must be addressed and responded to.

Most of us see through a mirror dimly. Most of us remain convulsed in a daily busyness that exacerbates our inability to see ourselves and our actions objectively. But, now and then, voices rise out of our rushing schedules to remind us of our spiritual, emotional, moral, or ethical neglect. Listen for those voices today. What do you need to see more clearly? To hear with wisdom? The choice you make in the present will, one way or another, serve the present of tomorrow.

> "Humankind has always realized there is something fearful about the flux of time, a riddle which we cannot solve, and the solution of which we could not stand. We come from a past which is no more; we go into a future which is not yet; ours is the present."
> — Paul Tillich

FRIDAY

For now we see in a mirror, dimly, but then we will see face to face. Now I know only in part; then I will know fully, even as I have been fully known So faith, hope, love abide, these three; but the greatest of these is love.
(I Corinthians 13:12).

With these words, Paul was addressing a rowdy group of new Christians in a wild city called Corinth. More will be said of this later; for now it is enough to know Paul was writing to a church in turmoil. Among the many problems confronting this audience were divisions of ethnicity, class, language and issues of jealousy, bitterness, greed, haughtiness, and immorality.

In the midst of this interpersonal friction and ecclesiastical tension lived a highly dysfunctional spiritual confusion. The motivations at work in their lives and interactions had less to do with a desire to fulfill God's hopes and more to do with small-minded competition. What was true then is equally true now. Such attitudes and actions in both settings stem largely from *personal insecurity*, not social or spiritual superiority.

In fact, Genesis 4 and the classic and highly insightful, but sometimes confusing, story of Cain and Abel recognizes that insecurity and competition potentially serves up a deadly brew of foolishness.[9] We naturally cope by tuning our channels to suit our own needs while tuning out the needs and hopes of others. This was the toxic mix in the Corinthian Church.

The remedy the Bible recommends? We desperately need faith and hope, these indispensable elements of the Christian life. But even more vital is the grace God gives to us and the grace we are expected to share with others: God's love. It is the one remedy that allows us to see, if only briefly through the mist, that God's love lives in us, flows through us.

Just as you exercise to strengthen your muscles and increase your stamina, so also today, exercise your love. In doing so, may

---

[9] See my book, *Subversive Words: Biblical Counterpoints to Conventional Wisdom* for more on this fascinating and important biblical warning concerning the dangers of selfishness, insecurities, and the potential negative dynamics of competition.

you increase your capacity to live in community, expand your ability to share your life fully, and enlarge your circle of deep and meaningful relationships.

> "Living in community is not easy. Sometimes we are able to live together faithfully only when we remember that God is there with us, and that it is God's love that binds us together into the body of Christ."
> — Rueben Job

SATURDAY

Just as the breath you breathe in originates from the same atmosphere as for all humans, so also are we joined in a divine connection. That is why we can say "the ground at the foot of the cross is always level" for all of us.

Relax your mind and body today, and visualize all the possibilities for the upcoming week.

MARCH
Waging Peace

The Romans originally began their year in March. It was the turning of the seasons when the weather became more appropriate for armies to march and for wars to be waged. The ground was beginning to dry, and generals no longer needed to be concerned about troop movements getting bogged down in the mud of winter or eclipsed by the fog of changing temperatures.

Instead of war, let us use the scriptures of our March section to challenge our understandings of how to treat others constructively, gracefully—and biblically. This month, we will explore in depth the biblical basis for hospitality, forgiveness, compassion, and humility.

The First Week:
Malta and Hospitality

After we had reached safety, we then learned that the island was called Malta. The natives showed us unusual kindness. Since it had begun to rain and was cold, they kindled a fire and welcomed all of us around it (Acts 28:1-2).

I had taken a group from our church on what was presciently called "The Fourth Missionary Journey of Paul." The idea was to trace Paul's travels by ship as closely as we could across the Mediterranean in the direction of Rome. Instead of leaving from Caesarea like Paul did, though, we left from Athens. We would travel south, stop at Malta[1], Sicily, Naples, and Rome, and then return to Athens. It didn't occur to us we'd be following Paul's Fourth Missionary Journey almost literally, which was a disaster and involved a shipwreck.

This item was not officially listed in our itinerary, but it should have been. Thankfully, we didn't have a shipwreck. But at one point during our second night onboard, I was fairly ambivalent about death. By three in the morning, I was so sick that dying would have been an improvement. The up and down movement of our ship (smaller apparently than it should have been for traveling that time of year in the Mediterranean) created the feeling of cresting the hill of a roller coaster, with my stomach ending up somewhere in the vicinity of my throat, falling, and then starting over again. This happened repeatedly throughout the night and well through the following day and evening.

I had been so looking forward to the good food of our cruise ship. But climbing the stairs or even getting out of my cabin, caused more nausea and discomfort than I was willing to endure. The thought of food was not relevant, we discovered later, since the kitchen was in shambles—as was the infirmary. You get the picture. So, I found at the beginning of the third day a lovely word that will forever remain close to my heart: "Malta!"

---

[1] Also known in Roman times as Melita, see Acts 28:1-11. Paul's shipwreck near there likely occurred in roughly 60 A.D. Mine almost occurred in 2007.

There it was, just as the sky was clearing and the wind calmed, at first a speck on the horizon. Then slowly, land rose out of the sea, high hills appeared. The waves began to diminish and, finally, we sailed into the vast and impressive harbor of high cliffs, ancient fortresses, palpable history, all gazing down on a deep and natural anchorage well used for international shipping since the earliest of times.

The Phoenicians, Greeks, and Carthaginians controlled this island cluster before the Romans and the time of Paul. During Rome's Punic Wars with Carthage, Malta became a Roman territory and remained so throughout the New Testament, Early Church, and Byzantine periods. The Arabs came in 870 A.D.; the Normans of Sicily threw out the Arabs in 1090 A.D.; and as the nastiness of the crusades was giving way to the Renaissance and the Reformation in 1530, Charles V of the Holy Roman Empire passed Malta over to the Knights Hospitalers. Also known as The Knights of Malta, these soldier remnants of the crusades built enormous fortifications to defend the island against the strong and expanding powers of the Ottoman Turks. As the name of these knights indicates, they ran a hospital on Malta that was second to none in all of Europe.

Malta, for us, turned out to be beautiful, fascinating, and exceedingly hospitable.

> Lord, help us to be hospitable people. We sometimes lean in the direction of suspicion. Allow us wisdom to see the hearts of our brothers and sisters on this earth and understand. May compassion outweigh circumspection. Let our trust not be foolhardy, but a reasonable and holy attempt to emulate your concern for all the families of the earth. Strengthen our ability to welcome the stranger in our midst. And let us recognize in each other your spirit of grace and truth. Amen.

REFLECTIONS FOR THE WEEK

MONDAY

Let love be genuine; hate what is evil, hold fast to what is good (Romans 12:9).

Today, consider what it means to be genuine in love. The people of Malta seemed to have discovered an authenticity in their hospitality. Authentic, or genuine, love—love of others with no preconditions or expectations—is truly a tall order. And yet, as we become more familiar with the scriptures, we begin to hear this type of expectation consistently: "Let love be genuine." Love another person for who they are, not what they can do for you.

Archbishop Desmond Tutu of South Africa speaks about "ubuntu," a word people of southern Africa use to describe the deep interconnectedness of human life.[2] The concept in that culture pulsates with this biblical ideal: one cannot be fully human without being in relationships. The result, he says, is an abiding genuineness in love, authentic hospitality, nurturing kindness, and deep, interconnected, authentic relationships. Try today to be as authentically loving as you can and see what happens.

> "I am what I am because of who we are."
> — Archbishop Desmond Tutu

TUESDAY

Love one another with mutual affection (Romans 12:10a).

"Loving one another with mutual affection" doesn't come naturally. Yet, as with genuine love, this biblical mandate must be tried to be fully understood. And to be aware and accepting of God's love for us is the best starting point. This was certainly the

---

[2] From the Bantu family of languages of which Zulu and Xhosa are a part. Pronounced "oo-boon-too."

case for the early church. The power of God's love in the life of individuals propelled this vast and transforming movement of everyday people. They gave themselves to the cause of Christ because they felt completely loved and accepted by God. And it was and is from this beginning that we can proceed to love one another—because this is the way God loves us. Let it be so for you today: to love and be loved with mutual affection.

WEDNESDAY

Outdo one another in showing honor (Romans 12:10b).

Honor is such a strong, mysterious, heavy word. And, over the centuries, the concept of honor has done considerable damage. "Honor killings" as the result of blood feuds come to mind. On the other hand, the biblical idea of honor is filled with richness and is intimately combined with blessing. I honor you when I bless you; I bless you when I honor you. I lift you up, hold you in high esteem, give you gifts, offer you praise. This is more than about just another person. The scripture is concerned with a lifestyle that competes in the arena of grace, goodness, righteousness, hope, faith, and love. So, today, how about a little competition? Outdo (with no fanfare, please) another in showing honor. And meditate on the following quote by E.B. White: "I arrive in the morning torn between a desire to improve (or *save*) the world and the desire to enjoy (or *savor*) the world. That makes it hard to plan the day."

All we can do is the best we can do. Give today your best, and that will be enough.

THURSDAY

Do not lag in zeal, be ardent in spirit, serve the Lord (Romans 12:11).

Despite invasions, bombings[3], and its consistently vulnerable island position, Malta has remained true to its biblical legacy of

---

[3] During the early years of WWII, German and Italian planes bombed Malta mercilessly, since it served as a vital lifeline for British and Allied ships in the Mediterranean.

hospitality. From the welcome and assistance to the Apostle Paul in Acts 28, to the generous care for the sick and wounded at the hospital of Malta under the Knights Hospitalers, along with the generous and glad welcome I and my weary band of travelers received a few years ago, this continues to be a land of compassion and kind hospitality to the stranger.

Consider how you might serve the Lord today. The word "ardent" above simply means "passionate." What might you do to display your passion for a cause or concern about an issue or compassion for a particular group. During the cold months here in Charlotte, a large group of people from our church welcomes a group of homeless men to our Mission Center. Every Saturday night, this dedicated gathering serves the Lord with a passion for these new friends who happen to be without a place to live for the time being. How might you be passionate about serving God by serving others? In what new ways might you become hospitable? As you take your walk or exercise in some way later today, reflect upon what you did and how you did it. And remember Paul's experience on Malta.

FRIDAY

Rejoice in hope, be patient in suffering, persevere in prayer (Romans 12:12).

Let us take the middle phrase as our starting point for today: "be patient in suffering..." To be patient is one thing. But to suffer and be patient in that suffering is quite another. These are hard words, particularly in our society. "Stand up for yourself," "don't let anyone push you around;" "I'm not going to take that lying down!" These are the more familiar catch phrases of our day, just as they were in Paul's day. The first century was steeped in plenty of this same kind of bravado and self-preservation. There is nothing new under the sun.

But this patience in suffering rested upon a theological perspective: God is with us in profound ways in the midst of our suffering: "Because he himself was tested by what he suffered, he is able to help those who are being tested" (Hebrews 2:18).

Whatever your situation today and the rest of this week, know that you are not alone! And offer others support as you accept support from others.

SATURDAY

Contribute to the needs of the saints; extend hospitality to strangers (Romans 12:9-13).

Hear again the words of Paul from earlier in the week and our reminders of Paul on an island after a storm: "the natives showed us unusual kindness…" Now enjoy this Saturday. It is the perfect day to share hospitality.

The Second Week:
Forgiveness and Transformation

Then Jesus said: "Father, forgive them, for they do not know what they are doing" (Luke 23:34).

His given name was Patricius. Born into a wealthy Roman family in Londinium[4], he was kidnapped by pirates and taken to the dark and distant island the Romans knew as Hibernia. He was sold into slavery, made to work as a shepherd, and kept in isolation. In a foreign land and too young to have really been schooled in learning or faith, he was completely alone and left to his own devices. Except, so the story goes, God guided him one day to begin walking to the east.

After numerous adventures, Patricius, now probably a teenager, arrived at a port city and met a sympathetic trader who eventually returned him to his homeland. His family rejoiced and welcomed him home, only to be newly disconcerted. They heard him speak of strange things—a calling for what he would view as the inspiration for his rescue and something even more radical. He now felt he was being called to return to the land of his enslavement to preach the gospel of Jesus Christ—a gospel of healing, reconciliation, and love.

Important training in reading, writing, and the basics of the Christian faith made up for the education Patricius had never received as a child. But now he shocked and disappointed his family: Patricius returned to the very land of his slavery and began to preach to the kings and tribal leaders who had persecuted him for so many years when he was a boy.

Today, we know Patricius as St. Patrick, and the dark island of Hibernia we know as Ireland. St. Patrick's ministry changed the history of a divided, warring land. His followers became missionaries who carried the message of God to Scotland, Wales, England, and the rest of Europe at the very time when faith was

---

[4] Londinium was the largest city in the Roman province of Britannia, controlled by Rome from 43 A.D. to 410 A.D. London, England, is the modern descendant of this ancient city.

on the verge of being lost under wave after wave of barbarian invasions from the 400s to the 700s A.D.

Thomas Cahill, in his book *How the Irish Saved Civilization*, tells this remarkable story of St. Patrick and his ability to hear God's call with clarity. There were so many perfectly good excuses for not returning to the land that had persecuted him. His family couldn't understand why he wouldn't simply stay with them and rejoin the aristocratic life he had been so tragically ripped from. But the power of God's reconciling hope and the pull of God's redeeming grace changed Patricius, as it can change us. For those willing to hear God's sometimes discomforting, sometimes confusing call, to forgive in the face of hatred, to reconcile in the throws of hostility, to trust against the odds in the holy, risky love of God, the rewards can be transformative.

You may need to take a risk this week. Let God use you to make a difference. Listen, respond, and live in the hopes and dreams of God for positive change in you and those around you.

> You have forgiven us of much, O God. To us, your grace is a merciful gift. Now, let us recognize our responsibility. Like with St. Patrick, give us the strength to offer the same grace and forgiveness to others that you have given to us. Help us to cut through the petty and sometimes vicious cycles of anger. Transform our hearts; renew our minds; and give us strength to forgive others this week with your magnificent grace. Amen.

REFLECTIONS FOR THE WEEK

MONDAY

Then Jesus said: "Father, forgive them, for they do not know what they are doing" (Luke 23:34).

I was in seminary back in 1984 when the people of South Africa still suffered terribly at the hands of the white-run Apartheid regime under then-president Pieta Botha. There was much discussion about what would happen there and how, if ever, the terrible situation would be resolved. At the time, I had a friend from there, a white South African who hated what South Africa had become, was sympathetic to the plight of black South Africans, and wanted very much for there to be justice in the land. Yet he was pessimistic that change would ever come. I'll never forget what he told me in those days: "David, you must understand, there are weapons, incredible numbers and of all types, stockpiled in caves, homes, businesses ... If the blacks of South Africa attempt to take power in my country, I tell you, there will be a blood bath as you have never seen. So change, it will not happen, Apartheid will not be dismantled. Whites will hold power no matter what it takes."

Six years later, on February 11, 1990, Nelson Mandela walked out of the Victor Verster Prison a free man. Imprisoned, often in isolation, for more than twenty-seven years, his release signaled a new day in South Africa. Then an even more amazing thing happened. Thanks in part to enormous world pressure and disinvestment in the South African economy but mainly thanks to the immense courage, tireless work, deep prayer, and persistent commitment to peace and justice from regular people and from leaders like Nelson Mandela, Archbishop Desmond Tutu, and the white South African leader, F. W. de Klerk, the blood bath predicted never happened.

The fear of violence and widespread chaos reflected in my friend's perspective materialized in only isolated cases and among surprisingly few communities. On April 27, 1994, Nelson Mandela was elected president of the country of South Africa and, on May 10, 1994, he was sworn in. This stands as but one example of the power of people working for justice, committed to peace, and holding fast to the transforming power of God's love, one so strong that even enemies are caught up in its redemptive web of grace and forgiveness.

The world continues to need forgiveness, for loving those who once were enemies. Nevertheless, the peaceful transition of governmental power in South Africa was nothing less than miraculous. Desmond Tutu still contends this transition only occurred because of deep faith, ardent prayer, and ongoing forgiveness.

Consider today who in your life needs forgiveness and what you need to do to forgive them.

> "To white-capped waters of rage, forgiveness whispers, 'Peace, be still.'"
> — Randall O'Brien

TUESDAY

Then Jesus said: "Father, forgive them, for they do not know what they are doing" (Luke 23:34).

We are not leaders of a large country, nor, thankfully, are we part of a society on the verge of widespread violence. But we can control the influence we have in our personal lives and the relationships that surround us. Our circle of influence, and that which influences us, ripples through a strategic community that overlaps with others and constitutes a far larger effect than we might think. Facebook and other internet technologies offer only a glimpse of this web of influence and power.

Archbishop Desmond Tutu declared the new beginning in South Africa successful because of the power of praying people, faithful churches, and the grace of God. Committed, interconnected communities made the difference. People united to bring about peaceful change.

You have more power than you might imagine. Who knows what change might occur by your wisdom, humility, courage, and forgiveness. Now comes perhaps the more difficult part of Jesus' teaching: there is someone in your life who needs to forgive you for something. Meditate for a moment on who and why.

> "We may not be able to will forgiveness, but we certainly can will the steps that lead to forgiveness."
> — Randall O'Brien

WEDNESDAY

Then Jesus said: "Father, forgive them, for they do not know what they are doing" (Luke 23:34).

There are many gray areas when it comes to giving and receiving forgiveness, and the task of forgiving and being forgiven is rarely simple or easy. But there is always hope and wisdom available beyond ourselves. George MacLeod, Scottish soldier and clergyman, wise Christian, teacher, preacher, poet, and founder of the Iona Community in Scotland, once offered these words of wisdom:

THE GLORY IN THE GREY
Almighty God...
Sun behind all suns,
Soul behind all souls...
Show to us in everything we touch
And in everyone we meet
The continued assurance of thy presence round us,
Lest ever we should thee absent.
In all created thing thou art there.
In every friend we have
The sunshine of thy presence is shown forth.
In every enemy that seems to cross our path,
Thou art there within the cloud to challenge us to love.
Show to us the glory in the grey.
Awake for us thy presence in the very storm

Till all our joys are seen as thee
And all our trivial tasks emerge as priestly sacraments
In the universal temple of thy love.

Today, and the rest of this week, may you find "glory in the grey." Try to see past those debilitating seasons of bitterness, anger, even hatred—and those times of indecision and insecurity. Find God's presence in the midst of these storms and "...emerge as priestly sacraments / In the universal temple of thy love."

This evening, exercise before or after a light and healthy dinner; allow your beating heart, invigorated muscles, and God's broader wisdom to surprise you with new insight and better perspective for tomorrow.

> "If God were not willing to forgive sin, heaven would be empty."
> — Randall O'Brien

THURSDAY

Then Jesus said: "Father, forgive them, for they do not know what they are doing" (Luke 23:34).

Forgiveness is easier for some than others. I've known people who insisted what someone else did or didn't do constituted a violation of their freedom, control. There's no question our call to forgive is rarely easy, but keep in mind Jesus speaks these words as he hangs from a cross. His call for divine forgiveness is in the depths of his humanity and at the peak of his pain.

Crucifixion was state-sponsored terrorism. The Persians invented it; Alexander the Great improved it; Rome perfected it. The whole point was to postpone death while inflicting maximum suffering. It was both horribly personal and horrifically public. A criminal or subversive was raised high before the gathered community. Offering utmost agony, often accompanied by others similarly convicted, crucifixion was an ideal punishment for the alleged perpetrator and his supposed system of support. It sent the powerful message of Rome's authoritative control; it squelched any desire to foster further discontent.

In Jesus' case, the religious leaders played a crucial role in his suffering and death. And even his followers were unable or unwilling to stand with him in his time of trial—they were asleep in the garden, absent at the cross, disconsolate at the end, disbelieving of a future. His entire community collapsed before his eyes. And yet, despite the potential combined weight of multiple disillusionments, intense cruelty, and blatant betrayal, Jesus prayed for their forgiveness. And so must we.

Give some quiet meditation to the dynamics of Jesus' death and the depths of Jesus' forgiveness. Remember interactions from your week so far and look for ways to continue and improve your ability to forgive.

FRIDAY

Again from the words of George MacLeod:
> In every friend we have
> The sunshine of thy presence is shown forth.
> In every enemy that seems to cross our path,
> Thou art there within the cloud to challenge us to love.
> Show to us the glory in the grey.

Contemplate the words above. What have you learned this week about your own "enemies." What cloud has passed over you? Where in that cloud is God's presence? Challenge yourself to understand selfless love and see "the glory."

> "We cannot be born anew if the power of the old is not broken within us; and it is not broken so long as it puts the burden of guilt upon us. Therefore, religion, prophetic as well as apostolic, pronounces, above all, forgiveness. Forgiveness means that the old is thrown into the past because the new has come."
> —Paul Tillich

SATURDAY

Continue your contemplation on MacLeod's words:
> Awake for us thy presence in the very storm
> Till all our joys are seen as thee
> And all our trivial tasks emerge as priestly sacraments
> In the universal temple of thy love.

In some way during your day today, enjoy the good and resonating truth of God's presence in whatever storms arise. Even in your most trivial tasks—those potentially mundane pieces of life and work that too easily are cast off as extraneous—let God's light shine; let them be transformed so they "emerge as priestly sacraments in the universal temple" of God's love. Today, reflect on your efforts this past week and be aware: is there any joy or wonder awakening in you?

THE THIRD WEEK:
The Holy Grail and Compassion

To them God chose to make known how great among the Gentiles are the riches of the glory of this mystery, which is Christ in you, the hope of glory (Colossians 1:26-27).

Christ. Is. In. You.

In *The Da Vinci Code,* Dan Brown played with a creative idea that captivated much of the English-speaking world. His adaptation of myth in his novel, which became a film of the same name, made him millions. Brown's plot dealt with an earlier assertion, later debunked, that Jesus and Mary Magdalene had a child hidden away from church authorities in southern France. The descendants of this alleged relationship were part of the Merovingian French royalty whose genetic line was alive and well in the conveniently lovely, intelligent central character, Sophia. She was the grail, the living embodiment of Jesus' DNA, according to Brown. But this was not what the Bible or later authors had in mind. Nor was it even close to what we think to be the first mention of a grail.

In fact, there is no such thing in the Bible. The phrase is never used. The original idea for the grail and the quest to find it began with Chretien de Troyes and his *The Story of the Grail*, also known as *Perceval*. Written sometime between 1180 and 1190 A.D., this medieval story weaves a romantic saga of Perceval's quest to become both a knight and a disciple of Jesus.

For Chretien, these concepts were inseparable. To become a knight necessitated a genuine and humble faith. One had to constantly move in the direction of discipleship, humility, kindness, and compassion. The twists and turns of Perceval's journey echo the foibles, inconsistencies, misunderstandings, and gradual wisdom that ought to be part of all our lives. The grail plays only a metaphorical role, serving as simply a way to convey a parallel in the human experience.[5] Perceval starts out knowing nothing about knights and their weapons, God and spirituality,

---

[5] Professor Monica Brzezinski Potkay, The College of William and Mary, in her lecture series *The Eternal Chalice: The Grail in Literature and Legend.*

or how to interpret what he sees and hears in relation to what is sacred. The story chronicles his quest for deeper faith and selfless, knightly devotion. His growth results from authentic humility and admirable inquisitiveness.

In Chretien's story, Perceval finally becomes a highly respected member of King Arthur's court and a true follower of Christ. He ultimately learns the essentials to loving God and neighbor, the basic tenants of the Christian life. And the grail, this container in the story, serves as a metaphorical vessel, a symbol for our own bodies, our own call to be the containers of Christ's spirit. We are the vessels of God's blessing, not to be held for our own benefit but to pass on what God has so generously given. This was Chretien's message.

And so it is with Paul's message in Colossians: "the mystery that has been hidden throughout the ages ... the riches of the glory of this mystery, which is Christ in you, the hope of glory" (Colossians 1:26-27). May you live this week in full knowledge that you are not on your own. There is something in you fully sufficient and more than you need. You are the holy vessel of Christ. Live, then, with reverence. Be humble and compassionate. And pass on the blessing.

> Let us, in true reverence, claim this awesome gift, O God: that your presence is alive and well in us in the spirit of Christ. This is sufficient for all that we need and all that we can ever hope. Allow us to relax in this great truth, and to know that all is well and all shall be well, not because of our own sufficiency, but because Christ is in us this day and every day. That is enough. Amen.

REFLECTIONS FOR THE WEEK

MONDAY

...Christ in you... (Colossians 1:27).

From our devotion in week two, we are reminded of God's transforming power in the lives of everyday people. St. Patrick, or Patricius, was an ordinary person thrust into tragic circumstances. His response could have been bitterness. Instead, he discovered the life-changing power of a Christ-centered life. And his personal transformation motivated the remarkable return to the land of his slavery, to the very people who had so mistreated him. And he, through the love of Christ in him, shared the truth of God's love. As a result, *his* transformation resulted in *their* transformation.

So, from the deep spirituality and mystic beauty of Celtic Christianity, let these words from an Irish poem go with you through this day as an emphatic reminder:

> **Breastplate of St. Patrick**
> Christ with me, Christ before me, Christ behind me,
> Christ in me, Christ beneath me, Christ above me,
> Christ on my right, Christ on my left,
> Christ where I lie, Christ where I sit, Christ where I arise,
> Christ in the heart of everyone who thinks of me,
> Christ in the mouth of everyone who speaks of me,
> Christ in every eye that sees me,
> Christ in every ear that hears me.[6]

Notice today if there is any difference in the way you greet, interact with, and react to others. Christ is in you. And that makes all the difference.

> "The true miracle is that I want to love others the way I am loved. Christ is contagious."
> — Randall O'Brien

---

[6] "Breastplate Prayer of St. Patrick" as quoted in Richard J. Foster's *Prayers from the Heart*, p. 84. Adapted from "every man" to "everyone."

TUESDAY

...Christ in you, the hope of glory (Colossians 1:27).

The quest for the Holy Grail is now complete, the mystery solved. You are the container of God's great gift. The ancient hope for a Messiah is fulfilled, but not only in the coming of Jesus. The word *Messiah* is a Hebrew word which simply means "God's anointed." The word *Christ* is a Greek word that means the same thing. So, when the Bible talks about the resurrected Jesus being alive in you and me, and of Christ being "in you, the hope of glory," this is a proclamation of radical importance. Before Jesus, the idea was for the anointed of God to do away with poverty, exclusion, war, disease, famine, etc. Jesus has come, yet clearly these things continue.

Many would contend, then, the simple assertion that Jesus was not the Messiah. And the point is a good one—unless we can understand what the early church came to realize and Paul began to teach: Jesus' earthly life spoke, taught, and lived the necessity of a community of faithful to carry out the preaching, teaching, healing, and loving that he began. His resurrection underlined the imperative and transferred responsibility to us. The mission of "healing the world"—as our Jewish brothers and sisters call it—is to be done as "little Christs" (the literal meaning of "Christian"). It is Christ's ongoing ministry of compassion and transformation in us and through us that has, does, and will offer ongoing, positive, and sacred change to the world.

Today, there is a job that needs to be done, and you are called to do it. Christ is in you. Go then; touch lives. Be passionate about Christ's presence in your life. Be *compassionate*.

WEDNESDAY

Christ with me, Christ before me, Christ behind me...
(Breastplate of St. Patrick).

We enjoy a special place in history, living in these times that continue to confound expectations: ever-new technologies, insights into ancient mysteries, discoveries unimaginable only a few decades ago. New possibilities emerge every day that lift hope for an end to a dreaded disease, or offer an alternative energy source, or provide new perspectives on technological advancements. An astounding array of options rises before us. More than ever before, it seems, we deal with massive change. As Heraclitus said long ago, "Nothing endures but change."

And there's financial uncertainty; increased concern about the environment, widening divisions between rich and poor; even the way we view life and faith, moving from "modern" to "post-modern" to now, what sociologists like Peter Berger are calling, "pluralistic"[7]—none of this particularly bodes well for an optimistic world view.

While we experience sweeping shifts in the way life works and how people interact, the old adage is still true: "The more things change, the more they stay the same." In spite of monumental change, we are no less susceptible to the consequences now than were our spiritual ancestors in the early church and the manifold adversities they faced. It was in such circumstances that they spoke truth to power, gave of themselves freely, shared resources generously, and cared for each other compassionately. We will explore this further tomorrow. For today, breathe deeply and remember how to be compassionate.

> "Our culture says that ruthless competition is the key to success. Jesus says that ruthless compassion is the purpose of our journey."
> — Brennan Manning

THURSDAY

...Christ in me, Christ beneath me, Christ above me...
(Breastplate of St. Patrick).

The New Testament book of Revelation is hard to read; it is also hard to teach. Sadly, it is probably the most overused

---
[7] See Peter Berger's book, *In Praise of Doubt.*

and misunderstood book of the Bible. We have no time or space to deal with fascinating truths that lie beneath the multitude of misinterpreted passages. Misconstrued by some ill-informed preachers and teachers, it continues to be misused to map out some kind of secretly coded scenario for the end of the world. This is not and never was the case.

What *is* the case stands in clear evidence: the church in the Roman Empire suffered under the tyrannical and increasingly paranoid reign of Domitian, Caesar of the Empire. At the time John wrote Revelation, the churches he loved and who knew him well were coming under increasing pressure to heed the demands of Rome and acknowledge Domitian as *dominus et deus*—"Lord and God."

The faithful faced a daunting choice: give in to the imperial command and be unfaithful to God and the Christian stance or refuse the command and risk, at least at first, crippling economic consequences. No one wanted to shop at a store whose owner appeared to be of questionable patriotism to the emperor and loyalty to the empire.

Yet John's repeated image throughout his grand work of apocalyptic literature provides a rallying cry for then and now: *Christ is in the midst of us.*[8] And earlier, from Paul, there is "nothing else in all creation that can separate us from the love of God that is in Christ Jesus our Lord" (Romans 8:39).

Claim this truth today. *Christ is in you.*

> "Compassion is expressed in gentleness."
> — John E. Biersdorf

---

[8] See Revelation 5:6; 14:1;19:11-21; also, what I think is one of the most misunderstood passages in Revelation, 14:17-20 refers to the "great wine press of the wrath of God." But closer investigation into John's imagery just might indicate *not* the gory death scene often depicted but the *opposite*. The "blood flowed from the wine press, as high as a horse's bridle, for a distance of about two hundred miles," might well, in fact, be one of the most redemptive and healing communion images in the Bible.

FRIDAY

Today, be reminded of the Celtic perspective from earlier:

> Christ with me, Christ before me, Christ behind me,
> Christ in me, Christ beneath me, Christ above me,
> Christ on my right, Christ on my left,
> Christ where I lie, Christ where I sit, Christ where I arise...

You are surrounded. In every good way, and with every good reason, you have available a resonate strength for good and compassion. For it is not you alone, but Christ in you, with you, before you, and all around you. So, may the truth of this presence in your life offer an entirely new perspective this day.

> "O Lord, I called you and longed to enjoy you, and I am prepared to give up everything for you. Let my mouth, my soul and all creation praise and bless you. Amen."
> — Thomas Kempis

SATURDAY

You are the container of God's hope for the world. In and through you and me, God's work can and must be done. If we fail, there are other vessels of God's goodness and blessing. But what a privilege to be the ones to carry out God's sacred mission of blessing others and of being blessed ourselves in the process, through and with their blessing. So today, gladly interact with those who cross your path. And may there be:

> Christ in the heart of everyone who thinks of me,
> Christ in the mouth of everyone who speaks of me,
> Christ in every eye that sees me,
> Christ in every ear that hears me.

May this sacred reality allow you to be compassionate. For Christ is in you—this day and every day.

The Fourth Week:
Lessons in Humility

Blessed are the meek, for they shall inherit the earth (Matthew 5:5).

Ulrich Zwingli (1484-1531) led the Swiss Reformation during the period we know today as the "Protestant Reformation."[9] This reformation occurred in a parallel universe to Martin Luther's Reformation in the German states. Zwingli and Luther were concerned about many of the same things; they preached, taught, and wrote very similar proclamations; they were equally adamant about the abuses, materialism, and increased secularism in the Roman Catholic Church of that time. They were passionate about the same Gospel, preached in the same language, used the same Bible, and inspired similar crowds to their respective movements. Ironically, they couldn't stand each other.[10]

Zwingli had numerous positive traits, not least of which was the power of his voice and vast import in translating the Bible into German, the first of its kind—even before Luther. This translation widely influenced the creation of a new sense of Swiss identity: the people could finally hear the Gospel in the language of the people, the language they spoke. Remember, masses were conducted in Latin, the official language of the church at the time.

Zwingli was a Swiss patriot and proud "protester" (thus the term would later become "Protestant"). He was a student of Erasmus, a spiritual and strident, even cynical, Dutch humanist.[11]

---

[9] Zwingli's Swiss Reformed church would ultimately serve, with Calvin's work in Geneva some years later, to form the basis of the Reformed theology of today's Presbyterian and Reformed churches.

[10] They both had exceedingly large egos. Sadly, a similar dynamic exists today with big name, outspoken preachers (and politicians). Oversized egos tend to get in the way of humble service and kind cooperation more than we would like to admit.

[11] Erasmus wrote *In Praise of Folly*, a lighthearted but stinging rebuke of the Catholic Church and its abuses, pettiness, and poor theology.

He learned well and adopted a similar tenacious wit and insight; however, he also had a zeal that would come to haunt him—his tunnel vision and passion for the Gospel done his way and no other (yet another ironic parallel to Martin Luther). And his love of the Swiss way of life also created in him an inability to see beyond his own reforms. He was a patriot, an early Protestant, and a preacher so passionate that, eventually, his cause would *cause* more harm than good.

> Lord, help me to learn humility this week. Allow me to see in others the face of Jesus, and to treat them as I would treat him. Give me patience, endurance, kindness—but keep before me—and in me—a humble spirit. Amen.

REFLECTIONS FOR THE WEEK

MONDAY

When pride comes, then comes disgrace, but with humility comes wisdom (Proverbs 11:2).

Protesters sympathetic to the kinds of faith issues Zwingli espoused became convinced faith should be proclaimed openly by consenting adults through public baptism by immersion. This was simply an imitation of Jesus' baptism in the Jordan River by John the Baptist. But, because of this theological stance, this group (derisively called Anabaptists, or "baptized again") was actively persecuted. To Zwingli and others, a civil society could not allow individuals to believe whatever they chose just because their conscience dictated it; that would create chaos, and the church and civil society could *lose power*.

Thus began a tragic century of persecution of believers looking for what the first American Baptist, Roger Williams, called "soul liberty." These Anabaptists continue today as Mennonites and in some branches of the larger Anabaptist family. Though not traceable to these first protesters, the first Baptists in Holland and England were, through theological "cross pollination," profoundly influenced by Anabaptist thought and theology.

Today, consider what it means to be humble. There are many who will tell you what to believe and why, sometimes loudly. Humility, though, is quiet. What you believe should be a gently growing sense of presence, love, wonder, gratitude—and increased inquisitiveness. Biblically, it is clear our spiritual journeys must be woven with a humble sense that God is at work in us—and in others. Live today with that perspective in mind.

TUESDAY

Blessed are the meek... (Matthew 5:5).

The Anabaptists had no power; they were regular people. And because of Zwingli's leadership and the desire of city fathers to maintain control of civic and religious affairs, the Anabaptists were labeled subversives. They were run out of Zurich following a horrible parody of their courageous stance. In March, 1526, four Swiss Anabaptists were given the choice to recant their belief in adult baptism. When they refused, stones were tied around their feet, and they were thrown into the river while people watched. The waters of this river are clear, so their tragic deaths were plainly visible. Yet their testimony still speaks to the invaluable truths of conscience, soul liberty, and a humble faith in God.

Today, live bravely—and with a similar humble faith.

> "I am certain of nothing but the holiness of the Heart's affections and the truth of Imagination."
> — John Keats

WEDNESDAY

...with humility comes wisdom (Proverbs 11:2).

Humiliation has often been part of the oppressor's strategy. To humiliate is to demonstrate control, to exert power and break down the psyche of the oppressed. The soldiers who mocked Jesus tried to humiliate him. But Jesus, with silence and dignity, remained true to his cause and firm in his resolve. So too did Martin Luther King, Ghandi, Mandela, the Anabaptists, and all who have believed that to live with humility was and is a vital part of God's hope for us and our peaceful co-existence.

This is *our* call, too: to live with kindness, gentleness, tenderness, and honest recognition that Christ is present, alive and well in our brothers and sisters, just as Christ is alive in us.

Today, find a way to demonstrate to others a genuine sense of *humility*—because you have a sense of Christ in others.

THURSDAY

When pride comes, then comes disgrace... (Proverbs 11:2).

Consider the faithful persistence of the Anabaptists and their clear, courageous understanding of biblical faith in the face of persecution and hardship. The threats they endured are hard to imagine today. The lesson might simply entail profound gratitude for those who have gone before and paved the ways of faith and freedom.

What in your life is worth the ultimate risk? What priorities are non-negotiable? In this lies the very real tension between passion and humility. One is occasionally necessary. The other is always called for. The first can easily turn into an ego trip. The other can certainly display personal enthusiasm but leans often in the direction of others and gladness on their behalf.

Do not be afraid to be passionate, as long as it is positive, life-giving, helpful, hopeful, in the name of justice and on behalf of others. But be on guard! In general, it is better to be humble. Today, strive to be glad for others. Enjoy laughter with, not at.

> "Lord! Give me courage and love to open the door and constrain you to enter, whatever the disguise ... even before I fully recognize my guest. Come in! Enter my small life! Lay Your sacred hands on all the common things and small interests of that life and bless and change them. Transfigure my small resources, make them sacred. And in them give me Your very Self. Amen."
> — Evelyn Underhill

FRIDAY

Blessed are the meek ... (Matthew 5:5).

Inordinate zeal about anything can create inordinate problems with everything. Such was the case with Zwingli and his followers in Zurich. His initial intentions were good, valuable, transformative. His broad scholarship, sharp intellect, articulate words, and cutting wit profoundly influenced the Swiss population and beyond. But fed by a large dose of ego and a broad slice of unchecked patriotism, his influence (like Martin Luther) led to widespread persecution, horrific torture, and mindless violence that would haunt the European landscape for centuries. Sadly, there are similar examples of unchecked emotions in influential people who propagate an ideology or a faith misused, misplaced, and inappropriate to the gospel of Jesus and humility.

Now consider the ways of Jesus and his words about who is blessed. It is not the brash, loudly insistent, authoritative, and cruel. Rather, *blessed are the meek.*

Take time today to be thankful—for those who have gone before and for those whose journeys we share in the present.

> "When I first encountered scripture, I had too much conceit to appreciate its simplicity, and not enough insight to penetrate its depths."
> — St. Augustine of Hippo

SATURDAY

It's that time of year when the basketball season moves toward conclusion and I am reminded of the years I had the pleasure of coaching teams for both my son, and then later my daughters and others from our church. I composed the following while contemplating my own basketball career and the sweet sound and feel of that winning shot:

A SWISH

Such music sounds as a ball
falls to earth
through knotted chords
and scores,
untouched by rim or board.
The ball feels only strings
and sings:
a quiet, intoxicating sound,
a whispered affirmation of skill
to thrill.

A ball launched
from fingers outstretched
arcs across empty space,
an ace flying through air
spinning and pausing
in glad destination
a proclamation
proud with rippled net,
in consummated wish:
a swish.

Today, enjoy the world around you, relax and be a good friend, and try a little tenderness.

APRIL
Resurrection

T. S. Elliot once called April the "cruelest month"—perhaps because in April we flirt with beauty and the opening of spring, yet we still have grey, cold days that pull us back into the grip of late winter. The Greeks and Romans likely had a sense of this, too. April was named after the goddess of love, Aphrodite (the Romans had the same idea but, for them, Aphrodite was called Venus). As we all know, romantic love can be a beautiful thing but can, at times, also leave us cold, left to wonder what went wrong and if things will ever be right again.

April moves us inexorably toward summer, greeting us with budding plants and spring green yet, even in North Carolina, leaving us always with the possibility of frost, cold, and disappointment. In April, we learn to live with the tension of the now, the expectation and endurance, disappointment and hope, death and resurrection.

THE FIRST WEEK:
Honest Appraisals

...As for me, my feet had almost stumbled; my steps had nearly slipped. For I was envious of the arrogant; I saw the prosperity of the wicked. For they have no pain; their bodies are sound and sleek ... when I thought how to understand this, it seemed to me a wearisome task, until I went into the sanctuary of God... (Psalm 73:1-4; 16-17b).

Confession is good for the soul. Here, right in the middle of our Bible, is a voice of compelling honesty and eternal relevance. The words remind us of a pulsating world of tempting possibilities and "sleek bodies." It is as if the psalmist is watching one of our modern, sensual commercials.

Everywhere we turn, there are good-looking models driving, swimming, drinking, and using whatever the marketers want us to believe will make our lives meaningful. If we purchase what they are peddling, our existence will be complete. If only.

But with biblical wisdom comes complete honesty. As the writer of the above scripture testifies: "my steps nearly slipped" (73:2). He, like us, was gravely tempted to believe that the kind of lifestyle he witnessed in these manufactured scenes of contentment and artificial constructs of easy living represented reality. The lovely faces and happy smiles came close to tricking him into believing that what he saw constituted an attainable goal he (and we) somehow deserved.

The billions of dollars Madison Avenue marketers spend to study how we think and what makes us respond positively to manipulative stimuli has been, for them, money well spent. But Psalm 73 awakens us again to the truth: there is more to a meaningful life than the inauthentic constructs of media campaigns. Nor is it necessary for us to look at others with envy. Instead, there is a time-tested remedy—and a saving grace for the psalmist almost taken in by the seductive world of the rich and famous.

"...I went to the sanctuary of God..." (73:17). He doesn't say what he did there. His awakened perspective comes, according to the psalm, by simply being there, in the presence of others struggling with similar circumstances, real insufficiencies, understandable anxieties, and natural uncertainties. Perhaps it was the very nature of this community of fellow strugglers, this place of refreshing truth that brought *insight* back to his sight.

Too often, what we see is not what we get. And what we want is not even close to what we need. Like the psalmist, going to church and being with others in a shared space of honesty and open appraisal is a redemptive opportunity that returns us to ourselves and realigns us with what is holy. Probably, this is why Luke makes certain we remember this about Jesus: "...he went to the synagogue on the Sabbath day, as was his custom..." (Luke 4:16). If it was good enough for the psalmist—and for Jesus—it is for us. Let us go to church and, in doing so, bring with our presence an openness to truth and an honesty about our condition that results in new perspectives on reality and commitment to truth.

> Give me the great gift of honesty this week, O God. Help me to recognize truth when I see and experience it—in myself and in what I encounter. Allow me to discern in myself, those things that need to be confessed, addressed, and changed. And give me the courage to admit my own shortcomings, and to refrain from envying—or blaming—others. Amen.

REFLECTIONS FOR THE WEEK

MONDAY

...As for me, my feet had almost stumbled; my steps had nearly slipped (Psalm 73:2).

April is a month for resurrection. We commemorate it at Easter, and we see it as the world around us returns to productivity and opens again to green. We continue to hope for it in our personal recognition of incompleteness. In her poem found in March, 2012, of *The Christian Century*, Bonnie Thurston says it well:

Broken Best

From where I sit
I see the celebrant's feet,
Black cap-toed brogues,
Dress shoes carefully shined,
Their ancient leather
Creased and cracked.

We bring who we are,
Our carefully cared for,
Often broken best.

He gives what He has,
Wine from broken feet
Which I would wash
With grateful tears,
Polish with my wild,
Unfettered hair.

Today, what is it that you offer? Consider the gift of who you are and what God has made you. Offer the best of yourself—to family, friends, colleagues, your job. If you feel broken, weary, discouraged, incapable, or unworthy, there is "wine from broken feet," a redeeming cross—for you—from Jesus.

TUESDAY

I was envious of the arrogant... (Psalm 73:3a).

The writer of this psalm is brutally honest. Telling the truth about one's envy of others takes courage. So does telling the truth about other feelings, especially when we are struggling with something as complex and potentially overwhelming as deep sadness or depression. Yet, just as confession is good for the soul, there is something quite liberating in telling the truth about ourselves.

When we consider the theme for April of resurrection and renewal, there can be no better reminder of the power of this than to place it in context with the struggles that come with certain conditions in life. Too often, through no fault of our own or those around us, we find ourselves plunged into emotional angst. As you have time today, read Psalm 88. Here is just one example of the emotional travails its verses reveal:

For my soul is full of troubles, and my life draws near the grave. I am counted among those who go down to the pit; I am like those who have no help, like those forsaken among the dead, like the slain who lie in the grave, like those whom you remember no more (Psalm 88:3-5).

If you have ever felt this way or know someone who has, there is consolation in knowing what the Bible knows—that God is aware of, understands, and stands with us in this part of the human condition. There are times in life when the coping mechanisms we rely on fail us and we find ourselves in what the psalmist calls "the pit." There are times when we wonder what our lives have become and if there is a reliable tomorrow.

As you go through the rest of this day, know that, for resurrection to take on the kind of vitality it must, and for life to be renewed, these times need to be recognized, remembered, embraced—and recast as a prelude to new understanding, a broadened perspective, and an entirely new claim on what it means to hope.

WEDNESDAY

I saw the prosperity of the wicked (Psalm 73:3b).

There are times when the redemption we seek and the renewal for which we hope is really there, waiting for us to claim. When Rick Warren, pastor and author of *The Purpose Driven Life*, came to the realization that he and many in his congregation were overweight and doing nothing about it, his confession led to his initiating a new focus on eating healthy foods. The model he utilized came from the biblical book of Daniel where the choice of vegetables and water over "royal food" becomes a sacred exercise.

Warren lost sixty pounds and encouraged his congregation to follow his lead. Sometimes, renewal comes by following our confession with a disciplined reading of the Bible—and doing what it says!

Today, make fresh, healthy, life-giving meals. Allow your discipline to grow from the good feeling of eating well.

THURSDAY

When I thought how to understand this, it seemed to me a wearisome task, until I went to the sanctuary of God (Psalm 73:17).

The taxi ride from LaGuardia Airport in New York across town to JFK Airport could have been an amusement ride at a fair. There was no rush. We had plenty of time. Yet our driver seemed to feel the need to weave, pass, dodge, honk, and generally create havoc for others—and heightened pulse rates for us. The frantic pace, though unnecessary, might well have been his strategy for more trips in less time. But I wonder.

There is something to be said for consistency, a steady pace, and gentle movement. But life has a tendency to tempt us into rushing, weaving, and dodging through our days. The psalmist above, however, learned the gift of being content, of taking time to visit the temple and seek community. There is no need to speed through life attempting to resolve all issues at once, or carry whatever burdens we feel all by ourselves.

If you have not already, make plans to join with others this week at some place of worship. For today, allow yourself to slow down, smell the roses, tend the garden, love your family, enjoy your friends. Take the time to soak in *your time*.

FRIDAY

...I have learned to be content with whatever I have (Philippians 4:11b).

Petra, Jordan, is a *World Heritage Site* and, in 2007, was elected one of the modern Seven Wonders of the World. To see it, to experience it, is to understand exactly why both of these designations have been made. This remarkable place exists in a desert with no natural water. After a hike of a mile and a half on sand and the remains of an ancient and uneven Roman road down a siq (narrow canyon), a massive and indescribable edifice looms out of the shadows and through a crack in the steep rock walls. There, before the hiker, is "The Treasury," the famous façade depicted in any representation of Petra.[1]

Carved directly out of the stone one hundred and eighty-one feet high and ninety feet across, this wonder of human ingenuity stands as a bold testimony to a civilization forged in the face of dramatic hardship and scarce resources. Once thought by locals to have held the riches of Egyptian pharaohs, it came to be known by its current name through mistaken hope and legend. In actuality, it held nothing but bones—and even those only temporarily, just long enough for the flesh to rot and the bones to be exposed.

Walk through the elaborate porch and façade today, and one sees only coffin-shaped holes in the stone floor of a large room. This was a temporary burial chamber for important people. Perhaps there was wealth that accompanied the dead to the body's place of rest, but nothing more. So these true marvels of monolithic architecture, this testament to artistic creativity on a grand scale—is empty.

Our psalmist discovers that this envy that so disoriented his perspective turns out to be much like these impressive

---

[1] I used a photo I took of this view for the cover of my 2011 book, *Subversive Words*, because it illustrated exactly what I wanted people to understand from reading my book on the Bible—previously narrow interpretations and assumptions should be opened up into broader, more exciting, and revealing understandings.

facades of Petra—pretty on the outside but vastly lacking on the inside. So, today, with the Apostle Paul, learn to say: *I have learned to be content with whatever I have.*

> "We mostly spend our lives conjugating three verbs: to want, to have, and to do. Craving, clutching and fussing ... we are kept in perpetual unrest."
> — Evelyn Underhill

SATURDAY

...I have learned to be content with whatever I have (Philippians 4:11b).

Relax today. Claim your Sabbath time of rest. Enjoy family and friends as much as you can at some point during the day. And plan on attending church somewhere tomorrow.

The Second Week:
Redeeming Lost Causes

I thank you that you have answered me and have become my salvation. The stone that the builders rejected has become the chief cornerstone. This is the Lord's doing; it is marvelous in our eyes. This is the day that the Lord has made; let us rejoice and be glad in it (Psalm 118:21-24).

Michelangelo was a genius consumed by creative passion. As mentioned earlier, he also struggled mightily in his personal life. Yet, over the ages, his sculpture, painting, architecture, and even his poetry continue to lift us beyond ourselves. His ability to see a loveliness of the "not yet" inspires awe. He envisioned grand possibilities from humble things—stone, pigment, plaster, paper, bricks... In his art, he consistently called forth magnificence.

It was 1502 in Florence, Italy, and there stood an immense block of marble in Santa Maria del Fiore Church. It had been a stone ready to become art but, sadly, some undiscerning craftsman bored a large hole through the very place where a figure's legs should have gone.

Piero Soderini, the mayor of Florence, sought several artists, including Leonardo da Vinci, to save the piece, but all agreed that the lovely marble had been mutilated beyond redemption.

But Michelangelo, hearing of the piece, traveled to Florence. After examining the marble, he determined it could indeed be salvaged. He simply needed to reconfigure the posture by adapting the pose of the figure around the hole.

From this seemingly unusable and soon-to-be-discarded marble, he created a young *David*, sling in hand, leaning slightly, and strikingly beautiful. Thus, the stone rejected by others was transformed into loveliness by the hands of a master.[2]

This is the theme of Jesus, the theme the Gospel writers want us to remember: Jesus was despised and rejected, discarded

---

[2] This story is related in *The 48 Laws of Power* by Robert Green. This "David" stands in marked contrast to the other more famous and earlier "David" sculpted 1502-04 now in Florence's Galleria dell' Accademia.

on the ash heap of history. And yet, God transforms rejection into redemption so the tragedy of the cross becomes the cornerstone of faith. This same theme replays itself in lives just like yours and mine. The redemption of lost causes continues. Do you ever feel like all is lost and hope is gone? Listen carefully to the good news of Jesus: redemption, rejuvenation, renewal, *resurrection* is at hand.

> Lord, remind me again of your redeeming, transforming power. You are making something beautiful of my life. Allow me the patience to wait, the wisdom to know, and the confidence to live with courage in the meantime. May the spring that surrounds me awaken anew the joy of your salvation and the reality of resurrection. Amen.

REFLECTIONS FOR THE WEEK

MONDAY

Have you not read this scripture: "The stone that the builders rejected has become the cornerstone; this was the Lord's doing, and it is amazing in our eyes" (Mark 12:10-11).

Disappointment is part of life. Perhaps right now is one of those times for you. Or maybe the memories of difficult times are still fresh and painful. The story of Jesus and the testimonies of the New Testament echo the same. What appears to be a defeat has another side: "The stone the builders rejected..." You cannot know what your experience of today will yield. You can hope for good things and glad victories. But if those glad victories do not come, there is still good in life. Take a moment and relax. Breathe deeply. Use your senses—sight, hearing, touch, smell—to feel what is around you in a new way. What message of hope might be emanating from what you notice? Remember the story of Michelangelo's rejected and redeemed stone—and of Jesus.

> "Every new beginning comes from some other beginning's end."
> — Seneca

TUESDAY

I thank you that you have answered me and have become my salvation. The stone that the builders rejected has become the chief cornerstone. This is the Lord's doing; it is marvelous in our eyes (Psalm 118:21-24).

Flying from New York to Istanbul not long ago, we crossed the Atlantic, then across Norway and Sweden, flew over the Baltic Sea, and then down across Poland, Romania, and Bulgaria. It was March. The northern countries were bleak and brown. Scattered lakes were frozen with frosted shores while vast cultivated tracks of farmland lay dormant.

Flying further south and over Turkey and the Black Sea, the March I had witnessed only an hour before was no longer in the thick of winter. Instead, the land displayed first hints then full bursts of green. From thirty thousand feet above, the change took only a couple of hours, yet the transformation from one state to the next was clearly evident.

For those in Poland or Romania, spring still hibernated, winter's grip apparent. This, too often, can be our outlook on life—lacking the ability to see beyond the present "cold." But there is a *spring thaw* just over the horizon. Out of sight and maybe too distant to imagine, it nevertheless is near. The reality of resurrection remains alive and well. Psalm 30:5 reminds us: "Weeping may endure for the night, but joy comes in the morning."

Today, let your mind be set free to rise above your circumstances. Allow your imagination to seek out what you envision to be God's hopes in the day before you. See the landscape of your life and enjoy the life-giving green of redemption. So, with the psalmist, you can say with confidence and joy: "I thank you, Lord, that you have answered me and have become my salvation."

> "It is spring again. The earth is like a child that knows poems by heart."
> — Rainer Maria Rilke

WEDNESDAY

This is the day that the Lord has made; let us rejoice and be glad in it (Psalm 118:24).

Each day lies before us in mystery. We have our schedule, generally. We begin with the morning routine. We view the accustomed scenery and mostly know what to expect. But there are always surprises, the unexpected breaking our routine. And yet, there is the pleasant reminder of the constant.

In Einstein's famous equation $E=mc^2$ (Energy=mass multiplied by the speed of light, twice). The "c" in the equation stands for "constant," or the speed of light. Regardless of all the other weird stuff that occurs in the universe, there continues to be one thing we can count on—the constant speed of light. The Theory of Relativity demonstrates in a physical way what the Bible wants us to know in a spiritual way.

In spite of complexity, craziness, and confusion, God's presence around us, in us, and among us continues to be the constant we can count on. Even when complications rise to the point of despair, the unchangeable nature of God's redemptive compassion always is. Claim this truth today, and recognize in all that you experience the sacred measure of what is and always will be. Now, remember and claim: "This is the day the Lord has made; rejoice and be glad in it." Tonight, enjoy your evening by taking a brisk walk and eating a light, healthy meal.

> "Life is like riding a bicycle—in order to keep your balance, you must keep moving."
> — Albert Einstein

THURSDAY

The stone that the builders rejected has become the chief cornerstone... (Psalm 118:23).

In case we have forgotten how the Bible story unfolds, let us remind ourselves. From Abraham, this "wandering Aramean," the biblical story moves from Isaac to Jacob. And Jacob, this troubled second son of Isaac and Rebekah, intends to marry Rachel. Instead, the clever and deceptive Laban, a kinsman of Jacob and father of Leah and Rachel, plays a trick on Jacob. In one of the more playful biblical twists, Jacob is unwittingly married off to Leah. She is the older sister, described whimsically with the Hebrew euphemism as having "lovely eyes." In modern times, we would say Leah had a "good personality." In other words, she wasn't much to look at.

Poor Leah is foisted upon Jacob, and he notices nothing whatsoever out of order throughout the duration of his honeymoon night until the morning sun peaks over the horizon. Only then does he realize with horror: "it was Leah!"

Rejection. Today, consider how it feels to be overlooked and left out. Has this been or is now a condition you experience? Notice those around you and be aware of anyone who might be the *Leah* of your surroundings. Tomorrow, we continue to explore this underlying and overarching theme of the Bible as told through her story.

> "I've been burdened with blame trapped in the past for too long, I'm moving on."
> — Rascal Flatts

FRIDAY

The stone that the builders rejected has become the chief cornerstone. This is the Lord's doing; it is marvelous in our eyes (Psalm 118:23).

Poor Leah. Jacob does marry Rachel as well, so he comes out fine—except that Rachel, in some kind of biblical poetic justice, is barren. Leah, then, becomes the mother of Reuben, who she poignantly names with her tragic hope woven into the name: "surely now my husband will love me" (Genesis 29:32).

Next is Simeon: "Because the Lord has heard that I am hated, he has given me this son" (29:33).

And Levi: "Now this time my husband will be joined to me because I have borne him three sons" (29:34). Notice, Leah envisions her identity through the eyes of Jacob. But, finally, she realizes God's gifts and says: "This time I will praise the Lord" (29:35). She names her fourth son Judah, which means "praise." She concludes, in spite of her difficult circumstances and in the face of rejection, "I will give God praise."

For both Christians and Jews, it is not the graceful, beautiful Rachel that becomes Jesus' lineage. Like the stone rejected and then redeemed in Florence, the heritage of Leah, the despised and rejected, eventually leads to redemption in Jesus.

Take heart as you enter this day. God redeems, making

hopeless cases burst with new life and hopeful possibility. Claim this for today. Add yourself to this faithful line of witnesses. Bear testimony to God and the glad openness the future holds.

> "Take hold of the life that really is life."
> — I Timothy 6:19

SATURDAY

This is the day that the Lord has made; let us rejoice and be glad in it (Psalm 118:21-24).

Relax today. Regardless of obligations, allow family and recreation (re-creation) to be your focus. Take time to be quiet and reflect on this past week: what do you have to be thankful for from your interactions? As you review, learn from your mistakes. Allow them to increase wisdom and add to humility. And rejoice in your victories, big or small, and learn from what you did well. In all things, recognize God's guidance and grace.

If you can, work in the soil as a partner with God. There is something very therapeutic about getting your hands dirty and helping something grow.

> "Something wonderful happens when you plant a seed."
> — Wangari Maathai

THE THIRD WEEK:
Corinth and Options for Renewal

My grace is sufficient for you, for my power is made perfect in weakness (II Corinthians 12:9).

A vibrant seaport, Corinth was a glitzy, glamorous place in Paul's day—international pizzazz integrated with an exciting can-do spirit. One might have compared it to our own San Francisco or New Orleans.

Newly built and strategically located between two natural harbors, Corinth quickly emerged as a financial and trading center for the vital mid-section of the Roman Empire. Consequently, it also served as a gathering spot and breeding ground for the strange and unusual. Sects, cults, and corporate preoccupation with the bizarre would create confusion in and competition for the nascent house church of Corinthian Christians.

The church birthed here with the help of Paul, Aquilla, Priscilla, Timothy, Sosthenes, and a host of others dealt with significant issues: inappropriate liaisons[3], competition between rich and poor, cliques arguing over whose baptism held higher status, spiritual snobbery, language issues, clashes between Jew and Gentile, along with tensions between men and women. This brief list alone implies miraculous survivability. Further, the depth and breadth of these problems allow for additional implications:

(1) The congregation must have been substantial numerically lest the weight of the number and gravity of these issues capsize the fellowship.
(2) The church wrestled mightily with both the blessing and the curse of diversity in ethnicity, language, gender, and religious backgrounds.

---

[3] Cultic prostitution provided a strange backdrop to the Corinthian church. Though Paul never explicitly addresses the cultic prostitutes of the temple in Corinth, he does clearly combat the ideas of "using" the sexuality of another person for your own selfish desires—also see I Corinthians 3:16-17 for what such behavior does to our own well-being and to God's good creation.

How this Corinthian church listened to Paul's advice and how thoroughly they discovered the kind of community God dreamed for them continues to be a matter of debate. Yet the preservation of these Pauline letters of I and II Corinthians tells us something. Had this Christian experiment in a pluralistic fellowship been a failure, there would have been little incentive for the early and later church to canonize these two letters from Paul to the church at Corinth. Instead, other churches from all over the Empire requested copies of this "Corinthian correspondence" for the edification of their own congregations.

No doubt, some claimed Paul's ministry to this bickering group was a waste of time. But Paul knew otherwise.[4] He saw in this struggling congregation a reflection of his own troubled history. And Paul knew through his own salvation that God's sufficient grace and power made all the difference.[5] And so it is for us.

> Lord, give me patience, wisdom, and courage so that I do not need to be afraid of strange ideas or things I do not understand. Fortify in me a calm discernment. And remind me again that, despite the many human differences among the family of nations, we all remain far more alike than different. You are and ever shall be the common denominator of all of life, now and forevermore. Why should I ever be afraid? Amen.

---

[4] Also in Corinth are the ruins of the synagogue and even perhaps the very bema, or platform in the agora (marketplace) where Paul preached (Acts 18:4-5). Walking through the ruins of the city today, one can still see the remains of that famous bema in the center of the surrounding archeological treasures.

[5] See II Corinthians 12:9.

REFLECTIONS FOR THE WEEK

MONDAY

...My grace is sufficient for you... (II Corinthians 12:9).

In Stephen Schwartz's *Children of Eden*, Eve discovers a curiosity that pushes and pulls, enticing her in directions that both thrill and terrify. Her cleverness, as portrayed by Schwartz, echo's the implicit tension in Genesis 3. The musical takes some liberties with the biblical text, but these are details the biblical writers expected us to figure out ourselves: what is knowledge—and why should we attain it if it is not to be valued and sought?

Eve laments and rejoices in the song "spark of creation" as she considers her newest vocabulary word "Beyond":

> Be-yond, Be-yond ... it sounds full of wind and mist, doesn't it?
> Father, why does my head feel this joy and dread
> since the moment I said, "beyond."

We, too, live in this tension, fascinated with the new, intrigued by what lies just out of our reach but also frightened by the unknown, that misty realm just beyond our understanding. We remain confined to the here and now while interested in and hopeful for something new and different—the next big thing.

Yet God reminds Paul: "My grace is sufficient for you..." What we have is all we need. Contentment continues to be a rare but indispensible mindset in our mobile, fast-paced, and materially driven society. But God's grace is enough.

Work today to discover peace with what is, an acceptance of who you are, and a thankful heart for what you have.

"Spring is the time of plans and projects."
— Leo Tolstoy

TUESDAY

...my power is made perfect in weakness...
(II Corinthians 12:9).

What do you have to fear? Those you see today share the same earth and air and resources. Like you, they are vulnerable to germs and are held in place by gravity. Like you, they live better when surrounded by community and others who care and call them by name. But most of all, they, like you, need a sense of sufficiency in their own humanity, a calm reassurance that all is well and all shall be well. As my mother and I have been working on this book together, she reminded me of these words in a song she once wrote and sang on her album:

> I feel your Presence like a wind upon my heart,
> refreshing as a breath of Spring.
> Blow through my being, let my sinfulness depart,
> and let my life take wing![6]

Today, as the early morning of spring begins to take hold, let your life take wing and feel a sense of presence that refreshes your spirit for this good day. Regardless of your perceived shortcomings, in spite of what feels like weakness, remember what Paul learned about grace and power through God's perspective in his life and ministry. There are times in our lives, when God can work most effectively through what we perceive as weaknesses. What is it that God might use in your life today? Be open to whatever surprise God's grace might facilitate.

WEDNESDAY

...be of good cheer; I have overcome the world (John 16:33).

In the Gospel of John, Jesus says to the disciples: "These things, I have spoken unto you, that in me, you might have peace. In the world, you will have tribulation. But be of good cheer; I have overcome the world" (John 16:33).

---

[6] From "I Feel Your Presence" on *It's a Good Life*, original songs written and sung by Diane Jordan, 1970.

What today do you feel needs to be overcome? What obstacles trouble you? Do you feel weak, inadequate? We are expected to demonstrate a willingness to learn, grow, work on those things we want to improve. But, as many of us have discovered over the years, sometimes those areas in our lives that need improving appear too vast, too broad, too confounding. Sometimes, our feelings of inadequacy and our need for improvement overwhelm our sense of potential.

It is to this breach of personal possibility and conflict that both II Corinthians and John 16 speak. Jesus reassures his disciples and us that we are not living on our own and only for ourselves. Others have gone this way before us—our ancestors in the faith fought the same battles, lived with the same uncertainties, dealt with similar adversities.

Whatever it is that lies ahead today, there exists an entire salvation history behind you. Live this truth today. And "be of good cheer," as Jesus says, "...for I have overcome the world."

> "You may be disappointed if you fail. But you are doomed to fail if you don't try."
> — Beverly Sills

THURSDAY

Whenever I am weak... (II Corinthians 12:10).

The Christian life and biblical trajectory fit this ultimate paradox: "when I am weak, then I am strong." In reality, of course, there are problems with how this pans out for most people. Our culture remains wedded to success and power. Who wants to be a loser? No one I know looks forward to failure, yet the Bible seems to be more realistic about us than we are about ourselves.

Paul's own condition is a good example. He was intellectually capable, spiritually vigorous, and emotionally strong. He was surrounded by a community of faithful friends and positive supporters. His effusive use of the words *joy*, *rejoice*, and *thanksgiving* in Philippians indicates a man in love with life and those around him. And yet he—along with Jesus, the psalmist, the writers of Ecclesiastes, Job, Daniel, Jonah, Ruth, the community of contributors to Torah, the prophets, and the Gospel writers— seem to agree that life can be exceedingly difficult; the human condition is unpredictable.

Too often, fear overcomes our sensibilities, selfishness overwhelms our intentions, and ingratitude overrides our appreciation. Far more than we would like to admit, we are weak, vulnerable, self-absorbed, distracted, unfocused. What can we do? Consider this as you move through your day and meditate on the scripture.

How do you handle your weakness and vulnerability? The truth is, most of us feel the need to hide our insecurities. We pretend. We distract ourselves. We self-medicate. But the Bible knows the truth: we are weak people and we need to hear and accept the truth. This is what finally liberated Paul—when he was able to accept the truth of his condition, he was most ready to be used by God in redemptive ways. What about you today? What weakness do you need to acknowledge? In what ways have you been fooling yourself? Are you ready to open yourself to God's grace, healing, and strength?

> "Reality is the leading cause of stress amongst those in touch with it."
> — Jane Wagner and Lily Tomlin

FRIDAY

Whenever I am weak, then I am strong (II Corinthians 12:10).

The self-help sections of bookstores are overflowing with personal improvement suggestions. Whether diet fads or meditation techniques, get-rich-quick schemes or exercise routines, there's never a shortage of marketing voices crying out for your curiosity, patronage, and money.

To help us, the Bible consistently evaluates our human condition realistically. Paul is clear there is much to celebrate in the very nature of being alive: "rejoice in the Lord, always, and again I say: rejoice!" (Philippians 4:4). But he also knows what it means to suffer, to struggle with physical maladies, to wrestle with personal losses, recover from betrayal, survive imprisonment, harassment, and accidents. (See II Corinthians 11-12 for an even more extensive list.) In spite of all this, Paul declares strength in weakness and hope in the face of suffering.

Pain, sorrow, loss never have the last word. There is more to who we are, what we share, and where we're going than our present ordeal or lack of strength. Today, know you are in good company if you feel less than positive about your ability to cope with all life has thrown your way. This is the real paradox: *when we acknowledge our weakness, we deepen our spiritual stability.*

The very admission of weakness garners strength. Out of genuine humility rises new liberation with the truth. This is but one of the reasons Jesus says: "You shall know the truth, and the truth shall set you free..." (John 8:32). When we free ourselves to be honest about who we are and who we are not, we expand our emotional capability, broaden our community of support, and further our reliance on God. This makes us truly strong.

Today, acknowledge your weakness. You cannot do it all or control everything, but you can admit the truth. In doing so, you are set free; you open yourself anew to God's presence, guidance, and abiding strength. You are stronger than you imagine.

> "In a just cause the weak will beat the strong."
> — Sophocles

SATURDAY

Relax today. Spend time contemplating the *nature* of nature and the growing world outside you. If you have a garden, enjoy working with your hands in the soil in partnership with God.

The Fourth Week:
Jesus and Claiming Your Potential

"When he came to Nazareth ... he went to the synagogue on the Sabbath day ... He stood up to read, and the scroll of the prophet Isaiah was given to him. He unrolled the scroll and found the place where it was written: The Spirit of the Lord is upon me, because He has anointed me to bring good news to the poor. He has sent me to proclaim release to the captives, and recovery of sight to the blind, to let the oppressed go free, to proclaim the year of the Lord's favor" (Luke 4:14-19).

Archeologists are exploring a recently discovered home in Nazareth that dates to the time of Jesus. There are countless ruins in Israel dating from that time. But, for the first time, we have not only the very stones, but a house Jesus would have seen and possibly entered. In his day, Nazareth was only a village of some fifty homes. The chances of his knowing the family and being in the house, perhaps even working on the walls himself, are considerable.

After all, Jesus did manual labor that was called, in Greek, *tekton*. This has been translated over the years as *carpenter*, but the better translation, according to scholars, is *workman*, *mason*, or *one who builds and moves things*.[7] Prior to his ministry, Jesus may well have built houses, and, in those days, the houses were built of stone. Very little was made of wood[8] because it was expensive and didn't last as long.

It is even possible those stones laying adjacent to the Church of Annunciation in Nazareth were put in place by Jesus himself. No one knows for sure; but just imagine if it were so...

> Lord, be with me through the journey of this new day. Inspire my vision with the eyes of faith. Just as Jesus carefully placed stones in the foundations of Galilee houses straight and true, may it also be so in me. May the foundation of my life be firm and strong. Amen.

---

[7] We get our word and concept for "tectonic" plates from this word in Greek.

[8] Window sills, a few pieces of furniture, roof supports...

REFLECTIONS FOR THE WEEK

MONDAY

The Spirit of the Lord is upon me, because He has anointed me to bring good news to the poor." (Luke 4:18).

In his musical, *Children of Eden*, Stephen Schwartz has the Storytellers, the chorus behind the main characters, remind the audience the evolving truth woven into and throughout:

> Of all the gifts we have received,
> One is most precious and most terrible.
> The will in each of us is free.
> It's in our hands.
> And if some day we hear a voice,
> If he should speak to us again
> Our silent father,
> All he will tell us is the choice—is in our hands—
> Our hands can choose to drop the knife.
> Our hearts can stop the hating—
> For every moment of our life
> Is the beginning.

Choice, that great life option and existential necessity dangles before us every moment of our lives, often between the beautiful and intimidating, the ecstasy and agony, the "most precious and most terrible."

Today, consider the stones Jesus must have carved as a young man. Imagine the planning and preparation necessary for each job. See in Nazareth a foundation made from the stones he fashioned, carefully fitting them in place, level and just so.

Now, imagine your own life as the structure on which Jesus focuses. Carefully planned, beautifully created, lovingly carved. Consider the choices that await you. Choose rightly. Claim your potential. The foundation of your life was created by the best.

"When you come to the fork in the road, take it." —Yogi Bera

TUESDAY

He has sent me to proclaim release to the captives, and recovery of sight to the blind, to let the oppressed go free, to proclaim the year of the Lord's favor (Luke 4:18-19).

Jesus' vision can be overwhelming. Too often, I feel perfectly comfortable feeling uncomfortable around others not like me. Let them do their own thing; I'll do mine.

My mother has written hymns and songs on many subjects, and one of my favorites was published for a celebration of the year 2000. This verse says what I need to hear on these occasions when my vision is limited and my thinking shallow:

> New horizons beckon forward,
> Shadow-filled yet bathed in light.
> Christ our Lord will lead us onward
> Toward tomorrow, through the night.
> Even though our past was driven
> By confusion, greed, and hate,
> In his cross we stand forgiven,
> By his grace we celebrate!
>
> — Diane Jordan, from "Welcome the Millennium's Dawning"

Let this day, though perhaps still in the shadows, gradually be bathed in light for you; let your understanding awaken to newness and grace. Translate that to those around you.

"Everyone has inside of him a piece of good news. The good news is that you don't know how great you can be! How much you can love! What you can accomplish! And what your potential is!"
— Anne Frank

WEDNESDAY

Jesus said, "Come." So Peter got out of the boat, started walking on the water, and came toward Jesus. But when he noticed the strong wind ... he cried out, "Lord, save me!" (Matthew 14:29-30)

Peter consistently struggled with great and, at first, unmet potential. He knew the outline Jesus was working from. The template from Luke, quoted by Jesus from Isaiah, was the well-known hope for all the workers in God's vineyard of life. Jesus lived it. Peter tried. And he demonstrated in this passage, miraculous possibilities. Below are my thoughts on the episode, his fine intentions, his burst of enthusiasm—and his (and our) limitations:

MIRACULOUS POSSIBILITIES

Enthusiasm overcame him. Leaping from the boat he discovered his miracle—temporarily: attention focused, faith unburdened, eyes uplifted, motivation directed— toward holiness. Unselfish and pure, filled with wonder, a lightness of being in surprise and joy. But temporary. Peter thinks too hard. He lowers his sight, ponders his faith and realigns his goals	From: Meeting Jesus To: Not sinking. And so it is with us. Except... When... Saved in spite of ourselves With deeper lessons and higher opportunities; to lighten the being and broaden the faith of others like ourselves... and Peter: Human beings better than we know, lighter than we believe... with the miraculous possibilities.

Today, may your experience of faith be in touch with the miraculous. Keep your eyes on Jesus. Don't worry about sinking. Think only of walking in his direction, step by step.

THURSDAY

When the wicked die, their hope perishes, and the expectations of the godless come to nothing ... The fruit of the righteous is a tree of life (Psalm 11:7,30).

Blaise Pascal was a famous French physicist, inventor, philosopher, and mathematician in the 1600's.[9] Following a powerful conversion experience, Pascal related his encounter with the holiness of God. He openly spoke about his Christian joy, faith,

---

[9] Pascal is reported to have invented the first primitive computer, or a glorified calculator, among other things. He was a truly remarkable man.

new understanding for the purpose, and reason for existence. And he was roundly criticized by colleagues for what they considered nothing more than superstition and strangeness.

As part of the defense for his faith, he developed a number of philosophical responses. One of the most famous has become known as "Pascal's Wager." It sounds very much like the simple truth that the psalmist shares above and goes essentially like this: if I live my life believing that God is—if I live for truth and conduct myself righteously, honorably, and with a sense of joy—and at the end of it all discover I was wrong and there was no God, I have not lost. For my life was good and righteous, joyful and meaningful. But if God indeed is, I have gained everything. Along with a good life in the present, I also shall be rewarded in the future.

On the other hand, if I live with no regard to truth, no concern for God, and no compassion for others—unrighteous, selfish, purposeless—and at the end discover God is, I have lost all.

Better, then, to wager that God is.

Like the psalmist and Pascal, live righteously today, enjoy the fruit of the tree of life, be with friends in compassion, community, and Christian fellowship. Better to bet that God *is*, and to live with all the gusto, joy, and love that such a wager entails!

> "Wonder, rather than doubt, is the root of knowledge."
> — Abraham Joshua Heschel

FRIDAY

The Spirit of the Lord is upon me ... To let the oppressed go free... (Luke 4:19).

We need not meet our daily struggles alone. We can face what confronts us on our own terms, with perspective, faith, perseverance, and a deep understanding of our true strengths and potential. Below is my mother's perspective from the hymn she wrote for the 2000 millennial celebration.

> Turn from yesterdays of anguish,
> Leave behind the painful past.
> Sin and strife one day will vanish,
> Christ our Lord will reign at last!
> Humbly now we ask forgiveness,
> Humbly now we kneel in prayer,
> Resting in his loving Presence,
> Trusting in is gracious care.
>
> — Diane Jordan, from "Celebrate with Joyful Singing"

Make this day one of calm reassurance. You need not feel oppressed by whatever it is that weighs you down. Your life is filled with unlimited potential—because you are not the only one in charge and Jesus has come to set you free. Claim this truth today.

SATURDAY

The Spirit of the Lord is upon me ... To proclaim the year of the Lord's favor... (Luke 4:14-19).

Gardens blossom, trees should be fully leafed out, and spring vegetables ought to be readily available. If not from your garden, see if, today, you can find fresh spring produce from a farmer's market or nearby store selling locally grown, fresh produce. Enjoy at least one meal on this day of rest and re-creation that is fresh, healthy, and local.

Plan at least two meals for the coming week with similar goals and shop accordingly. View these plans and your enjoyment of healthy eating and supporting local farmers as another opportunity to be in partnership with God for a more sustainable, more ecologically biblical world. By your actions, you, too, can proclaim "the year of the Lord's favor."

MAY
Beauty

Maius was the name for the goddess of Spring. These were sacred days in the early Latin understanding of the world as life blossomed and the fruit of the ground once again offered sustenance to the world. Hillsides began to shout with color, floral fragrances wafted over the country, signaling the full return of fertility.

Still today, many experience a new sense of energy and surge of hope as the world surpasses the awakening stages of March and April and opens fully to the newness of productivity. Spring crops offer a bounty of freshness and the first signs of summer reveal themselves to the world.

The First Week:
Working with Beauty

And God saw everything that he had made, and behold it was very good (Genesis 1:11).

IN SWITZERLAND, AUSTRIA AND SOUTHERN GERMANY: Not long after God called chaos into creation, this geographical area of today's Alps likely conveyed a primal beauty. But over the millennia, striking changes ensued in our modern Switzerland, Austria, and Bavaria. Movement from the earth's tectonic plates pushed the edges of enormous land masses into each other. Sliding gradually at imperceptible speeds, over and under, these colliding plates slowly pushed the land skyward.

For the Celts, some of the earliest recorded inhabitants in this area, the soaring mountains that would become the Alps presented impenetrable frontiers, hostile terrain, imposing peaks, and unpredictable, cascading waters. In spite of the difficult topography, however, those same inhabitants discovered lush fields and bountiful flowers, clear air and refreshing snows, pure water and incomparable vistas. Modern visitors continue to be welcomed with a feast for the eye, stimulation for the body, peace for the mind, and respite for the soul.

And visitors inevitably share a common verdict: the local inhabitants of the Alpine countries of Europe specialize in making God's natural beauty even more beautiful. Everywhere one looks, whether riding through the countryside or walking through the villages or along city streets, there rises the telltale signs of agricultural richness, botanical abundance, careful planning, and a commitment to cultivated beauty.

This week, keep your own senses attuned to the creativity of God's handiwork. And let yourself be used to enhance what God has so graciously given. We have inherited this beautiful world, and we are called to partner in God's good work. God's original verdict remains forever with us: it is not only "good;" it is "very good!" Like our friends of the Alpine regions, let us work to enhance the already-lovely. This is not an attempt to improve what God has done; it is to fulfill what God expects.

May this be your calling as you move through your week: work with the beauty God has given you, and with your help, loveliness shall continue to grow!

> Guide me this week, Lord. Awaken my eyes to beauty. Quicken my soul to the quiet gifts of loveliness, however hard to see. In spite of schedules, demands, pressures, and potential distractions, let me recognize beauty—and give thanks. Amen.

REFLECTIONS FOR THE WEEK

MONDAY

In the beginning when God created the heavens and the earth, the earth was without form, and darkness was over the face of the deep. Then the spirit (the wind, the breath) of God blew over the face of the waters, and God said: "Let there be light!" And there was light (Genesis 1:1).

Notice how this first verse of the Bible begins: "The earth was without form, and darkness was over the face of the deep." It is not so much that God created something out of nothing, but that God created *order* out of *chaos*. Think of times in your life when all you attempted seemed out of place or mired in difficulty. We only have to return to the resurrection themes of our April devotions to be reminded of the ongoing story of redemption and transformation that can take place in the lives of believers with proper perspective, patience, and faith. And yet, God's redeeming work calls for partnership in caring for, working with, and healing the world. This, too, was part of God's imperative from the very beginning.

> Our God of creation continues to reconfigure chaos and reconcile confusion.

Over the next few days, we shall consider this biblical theme of "Working with Beauty." As we do, we will explore not only awareness of beauty, but our call to wonder at, work with, and add to the beauty of God's world. For today, simply work on awareness. Look for something beautiful in God's creation. Give thanks and share the day in wonder. And, whether there is confusion or order, know that God is beyond, within, and overall the author of this good creation.

> "...God makes things beautiful from the inside out while we usually make things look good on the outside ... The down-deep interior of a redwood or a geode or the DNA molecule or, for that matter, our own body is a song of elegance."
> — Harold Best

TUESDAY

The Lord God took the man and put him in the garden of Eden to till it and keep it (Genesis 2:15).

We have explored this earliest part of our scriptures from the standpoint of our mysterious creation. Now, we will explore our responsibility as the created. We humans have been given an imperative to care for the earth and cultivate it. Like the earliest shepherds called to watch over the flocks and pastures with loving kindness and compassionate wisdom, we can be shepherds of God's earth, caretakers of God's world.

In one of the more poignant episodes of "The Andy Griffith Show," Opey accidentally killed a mother bird with his slingshot. Her death left a nest of three chicks without a mom.[1] Opey decided to care for the baby chicks until they were old enough to care for themselves. Then, at the conclusion of the show, Opey realized he had to set them free. The conflicting emotions he experienced in guilt over the death of their mother and the attachment he developed in taking responsibility for the chicks serve as potent reminders of our own compassionate responsibilities. The serious nature of Opey's life lesson remains with us every day.

Today, let us consider those things in our world that hinder beauty, rob us of goodness, and mar God's good, created order. Think as you go through your day about places you know that face environmental concerns. Consider what it is you might do inadvertently to contribute to environmental problems. What can you do with compassionate responsibility to begin to make things right? Drive less? Garden more? Use less energy? Use less plastic, less water, fewer damaging chemicals? Take seriously today what you can do to partner with God in caring for this sacred gift lovingly entrusted to us.

WEDNESDAY

And God saw everything that he had made, and behold it was very good (Genesis 1:11).

---

[1] From the 1963 episode: "Opey The Birdman."

Add to your reading list Barbara Kingsolver's *Animal, Vegetable, Miracle*. She spent a year living only on food her family farmed or from local produce. The joys, hardships, and insights offer tremendous food for thought—and inspiration for taking care of God's world seriously.

Today, do your best to plan and prepare a healthy meal with only local produce, either from your garden, from a local Farmer's Market, or from a store like Earth Fare that specializes in local foods. Sometimes, even chain grocery stores support local farmers—and will do so more if people like us ask them about locally grown produce. Give it a try.

> "The order, the balance and the beauty of creation are indeed a whisper ... They are a shadow, like the shadow of the earth on the moon, which speaks of the essence of God ... The beauty of God demands a response from us."
> — Michael Card

THURSDAY

And God saw everything that he had made, and behold it was very good (Genesis 1:11).

Today, as you go through your daily tasks, make an effort to be aware of trends and patterns of behavior—in yourself and those around you. What do you see, positively or negatively, about how our community is caring for the world around us?

In the Charlotte area where I live, there are encouraging signs with our recycling programs. For the first time in 2011, our area recorded that the monthly weight of recycling exceeded the weight of garbage and landfill materials.

Also, there is an interest in, and I hope increased commitment to, public transportation in the form of light rail and trains. The savings on gas, traffic congestion, and lower emissions can be huge. Trends like this are encouraging. And hopefully, what you notice today will be positive.

But don't shy away from seeing areas of concern, places of degradation, and perhaps even habits in your own routine that contribute to environmental difficulties. Be aware. Let your heart and God's words of "very good" resonate in the sacred spirit within you that connects you to all that is.

Today, consider this: you are God's very good creation; you are God's very important partner.

> "Around the world, we can see the results of exploitation which destroys much without taking future generations into account. Today, all ... have a duty to show themselves worthy of the mission given them by the Creator by ensuring the safekeeping of that creation."
> — Pope John Paul II

FRIDAY

The Lord God took the man and put him in the garden of Eden to till it and keep it (Genesis 2:15).

Gardening remains a popular hobby. But the word "hobby" implies it is nonessential. While enjoyable, working the soil in tandem with our creator is not something regarded today as essential. Yet, for centuries, gardening was necessary for most families. Even today, the majority of the world still grows at least a portion of their family's diet out of need.

In their book, *A Nation of Farmers: Defeating the Food Crisis on American Soil*, Aaron Newton and Sharon Astyk challenge their readers to return to the sustainable, biblical mandates of working together for the good of creation by reclaiming the biblical call to garden. Buying and eating locally grown food saves energy and supports local farmers. The food is fresher and better for us. It strengthens local economy and encourages partnerships with restaurants, farmer's markets, grocery stores, neighborhoods. If you have not already established your personal garden, do your best to buy locally grown food. Then eat fresher, tastier food while helping to preserve God's world!

It is not too late to begin your own garden. Ask neighbors if they might be interested in a community garden or in sharing different produce from their individual gardens.

> "When we first encounter God in the Bible, it is not as the awesome Lawgiver or the Judge of the universe but as the Artist."
> — Michael Card

SATURDAY

And God saw everything that he had made, and behold it was very good (Genesis 1:11).

Whenever I feel too busy to take the necessary steps to work on my own lifestyle or concerns for the earth, I think of my mom. For years, she cared for my father, every day all day. He suffered from Alzheimer's and, particularly near the end of his beautiful life, he was still quite mobile though very confused. Where they lived in Tennessee, they had not yet gotten curbside recycling. Yet my mother spent all week carefully collecting recyclable materials. Then faithfully, every Saturday, she loaded Dad into their van, with all the recycling, and headed to the county recycling center. She had so many other things to worry about, and yet this was important to her. Her concerns about God's world and her commitment to being a good steward of God's creation motivated her to keep doing the right thing, despite the extra hassle.

Today, make this a commitment in your life as you continue to enjoy and care for God's world.

> "I have learned that there are moments in human existence in which worship burns in our very bones, in which our spirits tremble and our reason quakes as we glimpse the molten center of life ... We have grasped the hand of God this day and found language insufficient save one word only: Yes."
> — Joy Jordan-Lake

THE SECOND WEEK:
Remembering Who You Are

After eight days had passed, it was time to circumcise the child; and he was called Jesus... (Luke 2:21a).

There is something sacred about your name. Much time and prayer went into dreaming about your birth, planning for your life, and imagining your personality. I don't ever remember not being called by my name; it has always been a part of me.

In many cultures, a name is more than just what the person is called. It corresponds with what that person will do and who he or she becomes. I remember a Nigerian family that belonged to our congregation when I was a pastor in D.C. Following the birth of their child, there came a "Naming Ceremony" similar to what might have occurred in the days of Jesus. The family gathered around the little baby boy; I held him up and was shown the first in a series of several names the parents had chosen.

The extended family had previously submitted suggestions—holy offerings, descriptive words imagining what this young boy would become and what he would contribute to the world. Once chosen, the child would be expected to live out the words of his name and fulfill the calling his family had claimed for him. As you might imagine, these were sacred, suspenseful moments; as I called out the name (there were about five), the family would gasp, and then clap and celebrate as though this little one had already lived out the hopes and dreams of his people.

"...and he was called Jesus..." It is the angel who tells Mary what the name is to be. The word *Jesus* comes from Joshua, the Hebrew word for "Bringer of God's salvation." This was the naming ceremony in Luke, and not only the naming of the baby who would change the world, but the claiming of that salvation as though it were already so. For Luke, God is bringing forth the miracle of Jesus, salvation for everyone everywhere: "Behold, I bring you good news of great joy for all the people" (Luke 2:10).

The way Matthew tells it, the good news at first is threatening: "Herod was troubled, and all Jerusalem with him..." Matthew also traces Jesus' genealogy in chapter one beginning with Abraham. This is the perfect place to start when attempting to underline Jesus' Jewish connections and ancestry. Yet Luke goes all the way back to Adam (Luke 3:23-38). For Luke, the connection to the entire human family is important. Luke's message is subtle but clear: if you are related to Adam, you are related to Jesus—and this good news is for you. And who is related to Adam? Everyone.

So, with Luke, the beginning is quiet, gentle, and universal. The name says it all: *Jesus*, and it changes everything.

> Help us this week, Lord, to live up to your calling in our lives. Just as our parents looked upon us with joyful anticipation of what we would become, you continue to hope and dream for the best in us to shine in good ways. Give me the strength, courage, and discipline this week to make you proud. Amen.

REFLECTIONS FOR THE WEEK

MONDAY

Let your gentleness be known to everyone. The Lord is near (Philippians 4:5).

Some years ago in the first church I pastored, we had a guest preacher who said something in her sermon that has remained with me: "I want to do things in my life that make God smile."

Think about that for a moment. As children, we make our parents smile in any number of ways. There are humorous moments of confusion, or discovery, or frustration. And there are tender moments of kindness.

I remember getting a call from my son's second grade teacher, Mrs. Gramlich. I was concerned, thinking there was a problem: "A young man in the class was being made fun of," she said. "Several boys had surrounded him and were saying hurtful things. Your son walked into that circle and over to the boy the others were tormenting and put his arm around him. He just stood there quietly talking to him. The other boys stopped making fun and walked away. I just thought you would like to know what a fine son you have."

This made me smile. And it made me thankful and proud. In that moment, I got a glimpse of what it is that God hopes for each of us—to do the right thing, to rise to the hopes and dreams of our own beginnings—to fulfill our callings. Today, meditate on what your calling is. And consider what you might do over the next few hours to make God smile.

TUESDAY

After eight days had passed, it was time to circumcise the child; and he was called Jesus... (Luke 2:21a).

In the Stephen Schwartz musical, *Children of Eden*, God leads Adam and Eve in a playful "naming." As all the animals rush past them, the man and woman call out alphabetical names from A to Z. It is fast-paced, great fun, and, in our church's rendition, took great effort and much practice to perfect the timing and rhythm.

Your naming—that moment when your mother and father imagined your future, wondered about your life, prayed for your health and safe birth, and chose a name for you—took tremendous effort. And that was only the beginning. There was the changing and the waiting, the feeding, the holding, the comforting, the playing, the teaching, the worrying. If you are now a parent, you don't need to imagine; you know exactly what your parents went through—and what Joseph and Mary went through.

Yet, just as Jesus rose to the essence of his name, today you have that great and renewed opportunity to remember who you are, to claim the essence and dreams of what your parents hoped, worked, and prayed for. Most of all, you have the chance to make God smile. In doing so, experience the joy of those who first celebrated your birth. Thank them if you can, and give thanks for them.

WEDNESDAY

Whatever is true, whatever is honorable, whatever is just, whatever is pure, whatever is pleasing, whatever is commendable ... think about these things (Philippians 4:8).

As we discussed before, Jacob's wife, Leah, gets a terrible deal. She is overlooked, unloved, left out. She is passed off to Jacob as a trick because her father, Laban, knows she will never be found worthy to be married.

Genesis 29 playfully unveils the trials, tribulations, and humor of Leah's story. But, within the text, there comes a dramatic discovery—and it has to do with naming.

Leah continued to long for acceptance after her marriage to Jacob. Each of her first three sons she names with this desire: Ruben, Simeon, and Levi are all names that reflect her desire to be considered worthy, loved by Jacob. In each case, the answer is no. Jacob remains consumed with himself, Rachel, and his own agenda.

But finally, in one of the more poignant and revealing moments in the Bible, Leah's fourth son needs to be named. For Leah—and us—this becomes a moment of self-discovery. The name she chooses no longer reflects her need to live through another person. She now looks past her loneliness and Jacob's self-absorption and names her son Judah, which means praise.

Today, make this your goal. Regardless of circumstance or condition, give God praise and dwell on those things that are most honorable, just, pure, pleasing, commendable—and purposeful. Your focus, your *life*, will be different as a result.

> "The purposes in the human mind are like deep water, but the intelligent will draw them out."
> — Proverbs 20:5

THURSDAY

I have learned to be content with whatever I have ... I know what it is to have little, and I know what it is to have plenty. I can do all things through him who strengthens me (Philippians 4:11-13).

The great paradox of the Christian story is this lineage of Jesus. His ancestry comes not through the popular "graceful and beautiful" Rachel. It comes through the unwanted, unloved Leah. And this continues to be the stance of a Christian—to remain faithful, to maintain hope, to gain meaning and purpose in life regardless of our life situations.

Too often, we search for our meaning through the eyes of others—friends, a spouse, or, as increasingly happens now in our culture, through the marketing forces that so inundate our lives. But the wisdom of the Bible cuts through these superficial views of existence. The sacred perspective to which you and I are called exists more substantively and flows more deeply. It is not through the whims or desires of another that we discover ourselves and the reason for our being. Our meaning to life and purpose for living comes not through distractions, recreation, work, success, friendship, relationship, or any earthly thing. It comes through the *Meaning of all Purpose* and the *Giver of All Life.*

In spite of the difficulties Paul faced, he discovered the gift of contentment in whatever condition he found himself.

Leah gave praise in spite of her hardships; in doing so, she saw her life with new eyes. She discovered a liberated self in the hands of a loving God. Make this your goal in the coming hours. Work to give thanks in whatever challenges come your way today. See those challenges as opportunities for growth, new faithfulness, deeper relationships, and partnership with God.

> "Stop leaving and you will arrive. Stop searching and you will see. Stop running away and you will be found."
> — Lao Tzu

FRIDAY

Therefore, since we are surrounded by so great a cloud of witnesses ... let us run with perseverance the race that is set before us, looking to Jesus, the pioneer and perfecter of our faith... (Hebrews 12:1-2).

Jesus had a name that he lived and claimed. He rose to the hopes and dreams God had for his life and fulfilled his purpose. In the same way, imagine a whole host of family and friends, those who have gone before and those who are with you now. In your imagination, see them rooting for you, cheering you on as you move through your day. Imagine each decision and obligation as an opportunity to make them proud, to gladly represent your heritage, to honor the memory of those who came before you—and to make God smile.

One way of concluding this week is to consider current priorities. Reflect on three things: (1) how you spend your time, (2) where you spend your money, and (3) who you share time and money with. What does this exercise teach you? What might you need to alter or change? Now, do your best to enjoy the opportunities that come your way.

> "We spread the call (of Jesus) because it is the call to every person in every period to receive the New Being, that hidden saving power in our existence, which takes from us labor and burden and gives rest to our souls."
> — Paul Tillich

SATURDAY

I have learned to be content with whatever I have... (Philippians 4:11).

Enjoy this day. Allow it to be one of rest for your body and re-creation for your soul. Reflect on your week and those who passed your way. See individual faces and remember specific interactions. Give thanks for the blessings, and consider whatever friction there might have been. Learn from your interactions. Deepen your wisdom.

> "Some friends play at friendship, but a true friend sticks closer than one's nearest kin."
> — Proverbs 18:24

THE THIRD WEEK:
A Call to Illumination

You are the light of the world... (Matthew 5:14a).

The rabbis in Jesus' day were referred to as "The light of the world." The same phrase also was used in conjunction with the Temple in Jerusalem. These familiar words are loaded with meaning. They imply: (1) sacred authority, as in the case of the rabbis, and (2) mystical power, as in the case of the Temple. When Jesus' audience heard these words, they understood their blessedness was unique. The thought that God could trust them—simple, country people—as conveyers of God's teaching, power, and connection would have been astounding for many. For others, the same identification would have been offensive.

While apparent at various points in the Hebrew scriptures, particularly in the prophetic injunctions to care for the least and potentially left out, this insight from Jesus comes as a natural extension and logical conclusion of previous Hebrew perspectives. Yet his elevation of regular people, even the peripheral and excluded, pushed the envelope of acceptability for his day.

We continue to wrestle with the limits of inclusiveness, but in these words recorded in Matthew, Jesus reclaims the sacredness of God's perspective from the beginning when God gazed on creation that, in the final phase, included "male and female;" and God said it was good. With the Sermon on the Mount, so does Jesus. This is the new law from the new Moses; this is the way it is to be because this was the way that God made it to be.

This week, take these words to heart: *you are the light of the world. Go out and shine!*

> Lord, use this week in redemptive ways. Allow your light to shine in my humble life so others might be drawn to your grace and truth. Amen.

REFLECTIONS FOR THE WEEK

MONDAY

And God said: "Let there be light"; and there was light (Genesis 1:2).

We constantly find hidden nuances in scripture, subtle connections that initial readings miss. We hear this text from Genesis with a sigh, little knowing that it serves as a foundation for what Jesus will expect. When God calls forth light as the initiating moment in creation, the universe blazes with physical illumination and sacred meaning. As we said in our January devotional, God's speaks, and chaos becomes creation.

With Jesus' message in the Sermon on the Mount, we now have a similar expectation and sacred imperative. Just as God orders confusion with an illuminating light, so also are we called into the task of illumination. "You are the light of the world," Jesus says. And from his description of us as this light, you and I have an implicit task. The very nature of light is to shine, to give life, to enlighten, to bring a sense of order to confusion.

Consider your role today and how you can be the "light of the world." Bring light into someone's life through a kind deed, gentle words of encouragement, a genuine smile. Allow yourself to be used in a way that will offer to another a new way of viewing the world. Live the way Jesus sees you. Go again today—and shine!

> "If we do not radiate the light of Christ around us, the sense of darkness that prevails in the world will increase."
> — Mother Teresa

TUESDAY

You are the light of the world ... No one after lighting a lamp puts it under a bushel basket ... In the same way, let your light shine before others, so that they may see your good works and give glory to your Father in heaven (Matthew 5:14a).

It's not just about you or me. We are the light, and this good news certainly involves us. But the real reason to live this as truth is to glorify God. It is not about us; it is about God.

Glorifying God and shining through "good works" makes a difference in us. We are different when we think differently. We change when our habits change. Our lifestyles are transformed when we reconfigure our attitudes. And our attitudes are profoundly affected when what we do remains in line with what is good, especially when we do so out of a reverence for God.

What we do shouldn't be done for reward or so we will feel better about ourselves. Rather, simply doing what we do because it is right and good and what is needed is redemptive and gives glory to God. Today, contemplate what it means to you personally to be a light in the world and act so others have a new appreciation for the goodness of God.

> "Love is not consolation. It is light."
> — Simone Weil

WEDNESDAY

A cheerful heart is good medicine, but a downcast spirit dries up the bones (Proverbs 17:22).

FROM DIANE:

When a Christian moves away from Christ—forgetting his or her commitment, struggling with temptation, not spending time in Christ's presence—the sense of a "light going out" becomes more and more noticeable. You can almost *feel* the darkness descending until the person returns to a closer relationship with God. Then radiance begins to glow once again from the person as Christ fills that person with light. Leslie Weatherhead reminds us of our need for God's help in being light-bearers with this prayer: "May Thy Spirit's radiance so fill and overflow my being that the lives of others may be cheered and blessed by every contact I make this day. Amen."

FROM DAVID:

It is true that, with one another, doing the best we can to bring light into whatever difficulties there are, whatever darkness there might be, is indeed the high calling of Jesus' followers. No one is expecting you to be perfect. Nor or we called to be inauthentic. But today, see what you can do to offer a cheerful heart to those around you. Look for the good and bring it to light. Instead of giving in to the temptation to complain and join with the lowest common denominator in your office, speak words that lift up and offer positive images. There are enough negative attitudes. And, since a "downcast spirit dries up the bones," you can be a redemptive light wherever you find yourself. Do your best to be the kind of light Jesus is talking about and discover for yourself: "a cheerful heart is good medicine."

THURSDAY

A perverse person spreads strife, and a whisperer separates close friends (Proverbs 16:28).

This book of the Bible we know as Proverbs often lies close to the heart of what Jesus taught. Without ever actually citing it, he often used it as the backdrop for his teachings.[4] Here, we understand that the nature of light is to illuminate the darkness and to eliminate shadows. Gossip, slander, even unkind words so detrimental to relationships and the broader community are part of what Jesus would consider *areas of darkness*. These pull down, rip apart, cause pain, create tension. Proverbs tells the truth: "a perverse person spreads strife." Jesus expects the opposite. A follower of Jesus, one who is the light of the world, offers kindness, friendship, compassion, hope, grace—all in a spirit of humility.

---

[4] See Proverbs 24:29 as an example for the backdrop of the Golden Rule (Matthew 7:12); and Proverbs 25:6-7 as the background for Luke 14:7-11.

Today, be determined to remain *light-hearted*—focused on having a heart filled with the light of God's presence, one called to pass on that light, to be a giver of light, a blessing to the world, a follower of Jesus. Only "a perverse person spreads strife, and a whisperer separates close friends." A follower of Jesus has the opportunity to be so much more! Today, follow the calling of Jesus.

> "We know the darkness is leaving and the dawn is coming when we can see another person and know that this is our brother or sister; otherwise, no matter what time it is, it is still dark."
> — Richard Foster

FRIDAY

The human spirit is the lamp of the Lord searching every inmost part (Proverbs 20:27).

George Fox founded what became known as the Quakers, or Society of Friends. Fox became deeply aware of what he described as an "inner light"[5]—an inspiration or inner presence that he interpreted as how God was working in his life and spirit. This same concept is at work in Proverbs 20: "The human spirit is the lamp of the Lord…"

Be aware as you move through today to search *humbly*, for you are on holy ground, yet *boldly reach forth*, for God's presence is with you and hopes to use *you*. Seek that "inner light" that gently guides, prods, inspires. The "lamp of the Lord" is at work in you, calling you, claiming you. Realize the sacred moving through your heart and soul; allow your awareness to move you to humble yet confident actions of goodness and love.

---

[5] George Harrison and the Beatles recorded George's song "The Inner Light" on side B of "Lady Madonna" in 1968. But I am referring here to the other George: George Fox, not Harrison.

> "These things I did not see by the help of (people), nor by the letter, but I saw them in the light of the Lord Jesus Christ, and by his immediate spirit and power, as did the holy (ones) of God by whom the Holy Scriptures were written."
> — George Fox

SATURDAY

Relax today. Enjoy fellowship of some kind at some point in the beauty of God's flowering world. Notice the interplay of light and shadow, if the sun is shining. See the vibrancy of color as the sun displays the glories of God's creation. If it happens to be cloudy, notice the absence of sunlight and search for what George MacCleod described as the "glory in the grey." How might the light of the world shine today in your life and friendships?

The Fourth Week:
Who Gets the Glory?

And whatever you do, in word or deed, do everything in the name of the Lord Jesus, giving thanks to God through him (Colossians 3:17).

In Bavaria, the marvelous alpine region of southern Germany, there are seemingly countless magnificent structures. One of them, a palace called *Linderhof*, was constructed in the late 1800's by a man who came to be known as The Mad King.

His real name was Ludwig II. He was rich and powerful, on the one hand. But by most accounts, he remained isolated, sad, and lonely. Not only did he appear odd, but he seemed unable to conduct the daily requirements of ruling the people of his kingdom. He squandered the bulk of his time and resources on these fanciful creations of space and beauty. Finally, when his Bavarian subjects could no longer tolerate his strangeness and palatial extravagance, he was deposed. Soon after, he met an untimely death—whether suicide or murder, no one knows.

His legacy lives still in palaces like *Linderhof* and castles like *Neuschwanstein*.[6] Ludwig's strange approach to life did allow for a particular kind of architectural exuberance to be passed on to later generations, but was the beauty worth the cost in life and resources? Did anyone but today's tourists and the mad king himself benefit from the extravagance of his imaginative experiments?

Sculpted in this same Bavarian countryside, *The Abbey of Ettal* and *Church in the Meadow at Wies* (or *Wies Kirke*) illustrate another approach to the wonders of human creation. These two sites represent the architectural styles of *High Baroque* and *Rococo*. Both are, like Ludwig's creations, extravagant in their elegance. Yet, the Abbey and the Church were created for reasons other than the pleasure of an unhappy king. They were constructed to the glory of God by craftsmen whose every effort was geared toward that end.

---

[6] This remarkable castle served as the model for Walt Disney's "Sleeping Beauty Castle."

Like with all things in life, there surely was an architect, an engineer, a sculptor, an artist or artisan at work on those projects hoping to make a name for themselves. This is human nature. But the overall goal of both artistic wonders was to motivate the human spirit, to direct the eyes, heart, and mind upwards in praise, to calm the soul and soothe a troubled heart in that sacred space.

Today and throughout this week, make the same true for you. With a grateful heart, let your deeds and words align with the high calling of Jesus' name.

> Give us wisdom this week, Lord, so that we offer what we do and say as a glad testimony to all that you have done for us. We want to keep our hearts grateful. We hope to keep our lives pure. And each day we need your help. Let us humbly receive it—and be a blessing. Amen.

REFLECTIONS FOR THE WEEK

MONDAY

...And whatever you do in word or deed... (Colossians 3:17).

Ambition is a dangerous thing. Often wrapped in humble words and a variety of garments, this dynamic of the human spirit is alive and well in our time. We tend to be ambitious people by nature. George Frederick Hegel, the great German philosopher, once speculated that all humans were driven by the deep-seeded desire for "recognition." This can be simply the recognition by and from another person. But ambition frequently emerges in our hope to be recognized in importance, achievement, popularity, acquisition, power, intelligence...

Today, consider carefully your motives for what you do. What kind of pull does ambition or recognition play in your actions and interactions?

TUESDAY

And whatever you do, in word or deed, do everything in the name of the Lord Jesus... (Colossians 3:17).

In their very important book, *God Is Back*, John Micklethwait and Adrian Woolridge offer some intriguing, even troubling, insights into the state of faith groups and the appearance of health and vitality. This is a provocative read on the reality of competition in the spiritual realm—for good and for ill. In the Christian faith, the positive responses from the competing marketplace of faith includes more vibrant and thoughtful worship which might incorporate a variety of styles, languages, and traditions as well as pulling from ancient traditions and liturgies from our ancestors.

Pastors are being pushed as never before to be creative, well prepared, and conversant in the latest trends. For many, this pressure, on top of the usual demands of pastoral duties, creates larger divides between competitive, cutting-edge congregations and those unable to compete for various reasons. It also lowers the possible prophetic stances pastors and congregational leaders can take—caring for God's world, for example. Too often, resources are stretched thin, concern for competing and surviving runs high, and the thought of working on justice or environmental issues seems peripheral and time consuming.

Today, take seriously what you do and why, not simply to keep up with what others are doing, but because what you do needs to be done in a way that conveys dignity to others and honor to God.

WEDNESDAY

And whatever you do, in word or deed, do everything in the name of the Lord Jesus, giving thanks to God through him (Colossians 3:17).

As we've discussed, there are countless challenges for churches now. Many congregations are learning quickly how to adapt, how to translate a challenging Gospel into a changing world, and how to build and grow disciples of Jesus. Yet, endemic are the superficial changes and simplistic marketing techniques used by many other churches to attempt to remain relevant. Whether in music, preaching, technology, or capital campaigns, churches sometimes lean in the direction of gimmicks over Gospel, and quick fixes over long-term discipleship. Learning about faith, spirituality, the Bible—and what all of this has to do with how we live and treat each other—too often gets lost in the desperate attempt to attract folks to worship.

In *God Is Back*, Micklethwait and Woolridge persuasively provide well-researched information and call upon us to dig more deeply into the why, the what, and for whose purpose we do what we do. Let us all attempt as best we can to do what we do with integrity. Today, make your passion for faith primary. If you are involved in a congregation, encourage depth, focus, and authentic compassion. Good things will happen as a result.

> "Take hold of the life that really is life."
> — I Timothy 6:19

THURSDAY

I hate, I despise your festivals, and I take no delight in your solemn assemblies ... take away from me the noise of your songs; I will not listen to the melody of your harps. But let justice roll down like waters, and righteousness like an ever-flowing stream (Amos 5:21-24).

The prophet Amos is hard to read, especially the part about God's feelings toward worship, assemblies, and songs—at least when attempted while others suffer or are neglected.

What might God be thinking of our festivals and solemn assemblies, or worship? What kind of justice needs to be done? What righteousness needs to be lived in order for our worship, songs, offerings, and gatherings to be more acceptable or justified?[7] Be aware this week of issues and concerns that your actions and words might help to change and make right. Consider what you might say and do to make a difference.

FRIDAY

Those who oppress the poor insult their Maker, but those who are kind to the needy honor God (Proverbs 14:31).

This is another one of those passages from Proverbs Jesus uses as a foundation for his teaching. Hear, for example, in Matthew 25:40: "Truly I tell you, when you did it unto the least of these, my brothers and sisters, you did it to me."

---

[7] Generally, in Protestant tradition, songs were composed for us. They were to teach, inspire, calm, and remind us what life and faith were all about and what our response should be. Notice, at least with the most famous hymn of all, to whom it was addressed. Not to God: "Amazing Grace, how sweet the sound, that saved a wretch like me." The response was gratitude—and humility.

Most of us have experienced what we perceive as "scams"—that is, we were "taken" by someone or "played" by somebody. Our tendency might be to "throw the baby out with the bathwater" when this happens, to refuse all charity because we don't want to contribute to delinquency or we don't like the idea of being taken advantage of. This reaction is understandable.

Yet, these scriptures are clear. Giving to those in need is not optional. We honor God best when we give to those most in need. Naturally, it is prudent to do so wisely, but giving wisely need not preclude giving generously.

Make a particular effort to honor God today by being kind, especially to someone who is not as fortunate as you. Find a good cause to contribute to today and help someone in need with no strings attached—except to give glory and thanks to God.

SATURDAY

And whatever you do, in word or deed, do everything in the name of the Lord Jesus, giving thanks to God through him (Colossians 3:17).

Be thankful today. Look around you as you move through the day and be particularly aware of the blessings in your life. Think of friends and family. Take joy in your efforts this past week and remember those who have gone before, teachers, church members, old friends, early mentors. Give thanks for their lives and for what they have meant to you.

Consider in your life anyone who might think of you as a mentor at some future date and give thanks for them, too.

JUNE
Passion

Juno was the principle goddess of Greek pantheon and the wife of Zeus. The month of June honored her as the goddess of marriage and the well-being of women. Still today, a majority of weddings are performed in June.

Our devotional thoughts for this month will explore the surprising presence of God in our lives, along with some issues Jesus was most concerned about: justice, inclusion, and truth.

THE FIRST WEEK:
Fire and Approach of the Presence

There the angel of the Lord appeared to him in a flame of fire out of a bush ... God called to him out of the bush ... "Remove the sandals from your feet, for the place on which you are standing is holy ground" (Exodus 3:2-5).

Each year, in the month of June, my family would visit my Grandmother's cabin in the mountains of North Carolina. This little house in the woods had no insulation; if you looked carefully, you could see the outside through the cracks where the boards met. We spent many cold mornings huddled in our metal bunk beds under wool blankets, trying to stay warm.

In the kitchen, there was a pot-bellied stove, big, black, and so old no one could remember where it had come from. While we shivered under the covers, my uncle would light a fire in that stove and, though it was far from the room where we slept, the radiating heat from that stove warmed the whole house before long. One fire, one stove, and lots of good warmth freed us from the prisons of our early summer Blue Ridge Mountain chill.

There is something special about fire—light, warmth, energy, and those lively flames. I remember campouts when I was in scouts, being mesmerized as we sat around those dancing flames, the coals glowing, sparks flying.

So, it is not surprising that a transformative moment in the life of a man as well as the early history of our faith is characterized by fire. For Moses, this divine fire that did not consume signified both a personal calling and a new era in the life of the children of Israel. This energy—God's presence—represented more than Moses could imagine. Understandably, he balked at the strange, new direction to which God was calling him. Like Abraham, Gideon, Jonah, Samuel, Isaiah, Zachariah, and a multitude of others, Moses was shocked that life could be different, that he could be any different than what and who he was.

We have a schedule to keep, things to do, people dependent upon us, bills to pay. Moses had his list. And he had some decent excuses. The best may have been not being able to speak well. This probably wasn't a speech impediment like many of us believed growing up. His "slow of speech" comment likely had more to do with growing up in the palace of the pharaoh speaking the language of the empire, Egyptian, not the language of servitude, Hebrew. A very good excuse: "I can't speak the language very well. How can I say and do what you need?" But God had it all worked out. Aaron, Moses' brother, spoke to the Hebrews for him. Moses, while still practicing his Hebrew, communicated with the pharaoh. But God's response is the most telling: "I will be with your mouth and teach you what to speak" (4:12). God is clear that he will be with us, providing the light of His presence; the fire of His power.

Luke describes the birth of the early church using the metaphor of fire: God's spirit came upon them "...divided tongues as of fire, appeared among them, and a tongue rested on each of them" (Acts 2:3). And the transformation that occurs in that fellowship changes the course of history. God is with us.

So, fire is an apt image; fire changes things. It can change a cold cabin into a warm home; it can take a broken man and transform him into a liberator. The fire of God transforms tentative and frightened followers into courageous witnesses for God's new era of good news in Jesus.

And what about you this week? The energy of God's spirit, the fire of God's love, the approach of God's presence all remain available to you. May you awaken to that warmth and power as never before—and sense God's approaching Presence.

> Awaken us with the fire of your presence this week, O God. Give us passion for your ways, enthusiasm for your justice, and enlightenment from your wisdom. Warm us with the flames of your love so that we radiate the same warmth and share the same light. Amen.

REFLECTIONS FOR THE WEEK

MONDAY

The Lord went in front of them in a pillar of cloud by day, to lead them along the way, and in a pillar of fire by night, to give them light, so that they might travel by day and by night (Exodus 13:21).

Deserts can be beautiful places in the daylight hours—far-reaching horizons where the golden sand and grey or dark red rocks meet the blue of the sky. But this same scenery, at first so intriguing, can soon become monotonous. The limited range of color schemes often turns even the most patient travelers into whiners. And this is exactly what happened to the Israelites.

Only weeks before, these wandering tribes lived in bondage. Now, they are free, but their destination is uncertain. Still, they have fire, a pillar rising in the night, a lingering symbol they are not alone on this unfamiliar journey, *so that they might travel by day and by night.*

We, too, wander sometimes, whether exploring new vistas or traveling familiar pathways. Life, like the desert, can be beautiful; it can also be an odd journey with disconcerting dips and turns. For the early biblical actors, this trip from Egypt followed a similar trajectory: from bondage to freedom, moving away from the slavery of sin and the captivity of selfishness toward a community of compassion and interconnectedness. For us, too often this remains hidden and untapped: the spiritual potential that God offers to each of us.

Like the metaphorical pillar of light to illumine the darkness, *to give them light,* we have available more spiritual strength than we realize. Today, imagine yourself living part of God's dream for your life and community. In the process, may you sense that Presence, that column of fire, that emerging awareness that all is well, that your journey will be good, compassionate, and filled with the light of God's presence. You are free to be good, righteous, loving, joyful, and filled with God's light.

> "God is our refuge and strength, a very present help in trouble."
> — Psalm 46:1

TUESDAY

There the angel of the Lord appeared to him in a flame of fire out of a bush ... God called to him out of the bush ... "Remove the sandals from your feet, for the place on which you are standing is holy ground" (Exodus 3:2-5).

The fires of Exodus and Moses' burning bush experience demonstrated both energy and potential. As would be true later with the early church and its remarkable transformation, the fire of the Bible, the fire of God, also represents the latent spiritual potential in us.

John Wesley, an Anglican preacher in the 1700s, was an English evangelist who experienced God's warming fire. He founded the Wesleyan Methodist Church. A disciplined man in every phase of his life, deeply committed to sharing the Gospel, concerned about the vast numbers of poor and oppressed, outcast and unfulfilled people, he devoted his life to preaching and teaching the Gospel. Yet, throughout his early ministry, he confessed to a deep confusion and an inner and unmet longing.

All that changed on the evening of May 24, 1738. The following experience Wesley recorded in his journal:

> In the evening I went very unwillingly to a society in Aldersgate Street, where one was reading Luther's preface to the Epistle to the Romans. About a quarter before nine, while the leader was describing the change which God works in the heart through faith in Christ, I felt my heart strangely warmed.

Fire transforms. And the fire of God's presence is alive and well. In the midst of our confusion, God uses the energy of new hope and the warmth of growing love to power your spiritual potential. So, make this day one of discovery, of change, of new direction through new insight and inner transformation. Let

Approaching the Presence

the fire of God burn in you and bring about change that makes a difference. Your heart, too, will be *strangely warmed.*

> "Someday, after mastering the winds, the waves, the tides, and gravity, we shall harness for God the energies of love, and then, for a second time in the history of the world, we will have discovered fire."
> — Pierre Teilhard de Chardin

WEDNESDAY

The fire on the altar shall be kept burning ... Every morning the priest shall add wood to it, lay out the burnt offering on it, and turn into smoke the fat pieces of the offerings of well-being (Leviticus 6:12).

This fascinating and rather odd part of the Bible acquaints us with an additional discovery and new symbolism for today. Early people learned that, as fire burned, it created heat. And this heat generated warmth, gave light, cooked food, and sanctified offerings. In the case of this particular series of scriptures in Leviticus, the fat of the offering changed from a solid into smoke: "The priest shall turn them into smoke on the altar as an offering by fire to the Lord" (Leviticus 7:5). Further, there is a repeated phrase regarding this transformed offering, that it would be "a pleasing odor to the Lord."

At work in the scripture is both the transformation of the fat of a dead animal into smoke and the pleasing smell created by grilling meat (anyone familiar with cookouts can attest to this). As the smoke goes up, and the smell, presumably, so also do the prayers that would accompany the offering. This would please God and, therefore, the prayers stood a better chance of being answered. Such assumptions seemed to be behind these rarely read but instructive passages in Leviticus.

The point here is not to evaluate the validity of early sacrificial practices but to recognize what the Israelites saw in the properties of fire and the nature of God. Both were mysterious forces that could bring change. Fire, almost magically, could transform things. As such, it is very practical for the Bible to present the reality of God's presence through fire.

Today, take this metaphor of fire a step further—beyond a warming of your heart to the changing of your outlook. No longer do we need the priest to place the sacrifice on the fire of the altar. Your life today can be the sacrifice—not in or through death but in and through the goodness and grace of God. That itself is pleasing to God.

> "Present your bodies as a living sacrifice, holy and acceptable to God..."
> — Romans 12:1

THURSDAY

Let us know, let us press on to know the Lord; his appearing is as sure as the dawn... (Hosea 6:3).

The history of inventions is a fascinating study filled with discrepancies. For instance, though widely thought, the first steam engine was not invented in the eighteenth century by James Watt.[1] Rather, it was a Roman playing with fire and water. Like many inventors, this Roman likely stumbled on the additional energy fire could create. In essence, the Romans first discovered that, by boiling water, steam was generated, and keeping the steam enclosed created pressure that could make things move.[2]

So, too, is the history and understanding of certain Bible stories open to reinterpretation and new understanding. Hosea assured his people that the Lord's appearance was as sure as the dawn. Similarly, the early church experienced a dawning,

---

[1] James Watt, in the eighteenth century, merely improved and perfected ideas that two other British inventors developed in the seventeenth and early eighteenth centuries. The Romans predated them all by about fifteen hundred years.

[2] Interestingly, the Romans never used steam for anything other than their Roman baths, as a child's toy, and possibly a musical instrument similar to our pipe organ. Rather, they relied on the abundance of slave labor and were concerned any potential labor-saving device could create unemployment and discontent among the slaves.

an awakening to God's presence. It was a movement, a form of new and sacred energy at a time of the Jewish year called Pentecost. As Luke explains in the New Testament book *The Acts of the Apostles*, "...divided tongues as of fire, appeared among them, and a tongue rested on each of them" (Acts 2:3). Luke describes this scene in metaphorical fashion and yet depicts God's spirit clearly in a way most could understand. There was something new and exciting, unpredictable and powerful, unifying and transformative.

From all over the world and speaking a multiplicity of languages, those gathered heard—each in his or her native tongue. Thus, from this small and insignificant group whose leader had just been executed as a traitor, begins a movement that would change the course of history.

If, for some reason, you are feeling discouraged or insignificant today, take heart. Know that, from this very kind of dynamic, the reshaping of history begins—all with a little fire and the presence of God in your life. Like fire and water and steam, there is a good chance something just might start to move. Be open and ready; be prepared to receive whatever is in store for you today by the surprising, transforming fire of God, *for his appearance is as sure as the dawn.*

FRIDAY

Someday, after mastering the winds, the waves, the tides, and gravity, we shall harness for God the energies of love, and then, for a second time in the history of the world, we will have discovered fire (Pierre Teilhard de Chardin).

I presented this quote Monday, and I think it bears repeating. Chardin was a French anthropologist and strong Christian. As an anthropologist, he learned that civilizations tended to wax and wane. Humans made discoveries, progress, and mistakes.

As a Christian, he understood the gift of God's love, the power it conveyed, and where it came from. In keeping with the metaphor of fire, in many ways Chardin also recognized the significance of life-change, of discovery. To finally get it right, finally to understand and to live out the blessedness of love, is the ultimate calling of every person. Just as the discovery of fire revolutionized the ancient world, the *fire* of today—the love of God alive in us—changes everything.

Today, begin small; take the fire of God's love in your heart and mind, and start a gentle revolution in your own spot: your home, your office, your school. Just a spark will do it. Love someone in an unexpected way, start a fire, tenderly fan the flames, and see what happens.

SATURDAY

Remember the Sabbath and keep it holy. Tomorrow could well be busy and time of rest and reflection might be fleeting. So, today, avail yourself of silence and the beauty of God's world. A walk through your neighborhood should offer you not only some silence and moderate exercise, but also opportunity for new observations. Notice what is blooming and take particular interest in the details: bees pollinating, new blooms preparing themselves for an unveiling of color and show. See the shape of leaves and arch of tree lines. If there are clouds, look for their contrast against the rest of the sky. Be aware of the small things. Notice the details. Give in to wonder. Give thanks.

THE SECOND WEEK:
The Quest for Justice

You have not strengthened the weak, you have not healed the sick, you have not bound up the injured, you have not brought back the strayed, you have not sought the lost... (Ezekiel 34:4).

Prevailing wisdom generally asserts that no one is truly altruistic; everyone has an agenda or is working some kind of angle for personal gain. And yes, sadly, it is also true we Christians often talk a better game than we play. But let's look at the biblical prophets for a moment. The cause they served and the messages they preached were largely on behalf of the overlooked—those who had no voice of their own. The above text from Ezekiel is a good example. And it is much of this thought and concern that also serves as the precursor to the cause of Jesus:

The spirit of the Lord is upon me, because he has anointed me to bring good news to the poor. He has sent me to proclaim release to the captives and recovery of sight to the blind, to let the oppressed go free, to proclaim the year of the Lord's favor (Luke 4:18-19 quoting Isaiah 61:1-2).

There was no money to be made or political influence to be peddled by such stances. These were not popular proclamations with those who controlled the power. Consequently, those who proclaimed them often met with less than desirable ends.

Similar perspectives rang out from the voices of Amos, Hosea, Jeremiah, and Micah. And, from the Christian perspective, their combined concerns were best and most fully embodied in Jesus. It has been God's desire from the beginning of Abraham's call (Genesis 12:1-3) that the same should be embodied in us—to humbly carry on the call, the perspective of the prophets, and the spirit of Jesus.

But the Bible is honest as well, and realistic. We hear less about heroes of the faith and those who succeeded with no struggles; we hear more about people like Jacob, Leah, Cain, and Adam and Eve. In other words, we hear about mistake-ridden people just like us.

We all can and should do better. But the failings of Christian people, all of us human to the core, never dull the flame of God's dream. From each generation, God calls new purveyors of hope and justice. There is much to be done—there continues to be much wrong in the world and in our communities. Too many are left out, too many are too busy to know or understand or care. But God's continual message echoes through time: "You have not strengthened the weak, sought the lost..." Followers of Jesus attempt to emulate his thought and action: "...bring good news to the poor ... proclaim release of the captives..."

This week, we will consider what this means, and how we might do a better job ourselves!

> Help us, God. Guide our considerations of lifestyle and pleasures; open our eyes to the world around us, both the beauty and the pain. Deepen our concerns; broaden our compassion; use us in kindness and humility to offer ourselves in your name. Amen.

REFLECTIONS FOR THE WEEK

MONDAY

The spirit of the Lord is upon me, because he has anointed me to bring good news to the poor. He has sent me to proclaim release to the captives and recovery of sight to the blind, to let the oppressed go free, to proclaim the year of the Lord's favor (Luke 4:18-19).

Have you ever been trapped? I remember vividly that feeling while reading Mark Twain's *Tom Sawyer*. Tom and Becky Thatcher became lost in a cave, trapped and far away from those they loved. It was dark and terrifying. I felt so anxious just reading about their dilemma and imagining myself trapped in the same darkness with no way out.

This is exactly how many in our world feel every day. There was a report not long ago about women and girls being kept as slaves, prostitutes at the mercy of those who controlled them *here* in America. Undocumented immigrants in this country work for less than minimum wage, are forced to live in inhumane conditions, and can't seek help because they fear the police almost as much as they fear their captors.

There are countless examples of people like you and me being taken advantage of. They are used, abused by forces stronger, more influential than themselves, made to work hard, live dangerously, and exist unfairly. They are *trapped* in a cycle of violence or oppression that Jesus came to expose. It was these people—the weak, dispossessed, fearful, and lost—that Jesus came to save.

What would it be like to be trapped in a situation you couldn't escape? Consider this today as you move through your day free and in relative control of your life. In this endeavor, use your imagination and empathy to follow Jesus' example by making yourself more aware and, where possible, help someone in need.

> "Justice is nothing more than love turned into social policy."
> — Tony Campolo

TUESDAY

...He has sent me to proclaim release to the captives and recovery of sight to the blind, to let the oppressed go free, to proclaim the year of the Lord's favor (Luke 4:18-19).

As followers of Jesus, we seek to live a life of common purpose with and for those less fortunate. As such, we should condemn injustice, expose exploitation, refute discrimination, and live righteously.

Our starting point is learning where the struggles are, what the plight is, and how your community can help. Ask questions. Share information. Seek your pastor or anyone in your church who currently works to help refuges, immigrants, the poor, the homeless. Look for those who advocate justice in general. Make yourself available and trust that God will guide you. Once you begin, don't stop there. Encourage others to join in your efforts. Help all be better followers of Jesus.

> "When I fed the poor, they called me a saint; when I began to ask what made them poor, they called me a communist."
> — Bishop Dom Helder Camara

WEDNESDAY

...What does the Lord require of you, but to do justice, to love kindness, and to walk humbly with your God? (Micah 6:8).

I have no words better than my own mother's to express the true meaning—and purposefulness—of justice. Inspired by Micah 6:8, Amos 5:24, and Jesus' overall concerns for justice, she wrote the hymn below. Today, study these words and determine what they mean to, and for, you:

Hear Again the Cry for Justice

Hear again the cry for justice, hear again the prophet's call,
"Like the mighty, flowing waters, let the streams of goodness fall."
May the words that God has given pierce our selfish apathy
'til, with joy, we turn to live them, 'til we heed the prophet's plea.

In a world of sin and anger, in a world where cynics scorn,
Millions weep in helpless hunger, refugees and orphans mourn.
Rise, O Church, to meet the challenge, lift the fallen, help the weak,
Change the laws that breed corruption, speak for those who cannot speak.

While we play in mindless leisure, feasting much and wasting more,
Others die, diseased and fearful, plagued by famine, greed, and war.
Yet God's call to right and justice echoes still, across the years,
"Turn from sin to joyful service, wipe away your neighbor's tears."

Hear again the words of Scripture, linger long at Jesus' feet.
Let the message grow within us 'til our prayers and actions meet.
May we listen, may we worship, then obey the Spirit's prod,
Doing justly, loving mercy, walking humbly with our God.

— Diane Jordan

Live today with these words echoing in your heart while you wonder: how can I help God help others?

> "The God of love is also the God of justice ... for in the Bible justice is the social form of love."
> — Dallas Willard

THURSDAY

You have not strengthened the weak, you have not healed the sick, you have not bound up the injured, you have not brought back the strayed, you have not sought the lost... (Ezekiel 34:4).

What a joy it is to watch others discover the power and joy of being used by God. A physician in our church shared his testimony not long ago of an event that occurred that week. A family at his hospital had just been informed of their loved one's death. There was nothing the doctors could do. In his testimony, this doctor said he felt so weak, so helpless to take away this family's suffering. And yet, something inside called him to ask the family if he could pray for them.

Through tears of awe and wonder, in the midst of terrible loss and incredible sadness, he recognized there was no way to repair the damage or bring back the loved one. But, in those moments, he said, there was such a powerful sense of presence, of healing, of hope in the middle of this tragedy. He had the amazing sense he was being used as an instrument of God's love, even as he felt helpless to stave off their loved one's death.

A couple of days later, he attended the funeral and was greeted by the deceased's loved ones like a member of their family; he was asked to speak during the service.

There are times in all our lives when problems loom too large, obstacles to reconciliation too numerous, evidence for hope too miniscule. And yet, God remains in the miracle business. We are part of a great family built upon hope *beyond* hope.

Think on this today. Look for opportunities to "strengthen the weak, heal the sick..." and offer hope through God's hope.

> "To take the God of love and justice seriously means to take justice seriously and to be aware that prolonged injustice has consequences."
> — Dallas Willard

FRIDAY

The spirit of the Lord is upon me, because he has anointed me to bring good news to the poor. He has sent me to proclaim release to the captives and recovery of sight to the blind, to let the oppressed go free, to proclaim the year of the Lord's favor (Luke 4:18-19).

In preparation for a medical mission trip to Honduras a few years ago, I made copies of the verse Jesus read from Isaiah and used as the initiation of his ministry. The verse was copied onto a strip of thick, bonded yellow paper, and each member of our team was given one to keep in their pockets throughout the trip. Our instructions were to take it out and read it whenever we could remember to do so, or whenever we felt a need for extra guidance.

In our debriefing after the first day, we shared and reflected on how this verse had become real to us—of the new perspectives the words had evoked as we experienced the incredible hurt, the vast needs of the good people we had met and attempted to treat. We discovered through our sharing that many of us had taken the verse out repeatedly during the day and reflected on its meaning—how we were and are followers of Jesus in the role of "bringing good news to the poor, proclaiming release to the captives..."

One of our group shared with us that he distributed free eyeglasses (used ones we had collected from various places back in North Carolina); this was the literal embodiment of our verse. He was overwhelmed as he witnessed those men and women, boys and girls, for the first time in their lives suddenly seeing with clarity the beauty and details of God's world through the miracle of discarded glasses.

Today, make it your personal goal to see with new eyes what God can give you, and believe that the Lord has anointed you to proclaim the "recovery of sight to the blind."

SATURDAY

Today, be still, rest, relax, enjoy those you love, and remember those who are in need of being remembered. And rejoice in how you, through God's assistance, have grown in spirit this past week.

> "You are not forgotten."
> — A note sent by Amnesty International to prisoners the world over[3]

---

[3] Written in English, French, Russian, Arabic, Chinese, and numerous other languages. Survivors often tell of almost giving up until a crumpled note with this message somehow would be delivered to their place of captivity.

THE THIRD WEEK:
Aliens and Jesus

When an alien resides with you in your land, you shall not oppress the alien. The alien who resides with you shall be to you as the citizen among you; you shall love the alien as yourself, for you were aliens in the land of Egypt: I am the Lord your God (Leviticus 19:33-34).

Someone said to me not long ago, "I am tired of all these illegal immigrants sneaking into our country, spreading crime, taking our jobs, freeloading on our schools and welfare system, and draining our economy…" I can understand how it feels that way; there are numerous negative reports in our media indicating there is truth in such concerns; however, the following facts from the Church World Service and Lutheran and Refugee Services (very reputable sources you should check out) debunk such fears:

(1) *All immigrants pay taxes; even undocumented immigrants pay sales taxes and real estate taxes (either directly as homeowners or indirectly through rent). In addition, the Social Security Administration estimates fifty to seventy-five percent of unauthorized immigrants pay federal, state, and local taxes, including Medicare. In 2005, undocumented immigrants contributed more than six billion dollars in Social Security taxes they can never benefit from, nor their families.*[4] *In other words, we benefit from their labor.*

(2) *Twenty-six million immigrants currently residing in the U.S. arrived after the age of eighteen and are of prime working age. They represent more than two and a half trillion dollars to the rest of us as U.S. taxpayers. Again, we receive the benefit of their labor without the cost of their education.*[5]

---

[4] Eduardo Porter, "Illegal Immigrants Are Bolstering Social Security with Billions," *New York Times*, April 5, 2005.

[5] "It's Tax Time! Immigrants and Taxes: Contributions to State and Federal Coffers," *Immigration Fact Check* (Immigration Policy Center of the American Immigration Law Foundation, April 2008).

(3) *Undocumented immigrants can get emergency medical care for their children but cannot receive welfare, food stamps, or Social Security.*[6]

From these statistics alone, we see the complexities of this tough issue; we can deduce how unfair generalizations and angry finger pointing do little good and possibly much harm. There are well-meaning people on both sides of this complicated conundrum. But, beyond the facts, there are biblical ramifications.

Just after the passage in Leviticus 19:18 that is so familiar—"Love your neighbor as you love yourself"—comes this: "Love the alien as you love yourself; for you were once aliens in the land of Egypt..." (Leviticus 19:34). The "alien" Leviticus refers to is one beyond the children of Israel. They were, indeed, aliens, undocumented and probably considered illegal. Also, there is the undocumented immigrant that crops up at various times throughout scripture, both in the Hebrew scriptures (Old Testament) and then again in the New Testament. Here are just three examples:

(1) Jesus begins his life as an infant whose parents are fleeing a localized holocaust in Judea perpetrated by Herod the Great (Matthew 2). They leave Bethlehem and rush into Egypt without documentation where they are at the mercy of the Egyptians. Fortunately, the locals are willing to overlook the illegality of their presence, the drain on the local resources, and the illegitimacy of whatever employment Joseph, Jesus' father, would find over the next two years.

(2) Later, in the midst of Jesus' ministry, he tells one of his most famous parables about the hero who is an alien, hated, despised, and understood by many to be the suspected equivalent of a modern-day terrorist. The question is asked of Jesus, "What must I do to inherit eternal life" (Luke 10:25). Jesus' deft merging

---

[6] "Separating Fact from Fiction: Refugees, Immigrants, and Public Benefits," *Immigration Fact Check* (Immigration Policy Center of the American Immigration Law Foundation, September 8, 2008).

of Leviticus 19:18 (love neighbor) and 19:34 (love alien) in this story reveals that how we treat others—all others—carries much weight in the eyes of God.

(3) Finally, at the other end of Jesus' life, there are some who conclude he died as an undocumented immigrant. Though Jewish and arrested in the Jewish capital of Jerusalem, his home was in Galilee, not officially a Roman province[7], as was Judea, though still a part of the Roman imperial system. Jesus wasn't a Roman citizen and not legally a citizen of Judea. Consequently, it is said that he was killed outside of the walls of Jerusalem in a fashion and place reserved for criminals, outcasts—and aliens.

There are clearly problems with our current U.S. immigration system. The good people of Arizona and Alabama have much to be frustrated about. But, in the ongoing debate, may we all seek to maintain a sense of decency and better perspective. Immigrants, documented and otherwise, have, do, and will continue to contribute much to the richness of this land, its bounty, and its people. God cares tremendously about those who, like Jesus in Egypt at the beginning of his life and then in Jerusalem at the end, are strangers in the land.

Charge yourself this week to gain understanding, sympathy, and empathy for those you would deem "aliens."

> Help us, Lord, when issues are less clear than we would like; when tensions are high and patience is low, give us wisdom. Allow us vision to see through the haze of anger and resentment. Let us seek your will and stand for what is right, not simply what is convenient. Amen.

---

[7] Galilee was under the reign of the puppet Jewish king, Herod Antipas, son of Herod the Great. Judea, on the other hand, was under the control of the Roman Prefect, Pontius Pilate.

REFLECTIONS FOR THE WEEK

MONDAY

In the subcontinent of India, the coconut often serves as a sacred symbol. Hard on the outside, it takes great force to cut through the outer shell. But, on the inside, there is a soft sweetness that gives sustenance. As such, it is used to represent the human heart.

The heart can be hard and unforgiving; it can be selfish and self-absorbed. But, once exposed to the love of God, the hard, outer shell gives way to tenderness. Kindness and patience are accessible. Generosity of spirit and compassion for others become the ready fruits of a softened heart. Like the heart of the coconut, the love of God facilitates a pliable center and offers refreshing, life-giving nourishment.

Today, allow your heart to be open to new realities. Imagine seeing the world through the eyes of one who is trapped in the web of illegal immigration. Imagine how easy it would be to become disillusioned, cynical, despondent. Think what it would be like to want to feed your family yet be constantly frustrated, desperate to find a way to care for those depending upon you. How might you view the world around you? What would it feel like? What would *you* be like?

Remember the coconut—is your heart hard like the shell? Or is it becoming soft, rich, and life-giving like the inside?

> "When we are clear about our inheritance as children of God, we also become clear that all of God's children are the objects of God's seeking and saving love. That is why we are called to do our part to leave this world a better, safer, and more equitable place."
> — Rueben Job

TUESDAY

In all things, do unto others as you would have them do unto you (Matthew 7:12).

This scripture—sometimes known as the "Golden Rule"—requires imagination. It means for us to ask ourselves how we would like others to treat us. How do we want others to think, feel, and be around us? The answers to these questions, then, determine how we treat others. In regard to our concentration around "the alien" this week, consider this: how would you feel if you had left your home country to get a job for better pay so that you could feed your family? What would you wish for? What would you want others to do? How would it feel to be unable to visit a doctor, or worse, be unable to take your child to a doctor for fear of deportation or jail?

To love God empowers us to love others. The love of God we experience is and should be channeled through us and to, for, and with others. In this loving, there arises an openness to the life and perspectives of others. In this kind of loving, we get a glimpse of what it is like to be the "other"—to walk in their shoes, to know what they know, to feel what they feel.

This is not our doing. To love God in the ways Jesus teaches is about being liberated to be ourselves more fully. To love others simply to be popular rarely works to anyone's advantage. But to love others because God first loved us—to feel in ourselves God's love resonating like a tuning fork, its sympathetic vibrations reaching out to the world—these are sacred moments.

Look for the holy ground of God's love joining you with those around you. And imagine those not immediately around you, those you might not know at all, people just like you, except they are struggling to survive in an unfamiliar land.

Love God; love others creatively, and let your heart soften in the process.

> "What greater thing is there for two human souls than to feel that they are joined together to strengthen each other..."
> — George Eliot

WEDNESDAY

They shall be to you as citizens ... In whatever tribe aliens reside, there you shall assign them their inheritance, says the Lord God (Ezekiel 47:22-23).

She saved me. I was lost in the subways of New York City, a college student in a foreign land. It was 1982, and I must have looked really goofy and out of place—an alien. I didn't know any better; I trusted a couple of scruffy looking characters who claimed they would show me a shortcut to the subway platform I was trying to find. I must have looked ridiculous, scared and lost, blindly following two ruffians. Then she appeared, an older, African-American woman with an umbrella and nice hat who looked like she was on her way to church. She stepped in front of me, aimed her umbrella at the two men I was following, and said: "Where do you think you are going with this young man?"

"Don't worry about it Grandma," one of the men said derisively.

She got in his face and, as she threatened him with her umbrella, said, "You get out of here and leave this young man alone, you hear!"

They obeyed her.

And to me: "Are you out of your mind following hoodlums like these two?"

"Yes," I said. "I mean, no. I mean, well—"

"Now, where is it you want to go? *I'll* help you."

Today, consider this story within your own context. Who can you identify in your community that might be struggling? What might you do to help? Here are a few suggestions: offer English as a Second Language; tutor a student; encourage an immigrant you know in their adjustment to this country; share clothes, eye glasses, shoes, blankets, furniture, dishes... Would you consider challenging your church or an organization you are part of to offer assistance? Thanks to a host of devoted volunteers in our congregation, we have been truly blessed by new friends who once were refugees from Burma, Latin America, and Africa. They have taught us, loved us, and shown us full and beautiful measures of God's love.

In God's eyes, we are all citizens of the same place.

> "Miss no single opportunity of making some small sacrifice, here by a smiling look, there by a kindly word, always doing the smallest right and doing it all for love."
> — Mother Teresa

THURSDAY

Love the alien as you love yourself; for you were once aliens in the Land of Egypt... (Leviticus 19:34).

Fear is a powerful thing. Marketers know this. So do politicians. Those who are in charge of selling us things, ideas, take full advantage of our fears—that we aren't keeping up with our neighbors; that we will get left behind socially, technologically, internationally, intellectually; that we are being taken over by "the other."

The Bible offers another perspective: "Love the alien as you love yourself..." For a moment, let's focus on the second half of the equation: "...love yourself..." What does this imply? It sounds conceited and self-absorbed—until we consider the context. We are to love another person who is not like us and who comes from a different place *as we love ourselves.*

We love ourselves in the sense that we care for ourselves. We brush our teeth, clean ourselves, feed ourselves. We care for ourselves in rudimentary and, occasionally, even pampering ways. We do so in part because we consider ourselves worthy of the trouble. We need to be cared for; we deserve to be cared for. To love myself as the Bible expects, then, is not vain. Rather, it is a normal part of God's expectations in the created order. In the image of God, I can love myself because God created me and first loved me. *And* I am to love my neighbor *and* the alien in exactly the same way. Today, do not be afraid. Instead, love just as God loves you—and as you (should) love yourself.

> "A child of God knows that he or she is loved. And because of that love, which exceeds our own love, we can move out to take risks..."
> — Markoto Fujimara

FRIDAY

There is no fear in love, but perfect love casts out all fear... (I John 4:18).

Not long ago, within the same week in our area of North Carolina, there were two tragic examples of fear and what it can do to otherwise thoughtful people. A U-Tube video of a pastor in Maiden, North Carolina, went viral. He was calling for gays and lesbians to be rounded up and placed in the equivalent of concentration camps.

Then, as if this wasn't bad enough, another small community not far away began proudly publicizing a KKK rally for "whites only." In the words and actions of these two incidents, fear seemed to be the prime motivator. "We are being taken over, and we have to do something! Round people up; hold a rally; circle the wagons; stand together against the enemy!"

Thankfully, the responses against this bigotry largely demonstrated not only disbelief but righteous anger and deep concern. Because our church, Providence Baptist in Charlotte, had a name very close to the offending church in Maiden, we received countless concerned, furious e-mails and calls asking the simple question: "How does this kind of attitude in any way reflect the spirit of Jesus?" It doesn't. It reflects the spirit of fear.

Today, make it your goal to *cast out all fear* within yourself and in others. Be aware of situations that can create such fear and strive to communicate God's perfect love instead.

> "This rejected, unknown, wounded Jesus simply asked, 'Do you love me? Do you really love me?' He whose only concern had been to announce the unconditional love of God had only one question to ask, 'Do you love me?'"
> — Henri Nouwen

SATURDAY

Reflect on this past week's lesson and your revised definition of "the alien." Rejoice in your awareness. Rest. Relax. Enjoy good friends. Revel in God's good world.

The Fourth Week:
Speaking the Truth Then and Now

Then Paul stood in front of the Areopagus and said, "Athenians, I see how extremely religious you are in every way. For as I went through the city and looked carefully at the objects of your worship, I found among them an alter with the inscription, 'To an unknown god.' What therefore you worship as unknown, this I proclaim to you..." (Acts 17:22-24).

Athens was the greatest of all Greek cities, the mother of democracy and philosophical home to Socrates, Plato, and Aristotle.[8] It was here that Herodotus birthed our tradition of recorded history, investigated other cultures, and recorded how their respective histories interacted with that of Greece.

In Athens, Sophocles created and perfected the tradition of drama; countless artists and artisans raised and beautified *The Parthenon* on the acropolis in what would become the "classic Greek style" above the city. This magnificence, along with a vast array of temples and public buildings, would influence western architecture for millennia.

And so the Apostle Paul, with all this history spanning before him, with all the accumulated centuries of wisdom and experience preceding his visit, has the audacity to speak of something new. These philosophers and city leaders did not yet have this particular knowledge at their disposal; neither the information about Jesus nor the transformation that accompanied his proclamation had yet become a part of their personal experiences.

To connect with these people, Paul intentionally speaks to the culture of the people of Athens. He refers offhandedly to the shrines he sees in the city labeled "to an unknown god."

This monument was a clever strategy by the Athenians, one we would call "covering all our bases." They had placated

---

[8] Aristotle was actually from Macedonia, a Greek area to the north that, under Phillip of Macedon and later his son, Alexander the Great, conquered and controlled Athens for a time. As a result, Aristotle was less popular in this Greek capital than were his predecessors.

one of the governing powers of life, the gods of the pantheon, "to an unknown god" as an emergency back-up plan. Think of it as an insurance policy against divine anger.

It is from this connection to what he has seen and heard that Paul proceeds to tell the story of faith. He compliments the Athenians on their devotion and search for truth. He quotes a Stoic philosopher: "...in him we live and move and have our being." He refers to an Epicurean saying: "For we, too, are his offspring" (17:28).

In other words, he knows well the culture, what the people think, and how they interact with reality. He doesn't condemn. He simply offers his understanding of what God has done in the world, why that is important, and what that means—and he does so in a manner that engages the people of Athens. He tells the truth, and he lets God touch the hearts. Some scoffed, but others believed.

This is our model for this week.

> Lord, help us to see deeply into our culture and care deeply about others; give us wisdom; keep us humble; use us today to speak the truth; and may we witness your grace as it touches hearts and minds—ours and those around us. Amen.

REFLECTIONS FOR THE WEEK

MONDAY

Telling the truth isn't always easy. But, even though Paul was confronted with people who scoffed at his conclusions about Jesus, even though he knew many would find it ludicrous that following Jesus' path could change them and the course of their history, Paul spoke the truth.

In doing so, he also demonstrated a cultural sensitivity that is instructive. First, as should be evident from the scripture in Acts 17, he had studied and understood the culture he was addressing. He was conversant enough with Greek literature, Roman philosophers, and Epicurean sayings that he could hold his own with some of the smartest in Greece. Not that he wanted to show off. Rather, the point for all of us should be a lesson in eager learning, attempts at genuine understanding, interest in cross cultural connections, and a quest for common ground.

In the case of those we work beside and interact with, regardless of where they are from or what they believe, we would do well to work for deeper relationships, better communication, and more conscientious understanding.

For Paul, there were some who rejected him outright. Others, though, appreciated that he knew something about them and their worldview and desired to hear more: "We will hear you again about this" (Acts 17:32b). And "some of them joined him and became believers, including Dionysius the Areopagite and a woman named Damaris, and others with them" (Acts 17:34).

Make a point of learning something new about those around you today. How does that affect your relationship with them? How does it affect your understanding of God's presence in your life—and theirs?

> "If I were a preacher, I would preach nothing but the practice of the presence of God."
> — Brother Lawrence

TUESDAY

Pilate asked him, "What is Truth?" (John 19:38).

In the Gospel of John, Pilate reluctantly gets swept into the vortex of Jesus' crucifixion. He summons Jesus to his headquarters. In the interview and strange interaction that follows, Pilate finds no case against him. Yet, for the sake of convenience, he goes along with the crowd of that time and place. It is in this context, surrounded by all the accoutrements of worldly power, that Pilate asks the question: "What is truth?"

He was likely less than happy with his position, a prefect in a part of the empire that wreaked of rebellion and was filled with what he felt were bizarre characters and odd beliefs. Nevertheless, his question echoes through time: *what is truth?* Rather than seek the answer, he avoided the question. Instead of advocating what was right, he accepted what was popular. He took the easy way out. And Jesus died.

Today, charge yourself with this same question. And consider what you stand for and whom you stand *with*.

WEDNESDAY

Jesus entered Jericho ... A man was there named Zacchaeus; he was chief tax collector and was rich (Luke 19:1-2).

Here, Luke introduces us to a character whose very name offers a hint of what he is supposed to be—and, sadly, what Zacchaeus is not. We also discover, hidden in the language of Luke's day, a double entendre about Zacchaeus' stature, both literal and symbolic, and we find a detail of his occupation that creates further insight into the encounter Jesus initiates. In fact, Jesus' *tough love* saves Zacchaeus, both literally and figuratively. To understand, let us look at this more closely:

His Name: Zacchaeus, or ZaKal, in Hebrew means "pure." But Zacchaeus, the man in the story, is nothing of the sort.

His Occupation: To be a sinner is bad. To be a tax collector is worse. This is a special class of sinner. For Zacchaeus, it is even worse: he was a *Chief Tax Collector*. Not only did he unjustly take money to support the occupying power of Rome, he also had authority as Chief Tax Collector to use a special group of soldiers to "invade" people's homes to collect taxes. Though explicitly forbidden in the Jewish law, Luke makes it clear that Zacchaeus ignored the law, disregarded the prophets, and got what he wanted without concern for others.

His Problem: Finally, Luke uses another wordplay to give us insight into what is about to happen with Jesus. Zacchaeus "was rich," says Luke, but apparently not satisfied. He still searched for something more than what money could buy. And he was "short of stature." Usually understood as physical height, the Greek word, *helikia*, can also be understood as *maturity* or *character*. One described in this way might well attempt to do whatever necessary to compensate for his shortcomings. His lack of character and *little* maturity implies the shortcut he has chosen: take from others to support the lifestyle he has come to expect.

Consider what in your life is less than it should be—your outlook, perspective, sense of maturity. If Jesus were to "call you down," what would it be for?

THURSDAY

Zacchaeus, hurry and come down; for I must stay at your house today (Luke 19:7b).

When Jesus enters Jericho, he notices not just a man in a tree but something *inside* the man in the tree. He recognizes an emptiness, an inner captivity, that needs to be freed. Zacchaeus needs to be saved from himself.

In one of the most overlooked and underappreciated moments in the Bible, Jesus confronts Zacchaeus with a classic expression of tough love: "Zacchaeus, you come down" has both a literal and figurative meaning—down from the tree, yes, and, as my mother used to say, *"Get down off that high horse of yours!"* Jesus' call to Zacchaeus was not one of gentle suggestion. It was a call for repentance. Jesus is "calling out" Zacchaeus on his immature character, his material greed, and his spiritual poverty.

Building on yesterday, consider again—and in more depth—what, in you, needs to be "called out." What hidden truth in your life needs to be confronted today? What is the truth that could be spoken by Jesus?

> "When God finds a soul that rests in him and is not easily moved, he operates within it ... giving to such a soul the key to the treasures ... and the joy of his presence..."
> — Catherine of Genoa

FRIDAY

Today, salvation has come to this house... (Luke 19:9).

The fact that Zacchaeus "wanted to see Jesus" implies he was looking for a way out of his spiritual dilemma. Jesus gives it to him: "I must stay at your house today." But the NRSV doesn't do justice to the real emotion of this imperative. A better translation might be: "Just like you have invaded the homes of those you took from, I am invading your house (and heart)..."

Today, we could call this an "intervention," a telling of the truth so that the truth could set him free. And Zacchaeus responds by repaying those he had cheated. The result of this story, after many hidden twists and turns, is "Salvation has come to this house." Finally, Zacchaeus lives up to his name: he is pure; he is whole; he is saved.

Today, contemplate how Jesus might respond to your everyday actions, to your "business," to your being. Take note that, if Jesus calls you down, it is to set you free!

SATURDAY

Reflect on how, this past week, you have worked to be truthful, to yourself and others. Rejoice in your learnings. Rest. Relax. Enjoy this day and the good things that will be part of it.

JULY
Insight

Originally known by the Romans as Quintillis, or fifth month, the name for this month changed during the reign of Julius Caesar. His reforms of the calendar in an attempt for better accuracy created additional days and months. As a result, and being the humble fellow he was, he named this month after himself.

July also holds the esteemed position for Americans as the month that marks our nation's independence. And July is usually an opportunity to vacation, relax, reap the benefits of all our gardening efforts, and enjoy fresh, local produce from stores and farmer's markets.

As we work through this month, we shall consider aspects of wisdom, common connections, and common ground.

The First Week:
Ancient Connections

And God said, "Let there be light." And there was light (Genesis 1:3).

I once did a revival service in a town near where I was going to seminary. After the sermon, people passed by thanking me for my words and sharing the requisite pleasantries, deserved or not, for what I had just said. But, as one woman approached, I could see her scowl—she was clearly upset about something.

"What translation of the Bible did you use?" she asked in an accusatory tone.

"I used the Revised Standard Version," I said.

She looked at me with disdain.

"Well, I only use the King James Version. If it was good enough for Paul, it is good enough for me."

She said this with a completely straight face. She was totally serious.

As most of you know, in Paul's day, there was no English. Paul spoke Aramaic and Greek, along with Latin (likely improved while he lived as a prisoner in Rome). Jesus spoke Aramaic and probably Greek. The English language had not yet evolved.[1] Here's an abbreviated story of how that happened—and why it matters.

The New Testament was written in Greek. That was the commercial language of the Roman Empire. Latin had been the administrative language of the empire, used for legal and governmental matters.[2] It was the language of Rome and became the language of the church as the Roman church expanded its influence and the Popes became more powerful. Missionaries carried the gospel to far-flung areas and, increasingly, Latin

---

[1] From the fascinating mix of Germanic languages, Greek, Latin, French, along with a host of loan words from other languages, including Turkish and Arabic.

[2] Geographically, Greek was also the primary spoken language in the eastern half of the Roman Empire; Latin tended to be spoken more in the western part. Even so, Greek remained primary in economic and business matters.

became the language of worship and scripture. After the political disintegration of the western part of the Roman Empire around 476 A.D., church institutions remained the sole facilitators of education. Therefore, Latin, the language of the church, became the language of learning, too.

Meanwhile, in the area where English would one day take hold, the former Roman province of Britannia became a melting pot and multi-linguistic arena of competing people and languages.[3] Slowly, the language of the Angles took hold among the vast numbers of the poor, but the church and the educated continued to read, write, and study Latin.

By 1066, another outside influence bore down on the land of the Angles and the Anglo-Saxon culture.[4] William the Conqueror, a Norman king from France, invaded and successfully took over and controlled the land. French became the language of the aristocracy. Landowners and the cultural elite either already knew or had to learn French in order to fit with the ruling class. Latin continued to be the language of education and church, but this Anglo-Saxon Germanic language persisted among the majority of the island, the regular working people, those who worked the land, worked with their hands, and kept the economy going.

Gradually, the languages began to fuse, to merge into an extremely useful and vitally flexible language that utilized Germanic structure and grammar with French and Latin vocabulary. Some estimate today that, at most, only twenty percent of English remains from the original and mostly Germanic "Old English."[5] But the resulting, highly adaptive combination we now have is

---

[3] See Tore Janson's *A Natural History of Latin* for more details, especially pages 93-95.

[4] The Angles and Saxons entered the British Isles at about the same time, in the 700s A.D. Though they were separate tribes and spoke different dialects (as did the Jutes who arrived with them), they have become fused into the cultural nomenclature of "Anglo-Saxon."

[5] Old English was the type spoken between 500-1100 A.D. *Beowulf* is an example. Middle English was from 1100-1500, an example being Chaucer's *Canterbury Tales*. Shakespeare's plays and poetry, and the printing of the King James Version of the Bible, took place on the heels of Middle English and at the beginning of Modern English. If you ever had trouble understanding Shakespeare or the KJV, that is why. The words are from an English over four hundred years old.

recognized worldwide as the most practical for trade, business, economics, and international relations.[6] And it was this interaction with and learning from other languages and cultures that led to the organic evolution of the English we know today.[7]

Though neither Paul nor Jesus spoke the English of King James—regardless of what the frustrated lady in Indiana felt—our language today still has grammar, vocabulary, and roots of words that can take us all the way back to the richness and depth of the Greek and Aramaic they spoke. The way we communicate, what we say, and how we say it connects us to a distant linguistic past from another day and time.

We also are connected to the words, acts, and life of Jesus because we are connected to the spirit of Jesus. When God said, "Let there be light," it was not only to activate creation; it was to begin a continuing enlightenment, ongoing insight, and renewed perspective. Just as the movement of language and the evolvement of our words is dynamic, fluid, and continuous, so is the movement, direction, and flexibility of God's spirit in an ongoing revelation over time. New insights emerge from experience—and inspiration. We will continue to explore these thoughts as we move through this week seeking God's light—and new insight.

> O God, this week, please teach us, grow us, and help us to be accepting of new things, generous with old things and always ready to learn something new. Amen.

---

[6] Some of this certainly has to do with British influence and the fact, in the late nineteenth and early twentieth centuries, Britain controlled as much as twenty-five percent of the globe. The United States and the power and influence it wielded following World War II also contributed to the broad use of English. However, the fact remains that English is widely spoken because it remains so utilitarian.

[7] We continue to borrow words (called "loan words") from other languages and drop them right into our own. We also make them up—every year and with almost every change in culture ("to Google" is a good example)!

REFLECTIONS FOR THE WEEK

MONDAY

There is no longer Jew or Greek, there is no longer slave or free, there is no longer male or female; for all of you are one in Christ Jesus (Galatians 3:28).

Families were devastated. The economy was in ruins. Major portions of cities and farms were wastelands. Resentment ran high and, in some portions of the land, there had been systematic acts of terrorism on both sides. Just Google "Kansas, Bloody Kansas" and you will be shocked at the horrors that exploded in Kansas and Missouri, as well as other parts of the south—acts of terror that would make the Middle East look tame. It was to this greatest national emergency that the president addressed his attention:

> *The dogmas of the quiet past are inadequate for the stormy present. The occasion is piled high with difficulty, and we must rise with the occasion. As our case is new, so we must think anew, and act anew. We must disenthrall ourselves.*

When Abraham Lincoln spoke these words on December 1, 1862, our American Civil War appeared intractable, tragic, and expanding. The country had to "disenthrall" itself. The bigoted, closed-minded attitudes of then we recognize now as antiquated, racist, classist, sexist, and fool-hearty.

Think on what perspectives you hold today that will need to be revised in the future. Expand that to include any aspect of society. What new insights are necessary now? Let us "disenthrall ourselves," as we consider carefully, evaluate fully, and live compassionately.

More importantly, consider what God's spirit, working in and with regular people like you and me, might be up to in our world today. As language works within the confines of culture and human perspective, it continues to change and adapt. Following the Civil War, many would now agree there was a gradual spiritual awakening as regular people opened up new realities. We now realize the immoral and anti-spiritual nature of slavery—and, finally, though still gradually, we have begun to see the destructive nature of discrimination and prejudice. Reflect on how God might be at work today, in you or in those whose voices you hear. Search for new insights emerging in your mind, heart, or surroundings.

> Open unto me—light for my darkness ... courage for my fear ... peace for my turmoil ... wisdom for my confusion ... Thyself for myself. Lord, Lord, open unto me! Amen.
> — Howard Thurman

TUESDAY

All the families of the earth will be blessed through you (Genesis 12:3).

Our family once had the privilege of hosting a kind and very wise doctor from India. Her name was Dr. Vina. She insisted on cooking for us, even though she was our guest. Each evening, she brought out these amazing spices from her suitcase and prepared cuisine the likes of which our family had rarely dreamed. We marveled at the dishes so expertly mingled in sight, smell, and taste. Every night, our home became a place of culinary delight fit for kings and queens—but all for us. Paradise.

I took her to speaking engagements where she told her audiences about her home, her family, her town and country, and what she did as a woman professional. Each time, she moved to the center of her speaking area, stood straight, smiled, placed her hands together just over her heart, and pointed upward in a position of prayer; with eyes kind and wide, she would say: "Namaste."[8] I wrote the following recounting our time together and the meaning of this most ancient and profound of greetings.

---

[8] Namaste, pronounced "Nam-as-tay" comes from the ancient language of Sanskrit and means: "All that is holy within me greets all that is holy within you." It is one of the most ancient of greetings.

NAMASTE: "All that is holy in me greets all that is holy in you."
"Namaste," she said; a word I had not known, but needed.
A word from distant lands and long ago repeated: fresh; essential.

"Namaste," she said; with hopeful smile and kind eyes.
A blessing from India that supplies: grace; gladness;

"Namaste," she said; and bowed with hands together to pray.
Which meant when she, gently speaking this word, was to say
"All that is holy in me greets all that is holy in you."
"NAMASTE."

Today, greet others with all that is holy in you, reach out and bless that too-often hidden part of another that is equally good and right and beautiful. And may you be lifted and feel loved as you do so.

WEDNESDAY

Whoever pursues righteousness and kindness will find life and honor (Proverbs 21:21).

There is, in the American character, an exceedingly hopeful and optimistic spirit. I believe righteousness and kindness are embedded in the hopes and dreams of this nation. Though sometimes twisted in irrational ways or hidden behind today's political climate, we continue to share, as Americans, a desire to *welcome the stranger*, to see the rejected of other lands as a new and potentially vital part of our own. Yet, because of various pressures and difficulties, that vision—that hopeful trajectory of a positive future—is threatened. In some areas of our country where crime and illegal immigration have appeared to increase in tandem, it is tempting to leap to associative conclusions.

The complicated dynamics of our current time should not be minimized, nor should the legitimate concerns of the many caught up in the maelstrom of confusing policies and inappropriate behaviors on all sides diminish the power and necessity of welcoming the stranger. At the bedrock of our nation's character (and inscribed on the pedestal of the Statue of Liberty) are these words from Emma Lazarus' "The New Colossus":

> Give me your tired, your poor,
> Your huddled masses yearning to breathe free,
> The wretched refuse of your teeming shore;
> Send these, the homeless, tempest-tossed to me,
> I lift my lamp beside the golden door!

These sentiments correspond well to what Jesus intoned in the face of harsh opposition as he continued to reinforce: "Love the alien as you love yourself; for you were once aliens in the land of Egypt..." (Leviticus 19:34).

The tendency for many, and the constant temptation for all, is to blame problems on those who are new or different or those we simply don't understand. Yet, consistently in this country and throughout Christian history, we remember the legacy of the stranger, the heroic actions of the unwanted, the new insights and contributions of disregarded and even despised.

Let us "pursue righteousness and kindness and find life and honor" and live out biblical wisdom—together—as we seek those new insights so necessary for our spiritual, intellectual, and emotional growth. Watch carefully around you today—at the store, in the office, around the neighborhood, on the news—and look for positive signs of compassion, openness, courage, and new insights about living together in harmony.

THURSDAY

But this is the one to whom I will look, to the humble and contrite in spirit (Isaiah 66:2).

Just as the Statue of Liberty represents the spirit of human hope and the ideal of this nation and democracy, this verse from Isaiah is a bold reminder of our biblical hope—and spiritual goal. God's expectation is for our humility to exceed our suspicion. Though tempted to criticize and look down on those not in our circle of friends, the biblical calling is to welcome, bless, and empower "the least of these" (Matthew 25:40). Expanding on our discussion from yesterday, let's look at the full text of Emma Lazarus' poem. Notice the echo of this biblical theme of humility and welcome while alluding in comparison to the ancient Colossus of Rhodes[9]:

> ### The New Colossus
> Not like the brazen giant of Greek fame,
> With conquering limbs astride from land to land;
> Here at our sea-washed, sunset gates shall stand
> A mighty woman with a torch, whose flame
> Is the imprisoned lightning, and her name
> Mother of Exiles. From her beacon-hand
> Glows world-wide welcome; her mild eyes command
> The air-bridged harbor that twin cities frame.
> "Keep ancient lands, your storied pomp!" cries she
> With silent lips. "Give me your tired, your poor,
> Your huddled masses yearning to breathe free,
> The wretched refuse of your teeming shore.
> Send these, the homeless, tempest-tossed to me,
> I lift my lamp beside the golden door!"

Give some thought today on what this means, not only in our churches and places of worship, but also in our nation as a whole. How wide is the door? How humble and contrite is our spirit? Consider the role of a Christian regarding the various social issues of our day, including ongoing controversies with immigration, emotional debates surrounding gay rights, relationships with the Muslim community, concerns about those without homes... These and many other issues remain highly charged within and outside the Christian community. Without a coherent and well-articulated message from active citizens who are also committed Christians, all of us will continue to struggle.

> "Lord, grant us the serenity to accept the things we cannot change, courage to change the things we can, and wisdom to know the difference. Amen."
> — Reinhold Niebuhr

---

[9] One of the Seven Wonders of the Ancient World. The statue stood over one hundred feet tall on a pedestal that was reported to have been over fifty feet tall. Built in 280 B.C., it was destroyed in an earthquake in 226 B.C.

FRIDAY

There is no longer Jew or Greek, there is no longer slave or free, there is no longer male or female; for all of you are one in Christ Jesus (Galatians 3:28).

All are one in Christ Jesus.

There was a time in our country not terribly long ago when Poles, Italians, and Irish were considered exotic aliens worthy of exclusion. They had too many babies, couldn't understand democracy, and would never offer allegiance to anyone but the Pope. Now, we know better. We still have much to learn as we confront the serious issues in our country both creatively and collaboratively. As Americans, we must be wise, considerate, flexible, and forward-looking.

In the same way, Christians continue to wrestle with how far we go in accommodating perspectives different from our own. But, according to Galatians, what Jesus has done changes everything. And whether we like it our not, we are far more connected with one another than we can imagine. Today, think about ways you can take this biblical statement and turn it into reality. Consider whom you come in contact with during the day. Make a concerted effort to treat them in a way that demonstrates what God has already done through Jesus: we are connected in deeper ways than we can imagine or fully understand. Live today with this reality at the heart of your interactions.

SATURDAY

So God blessed the seventh day and hallowed it, because on it God rested from all the work that he had done in creation (Genesis 2:3).

Allow this to be your good and restorative Sabbath day. Look forward to communal worship tomorrow; but for today, enjoy the freedom of rest as you reflect on your learnings and subsequent actions this past week.

The Second Week:
The Necessity of Wisdom

One who is clever conceals knowledge, but the mind of a fool broadcasts folly (Proverbs 12:23).

Syracuse was a Greek city established on the island of Sicily and settled originally by colonists from the thriving city of Corinth.[10] Syracuse was widely known in the ancient world as "the most beautiful and noble of the Greek cities."[11]

In addition to its magnificent setting and rich history, Syracuse remains valuable to history also because of its most famous son, Archimedes. This remarkable physicist/inventor/mathematician/scientist brought fame to himself and his hometown through the quiet, humble work of his amazing intellect. It is Archimedes who yelled "Eureka" ("I found it") and ran through the streets naked in his excitement. At the public bath house, immersing himself in a large tub of hot water, he noticed the "principle of Archimedes"—that a floating body loses in weight an amount equal to the weight of the water which it displaces.[12]

His sharp mind and wise observations also contributed to the courageous defense of the city from the Roman invaders in 212 B.C. As the power of Rome spread across this part of the Mediterranean, Syracuse rose as an irresistible target for Rome's expanding appetite. With a stronger navy and army, and with experienced soldiers leading the way, most observers expected a quick victory for Rome and total defeat for the beautiful but poorly defended Syracuse.

---

[10] The beginnings of the city are traced to 735 B.C.

[11] From the Roman historian Livy.

[12] p. 630, *The Life of Greece*, Will Durant. Archimedes had been assigned the task of figuring out if the gold in King Hieron's (King of Syracuse) crown had been exchanged for some silver so that the goldsmith could keep some of the gold for himself. This principle of Archimedes allowed the great thinker to determine the amount of water displacement from an equal amount of gold compared to that of silver. His discovery was that, yes, some of the gold had indeed been replaced with the less expensive and less weighty silver. The goldsmith was executed for his crime.

But few realized the value of Archimedes quietly working in the background of the rising conflict. He had become fascinated with fulcrums and levers. One day, when his fellow townsmen were struggling to pull a large ship out of the water into dry dock, he intervened. Claiming to the playful jeers of those present that he could pull the ship onto shore alone, all laughed and called him a crazy old man. He proceeded to construct a series of pulleys and levers, then sat on the beach, turned a crank with one hand, and the ship easily moved out of the water onto the shore. His amazed audience begged him to use his genius for the defense of Syracuse against the great ships and might of Rome.

This week, we will continue to contemplate this bit of history from early Syracuse and Archimedes, but more, we will consider the nature of "skillful living," of passionate work and play, of working to increase understanding, and of being at peace with our surroundings.

> Lord, give me passion for what I do. May I be so inspired by your calling in my life that I overlook the distractions and look beyond to the larger good. Give me wisdom so that I might see Jesus in others; and give me gentleness that others might see Jesus in me. Amen.

REFLECTIONS FOR THE WEEK

MONDAY

Be wise as serpents and gentle as doves... (Matthew 10:16).

Too often, people of faith put too little emphasis on deep thinking, hard questions, and how these vitally support the broader wisdom the Bible calls us to. It is clear from Jesus' words in Matthew that his was a call not only to humility and gentleness but to wisdom, even cleverness. The great thinker and crafty inventor Archimedes demonstrates some of these good characteristics.

A humble man of peace, Archimedes was against using his inventions for war or to make money. He was a gentle man. But he consented for the protection of his home and those he loved. At seventy-five years old, he supervised the construction of large catapults able to hurl enormous objects long distances. The stones raining down on the Romans from these created such panic that they retreated. Returning under the cover of night, the Roman ships, if not sunk by projectiles from the catapults, were now harassed by large Archimedean-designed cranes raising large rocks to great heights and then swinging them out over the channel by which the Roman ships were attempting to invade. The rocks and large loads of heavy objects would then be released onto the vulnerable decks of the Roman ships, sinking many and drowning countless sailors. His inventions captivated even his enemies, many of whom were certain they battled with gods, for who else would be capable of such strength—or cleverness.

In our day, to be "crafty" conveys negative implications. Yet, Jesus' call to be "wise as serpents" offers something of this— that we should not be naïve, nor should we be unaware of what surrounds us. We should be biblically astute and reliably conversant in whatever the emerging issues for our day might be. Biblically, we are expected to be discerning in what we believe, passionate in how we relate biblical principles to real life situations. Our opinions, still humble and contrite, ought to be based upon understanding cultivated over time and distilled from a variety of sources, including personal experience and an openness to the prompting of God.

Reading the Bible and studying scripture is vital to a growing faith. Make a priority today to add to that discipline—search for reliable, stimulating sources of additional information that will add perspective and depth to your understanding.

> "Study to make thyself approved unto God, a worker who needeth not be ashamed, rightly dividing the word of truth."
> — II Timothy 2:15

TUESDAY

When you come, bring the cloak that I left with Carpus at Troas, also the books, and above all the parchments (II Timothy 4:13).

This is a valuable verse. If there were ever any question that a person of faith should be a person of disciplined study, here is solid evidence of some of Paul's priorities. In spite of his difficult circumstances, he regards his books and parchments as essential for his continued pastoral responsibilities.[13] Learning, curiosity, study—always essential for spiritual growth and personal development—should remain priorities for us, too. Now, let us continue with the story of Archimedes and the Roman offensive on Syracuse.

Finally, as the Romans continued their assault against the city, additional cranes were constructed with long, thick ropes to which large hooks were attached and carefully strung across the bay where the Roman ships approached. As a ship crossed over the rope, the crank of the crane turned, the hook engaged

---

[13] Bound books as we know them were not yet in existence. There were collections of papyrii, the predecessor to our paper made out of pressed reeds, sometimes collected and sewn together in the middle so that, in shape and form, they would have been very much like our modern books.

the bow or stern of the ship, pulled it through, and ultimately out of, the water. The cranes literally dangled these huge ships in mid-air, their sailors falling helplessly into the sea.

Now sailors and soldiers were certain that Syracuse was inhabited by gods, not ordinary people, and they refused to fight against the city further. The Roman general, Marcellus, knew better. He decided not to push his men beyond their capacity for understanding, and settled in for a long and terrible siege. After eight months, the city of Syracuse surrendered. Though Marcellus demanded that Archimedes be spared so his brilliance could be used by Rome, an overly enthusiastic Roman soldier ran him through with a sword. Archimedes was too busy attempting to work out his next problem and refused to heed the soldier's call to rise and follow him to meet the general.

A man of immense inquisitiveness and broad discipline, Archimedes offers a prime example of one passionate about his craft of learning, generous with his time on behalf of his people, humble in spite of his brilliance, playful in the use of his intellect and skill, and focused on continued improvement in the quality of his understanding.

Search out ways today you can expand your knowledge, cultivate your curiosity, and deepen your understanding—and then be generous with what you can contribute, humble with how you share, and determined in your continued efforts.

> "If I have a little money, I buy books. If I have any left, I buy food and clothes."
> — Erasmus of Rotterdam

WEDNESDAY

Whenever you face trials of any kind, consider it nothing but joy... (James 1:2).

It was my third trip to Israel. One of the places I looked forward to experiencing again was the Mt. of Beatitudes, that place where tradition claims Jesus gave the Sermon on the

Mount in Matthew 5-7. It is a place of spectacular beauty and, the first two times I visited, I remembered it being a place of remarkable serenity.[14] I recalled sitting quietly on a bench below the chapel in a garden surrounded by herbs, roses, and the lilies of the field that Jesus used as one of his illustrations in Matthew 6.[15] But things had changed and, this time tour buses rumbled into the newly expanded parking lot loaded with noisy tourists from all over the world. I heard Spanish, Japanese, and Romanian; German, Russian and Korean; I saw a Polish flag, Ukrainian soccer jerseys, a New York Yankees baseball cap. This was not the serene spot I had previously enjoyed.

The bedlam of these disparate groups overwhelmed my patience—so much for spiritual focus. But what initially felt like an invasion of a sacred place gradually took on a different meaning. As I looked around, I literally saw what Jesus must have meant by *inclusion*—about welcoming the "other," those from different places and perspectives. Here I was part of the very community Jesus envisioned. *They* had become *we*. We spoke different languages and came from different places, yet we all gathered because of a common savior and through a common teaching, translated into all these languages that had so irritated me only moments before.

Today, look for those moments when you are most frustrated at the actions or inactions of others and try to find the blessing of God and new wisdom. Consider it "nothing but joy," for God just may be teaching you something new and valuable.

THURSDAY

Have nothing to do with stupid and senseless controversies; you know that they breed quarrels (II Timothy 2:23).

It would be nice to know exactly what controversies Paul was referring to with this statement. For it is clear, Paul did not

---

[14] Ironically, the chapel high on the hill overlooking the Sea of Galilee was built by Mussolini during his fascist rule of Italy in the 1930's.

[15] "Consider the lilies of the field, how they grow; they neither toil nor spin yet I tell you, even Solomon in all his glory was not clothed like one of these" (Matthew 6:28).

shy away from a wide range of controversial issues (read Galatians or I and II Corinthians). But, from our own family experience, I think I have a sense of what he intended.

Like many of you, as parents, Beth and I came to an early recognition that we had to "choose our battles." Often, what one of our children wore an a particular day mattered far less than how they felt about themselves or what they were most interested in or fascinated by. Through early mistakes and much wasted energy, we learned that some battles are just not that important.

For a Christian, this kind of discernment seems to be at the heart of II Timothy 2:23. This is no excuse to minimize passion for justice or concern for particular issues that *do* matter. It does mean we cannot do everything, change everybody, or make everyone think like we do. Nor would that be helpful or healthy. There are plenty of issues for which there are plenty of other passionate advocates. We are called to choose our battles wisely, to be discerning, understanding, open-minded, patient, humble—and well-versed in what we *do* believe to be vital, good, and central to faith.

Today, consider what these things might be for you—battles that need not be fought right now *and* issues that *are* front and center to your concern and passions at this time. Investigate ways your church or local gathering might be offering support and information for you and your interests. Look for others who share in your passion. Choose your battles wisely, and know what you are talking about when you do!

> "People demand freedom of speech as a compensation for the freedom of thought which they seldom use."
> — Soren Kierkegaard

FRIDAY

There is nothing better for mortals than to eat, drink, and find enjoyment in their toil. This also, I saw is from the hand of God (Ecclesiastes 2:24).

In Hebrew, the word for wisdom means "skillful living." The "Teacher" of Ecclesiastes expresses a particular brand of wisdom echoed in the philosophical teachings of Epicurus (We will discuss him next week). Seeking purposeful living, both Ecclesiastes and Epicureanism explore ways of looking at the world, with realism and with optimism. Like James and his wisdom in the New Testament, this imperative to "eat, drink, and enjoy your toil" is a reminder that all "is from the hand of God."

The Teacher here implores us to do more than endure life. Enjoy life with friends, with family, in community. Today, reflect on your toil, the job(s) you spend much of your life tending to. Whatever you do, strive to rediscover a sense of accomplishment and meaning by doing what you do with purposeful enjoyment.

> "I shall not say 'behold an hour of my life is gone,' but rather 'I have lived one hour.'"
> — Ralph Waldo Emerson

SATURDAY

Rest. Relax. Reflect on this past week's learnings. Enjoy some reading that has nothing to do with your daily routine, and have fun learning something new.

THE THIRD WEEK:
Recycled Stardust and Us

For he knows how we were made; he remembers that we are dust (Psalm 103:14).

Right now, you are experiencing a unique arrangement of molecular particles clustered in a way that will never again be. Consequently, what you understand to be *now* remains exclusive to this particular alignment of action, form, time, and space. The ancient Greek cosmologist/philosopher, Heraclitus of Ephesus said it a bit differently and much more succinctly: "You can never step into the same river; for new waters are always flowing onto you."

More strikingly, though, is the fact that you and I exist in the action, form, time, and place that we do at all. After all, we are largely recycled beings. All of us are an intricate accumulation of atomic material that has been around for all of history. We have, as the essence of our physical selves, the same substance as most of the universe: stardust.

The atoms that make up stardust, or carbon, and all the other elements of the universe, don't pass away with the cessation of our physical selves. Instead, by evaporated liquid, regenerated solids, and escaping gas, our bodies decompose into other usable forms to position themselves into other physical essences. What occurs when one of us dies ("from dust to dust...") is also what occurred when we came into existence.[16]

The psalm above refers to Genesis 2. In fact, the wording of 103:14 is fascinating: "...he remembers that we *are* dust." Not that we were, but we are. The very naming of humanity's beginnings in the second creation story cracks open a valuable shell of ancient wisdom.

---

[16] The ancient Greeks knew a version of this, believing that our physical selves returned to the dust of the earth. They could see this occur through observing the aftermath of the battlefield deaths. The soldiers left unclaimed and unburied eventually turned to dust and returned to the earth. They also sensed a divine connection, the psyche, known as the mind or soul, that somehow came from beyond the individual and his or her personal experience. Once death claimed the physical self, the mind/soul returned to the gods, or to some universal storage facility for the souls of future incarnations.

Somehow, the originators of our biblical tradition share vital, controversial insights into our earliest beginnings. They gained some providential inkling that, beyond the earthy stuff, we are infused with God's spirit, our substance comes from and is connected to something beyond our understanding.

"From dust we come; to dust we return..." and yet "the steadfast love of the Lord is from everlasting unto everlasting..." (Psalm 103:17).

> Let us have the vision this week to see beyond ourselves, O God. Allow us the wisdom to be at once, both humble in recognizing our physical makeup and honored in understanding our spiritual grounding. Give us patience in our interactions, serenity throughout our schedule, and sacred purpose for all our actions. Amen.

REFLECTIONS FOR THE WEEK

MONDAY

Consider the lilies of the field, how they grow; they neither toil nor spin, yet I tell you, even Solomon in all his glory was not clothed like one of these (Matthew 6:28).

There is something very humbling about being made from dust. The saying "you are nothing but dirt" may be derisive, but it also unveils a deeper truth. We are united with one another and with God's world in our *earthiness*. And this unity in our dusty origins *and* our unity in spiritual beginnings opens us up to broader philosophical questions. Ecclesiastes takes seriously the tension between these two realities: earthiness and sacredness. So does Jesus. Coming from the dust, we have as part of our makeup the same substance that nurtures the beauty of the earth, the fragrance of the flowers, the elegance of the blossoms, the sturdiness of the trees...

The majority of our lives, for most of us, is spent "on the job" in one form or another. Thus, we begin this week considering the role of wisdom and perspective in our everyday interactions. Jesus' concern in this passage from Matthew had to do with our tendency to worry, so his words were to facilitate a new and better perspective. We are to see God's hand at work in the little things, re-prioritize the peripheral, stay focused on what is good and honorable and right and true and beautiful—and remember our place in the universe. Honoring earthiness begins a valuable step toward embracing the sacred—and learning from Jesus.

> "It was a religious event when Meister Eckhardt pointed to the 'eternal now' within the flux of time, and when Soren Kierkegaard pointed to the infinite significance of every moment as the 'now' of decision."
> — Paul Tillich

TUESDAY

As for mortals, their days are like grass; they flourish like a flower of the field; for the wind passes over it, and it is gone, and its place knows it no more (Psalm 103:15-16).

My great-grandfather was a Baptist preacher (it runs in our family). He had been pastor of First Baptist Church of Decatur, Georgia, and was instrumental in the congregation's move to their current site. The building of that day had since been torn down and another erected in its place. But in my mind, he had surely played a crucial role in the life of that congregation.

I had the opportunity to worship there one Sunday not long ago and wondered if, by chance, there might be someone who remembered him. After the service, I targeted several elderly members and asked them if they knew my great-grandfather. I told them his name.

"Never heard of him."

"Who did you say he was?"

"Are you sure he was pastor *here*?"

All that work. Long hours laboring over sermons, committee meetings, pastoral care, mission work, and long-range plans—and nobody remembered him? Okay, it had been a long time. But still...

The psalmist above reminds us about the final outcome of our hard work: that we may flourish for a time but be forgotten later. Years from now, no one will remember how you almost killed yourself trying to finish that last project, trying to impress the boss, trying to make the stockholders happy, but *the steadfast love of the Lord is from everlasting unto everlasting.*

Contemplate what this means for you today; find peace and comfort in the bigger picture. And don't forget to smell the flowers, watch the clouds, listen to the birds, notice the laughter of children, and give thanks for quiet moments to be glad.

> "We have an interval, and then our place knows us no more."
> — Walter Pater

WEDNESDAY

The crown of the wise is their wisdom, but folly is the garland of fools (Proverbs 14:24).

Epicurus, like many famous Greek philosophers, encouraged those around him to think deeply, to experience wonder, to appreciate life, and to cultivate friendships. Like the Teacher of Ecclesiastes, he was realistic about life's difficulties and advocated facing them while finding the broader benefits in the cultivation of wisdom. The writers of Proverbs express the same.[17] There is a clear understanding throughout Proverbs that becoming wise doesn't just *happen*. Only fools stagger through life without considering the *why* and the *what for*. This is more than memorizing information. Wisdom is the integration of knowledge, experience, and understanding accumulated into *skillful living*. In such a perspective, curiosity thrives alongside integrity, humility, grace, and compassion. Together, these serve as food for the mind and strength for the soul.

Today, make it your personal goal to continue a biblical quest for wisdom, to live skillfully, to recognize the value in each new experience, and know that, in the words of Epicurus, "no age is too early or too late for the health of the soul."

> "Let no one be slow to seek wisdom when he is young, nor weary in the search of it when he has grown old."
> — Epicurus

THURSDAY

For he knows how we were made; he remembers that we are dust (Psalm 103:14).

I had the pleasure of leading a good-sized group to Israel and Jordan not long ago. We were from different churches,

---

[17] There were many contributors and multiple writers, none of whom we know. A few may have been collected during the reign of Solomon, others throughout Israel's history, and some we know even come from earlier Egyptian wisdom sayings.

denominations, different parts of the country, different political persuasions, and different ethnic groups.

There were fifteen from our group baptized in the Jordan River. We sang "Down by the Riverside" several times while the baptism took place. I noticed there were several Asian men not from our group standing over to the side watching us. In a pause during our singing, they began to sing "Amazing Grace" in their language. Our eyes met; they gave a thumbs up and grinned broadly.

They sang with joy for us, brothers and sisters from another place, united by this holy moment. Made from the same earthy substance, we claimed a common purpose, shared a common Savior, and celebrated an equal place before God in the sacred act of baptism.

Know that, today, you are far more than the mere collected parts that make up your physical body. God's spirit, breathed into you, animates and gives you the spiritual self that makes *you*. This remains the deepest part of yourself and is intimately woven together with those around you and far from you. Live accordingly; be more accepting, loving, patient. Live with gladness.

FRIDAY

So I commend enjoyment, for there is nothing better for people under the sun than to eat, and drink and enjoy themselves, for this will go with them in their toil through the days of life that God gives them under the sun (Ecclesiastes 8:15).

Here it is, the Teacher of Ecclesiastes blessing enjoyment.[18] And, as a follow-up on a previous passage, he tweaks the message. In chapter two, the imperative was to "eat, drink, and enjoy your toil." In chapter eight, the implication is different. "Eat, drink,

---

[18] It is worth noting that Isaiah 22:13 seems to both know of this perspective and condemn it. For him, the focus should be weeping and sadness over the people's selfishness and rejection of God's desires. Rather than contradicting Ecclesiastes, Isaiah's perspective is further evidence of the need for biblical interpretation and contextual understanding.

and enjoy *yourself*" for your job might be drudgery and you need to have something to spice things up. Or something like that. In other words, the Teacher understands how things work.

Ideally, we should enjoy what we do every day, lest we be miserable. On the other hand, sometimes jobs can be difficult. Every day might be a terrible grind. The office atmosphere could be tense, the boss could be self-serving or dishonest, the pressure could be too much. Understanding all this, there appears to be biblical permission to let off a little steam.

Today, have a good time—within reason, of course. The hope would be that all of us have enough sense to be appropriate, moderate our behavior, care for others and ourselves, be good stewards of the time, and still give ourselves a break. Enjoy!

SATURDAY

Rest. Relax. And consider what wisdom you accumulated over this week. Do you feel your living has become any more skillful?

THE FOURTH WEEK:
Imaginative Responses to Life

May you be strengthened with all power, according to his glorious might, for all endurance and patience with joy (Colossians 1:11).

"The hills are alive, with the sound of music..." So begins the opening scene of *The Sound of Music*, with Julie Andrews as Maria, the incorrigible nun, always late, a little flighty, filled with a nervous energy, wanting to break forth in song to the glory of God. Surrounded by the lovely land that is Austria in general, and Salzburg in particular, one can understand Maria's unquenchable thirst for beauty and irrepressible joy. The hills, the sparkling river, the colorful streets, the vibrant flowers, the creative gardeners, the talented musicians, the deep greens of the trees, and the bright blue of the sky are all testimonials to a higher power, a greater strength that fills, surrounds, awakens, and motivates. Maria was drawn to the abbey of Salzburg because of the creation she experienced around her. And she hoped to reciprocate God's love in creation and in her heart through devotion to the abbey.

But her restless spirit and boundless energy led her outward and beyond to a family in need—children and a new husband who would ultimately share her enthusiasm for life and faith.

For you, this week, may the hills, the flowers, all you see be "alive with the sound of music" and the glory of God. May you have a little extra endurance when you are tired, a little extra patience when you are stressed, and a little extra strength for your journey. In other words: *May you be strengthened with all power, according to his glorious might, for all endurance and patience with joy.*

> Lord, allow me to learn a new thing that will make me a better witness for your grace and goodness. Introduce me to a deeper understanding of those who have come before me so that I might learn from their courage and benefit from their faithfulness. Amen.

REFLECTIONS FOR THE WEEK

MONDAY

Praise the Lord ... Praise him for his mighty deeds; praise him according to his surpassing greatness! Praise him with trumpet sound; praise him with lute and harp (Psalm 150:1-3).

Like Maria, another native of Salzburg had an irrepressible spirit. In music, Wolfgang Amadeus Mozart possessed an energy and uniqueness parallel to Maria's joy of life. Mozart envisioned his compositions in much the same way as the psalmist describes: praising God according to his surpassing greatness. His imaginative responses to the great and broad influences of Bach and Hayden dazzled. His genius transcended traditional norms and burst forth in new, complex, confounding, joyous expressions.

Karl Barth, the great and influential Swiss theologian from the early to mid-twentieth century, used to write while listening to the recordings of Mozart. Barth's conclusion was that there was something about Mozart's music that cleared the mind and purified the soul.

So, on this new day of experiencing God's good creation, seek your own inspiration. Lifted and loved, may you, like Maria, experience an exuberance of inexpressible gratitude. And, like Mozart, may you express it with originality, joy, imagination. It also wouldn't hurt if you took time to listen to some of his music!

> "Neither a lofty degree of intelligence nor imagination nor both together go to the making of genius. Love, love, love, that is the soul of genius."
> — Wolfgang Amadeus Mozart

TUESDAY

May you be filled with the knowledge of God's will in all spiritual wisdom and understanding, so that you may lead lives worthy of the Lord, fully pleasing to him, as you bear fruit in every good work and as you grow in the knowledge of God (Colossians 11:9-10).

What a gift it would be to be filled, always, with the knowledge of God, spiritual wisdom, and understanding—lives worthy of the Lord and bearing fruit in every good work. Just as Mozart imagined an entire score of music in his head and then wrote it down, so can you utilize your own imagination. See the coming hours as good, right, truthful. Live today worthy of the Lord—the rest will follow.

> "It is a great consolation for me to remember that the Lord, to whom I had drawn near in humble and child-like faith, has suffered and died for me, and that He will look on me in love and compassion."
> — Wolfgang Amadeus Mozart

WEDNESDAY

...in him, all things hold together... (Colossians 1:17).

When you are feeling scattered, when life feels disjointed, take this verse to heart. In Jesus, all things hold together. Whatever life feels like today, or what happened yesterday, take a deep breath and remember: you have it all together. The Bible consistently offers us imaginative responses to what can go wrong. What God has done in Jesus makes all the difference. Regardless of how things seem and what life feels like right now, reality is deeper and larger and more profound than whatever stress you feel because *in him, all things hold together.*

Now, imagine this truth to be fully a part of your life and live today with confidence. Jesus has it all together—and so do you.

> "Imagination is what enables us to think with the heart and feel with the mind, a task Jesus seems intent on our learning to do."
> — Michael Card

THURSDAY

"...through him God was pleased to reconcile to himself all things... (Colossians 1:17-20).

When Mozart was thirteen, he went on tour with his father to Italy. While in Rome, he heard Gregorio Allegri's *Miserere* performed in the Sistine Chapel. Mozart returned to his apartment and wrote out the entire score from memory.

To have that kind of gift—that kind of focus—is both amazing and scary! The model of Jesus' ministry had such a focus, Paul says in Colossians. Through Jesus, God pulls together all disparate parts, jangling discords, loose ends. It was not to the power structure or those on the inside track of popularity and importance. It was to the lonely outsiders, to those who had made mistakes. So, just in case your week has been less than what you would like; if you are the lonely one, the one left out and overlooked, the one who made mistakes, here is the good news: in Jesus, all things (that includes you) are reconciled. You are on the inside, regardless of how others have made you feel. And this is very pleasing—to God and to us! Now move through the rest of this day without anxieties. You are not alone. And whatever mistakes you might have made yesterday do not define you now. Today is new, and your place in it is just beginning. You are free to begin again.

> "I live each day as if it were my last, and life, with all its moments, is so full of glory."
> — Helen Keller

FRIDAY

Mozart had an interesting sense of humor. Poking fun at those who never stop talking, he shared the following:

My great-grandfather used to say to his wife, my great-grandmother, who in turn told her daughter, my grandmother, who repeated it to her daughter, my mother, who used to remind her daughter, my own sister, that to talk well and eloquently was a very great art, but that an equally great one was to know the right moment to stop.

Live today with a glad sense of play. The ability to laugh with others and laugh at ourselves is always a good thing. Smile today, enjoy the company of others, and laugh. And remember when to stop talking!

> "Art comes to you proposing frankly to give nothing but the highest quality to your moments as they pass, and simply for those moments' sake."
> — Walter Pater

SATURDAY

Rest. Relax. Read. Listen to music, Mozart, if possible. And if you can and/or are willing, attempt to make some music—preferably with others.

THE FIFTH WEEK:
The Dead Sea and Stagnation

...give and it will be given to you (Luke 6:38).

I have never really been able to float. I can swim fine. But when I stop moving my arms and legs, I sink. This was never much fun when training for becoming a lifeguard. My trainer insisted we all participate in the "drown proofing" technique. The upper torso is to float on the surface, face down, relaxed with arms also floating and legs dangling easily and perpendicular to the surface. When a breath is needed, one gently strokes downward with the arms, lifts the head, takes a deep breath, and then returns to the original position. It sounds easy enough. And it almost killed me. My legs have no buoyancy—at all. While the rest of my body might float, my legs sink. So this drown proofing came very close to drowning me. Each time I wanted to take a breath, I had to swim back to the surface. And this, I came to learn quickly from my angry trainer, wasn't supposed to happen, especially to lifeguards.

So, I was very happy to discover the magic of the Dead Sea. Given that it has a salt content of around thirty percent, everything can float—even me. I was actually able to recline in the chest high water and hold a newspaper in both hands, read it casually, and still float effortlessly.

The water, you see, is trapped in the giant basin of this vast desert into which the waters of the Jordan River flow. From the sparkling clear, deep, and pure waters of the Sea of Galilee in the north, the Jordan River runs into the Dead Sea. With nowhere to go, since the Dead Sea is almost fourteen hundred feet below sea level, the water is left in what amounts to a giant puddle thirty-four miles long and between eleven miles at its widest to two miles at its narrowest. It is also fourteen-hundred feet deep.

Because of the unique conditions of this location, the only thing left for the water gathering here to do is evaporate. Further, high temperatures and exceptionally low humidity create the conditions for an evaporation rate that is one of the most rapid in the world. The result is this remarkably high salt content that allowed me to float as never before. But, for the water, the larger result is, literally, a *dead end*.

> Use me this week, Lord. Allow me to fulfill my potential. Let me pass along the blessings that you so abundantly give to me. Give me the recognition and the thankful heart I need for my own spiritual strength. And allow me the gift of generosity—help me to convey a sense of your blessing with a gladness that is both genuine and contagious. Amen.

REFLECTIONS FOR THE WEEK

MONDAY

...give and it will be given to you. A good measure, pressed down, shaken together, running over... (Luke 6:38).

The amazing geographic and topographic anomaly of the Dead Sea offers us an insight into what it is that God seems to be hoping for us. God has created us to be channels of blessing, not dead ends for grace. What we receive we are to pass on, not hold to ourselves. The Dead Sea is an apt metaphor for the dangers of spiritual hoarding. Without an outlet to allow the water to flow to the sea, this most essential element has no alternative but to evaporate, rising through the atmosphere back to where it began. This substance from God returns untapped, unused, and unfulfilled. Beware of this danger in your own life today. Share your blessings.

> "Gentleness, self-sacrifice, and generosity are the exclusive possession of no one race or religion."
> — Mahatma Gandhi

TUESDAY

...the measure you give will be the measure you get back (Luke 6:38).

In his book *The Life Cycle Completed*, Developmental Psychologist Erik Erikson speaks of our living in tension between two competing emotional poles at different times in our lives. During middle adulthood and midlife (ages forty to sixty-five), the tension is between what he calls "Generativity" and "Stagnation." We are generative, and generally more fulfilled, when we are creating things and contributing to others and society. Parenting and, usually, our most intensive and productive job years take place during this period. Creative and competent participation offers meaning, purpose, and fulfillment at this stage of life. On the other hand, stagnation results when we feel unproductive, fail to contribute, or are unable to offer our efforts to something or someone beyond ourselves. In other words, our lives become like a trapped body of water—*a dead sea.* According to Erikson, *and* the Bible long before him, if we are not generative then we are going nowhere; we stagnate.

> "Present your bodies as a living sacrifice, holy and acceptable to God..."
> — Romans 12:1

WEDNESDAY

...give and it will be given to you. A good measure, pressed down, shaken together, running over ... for the measure you give will be the measure you get back (Luke 6:38).

Every day, we are blessed by the gift of God's presence in our lives, grace for our journeys, and love for our relationships. None of these begin with us. And they are not supposed to end with us. We are conduits, channels for these blessings to and on behalf of the lives of others. But sometimes we forget, or get distracted, or stumble into selfishness. Then, like the Dead Sea— without an outlet for God's goodness—this vital resource in our hearts and spirits may *evaporate* for a time. Being miserly with God's blessings, damming up God's graces, shutting off the flow of God's love causes nothing but a puddle. In such an environment, nothing can live for long, let alone grow.

Know the consequences of spiritual hoarding. The water there is bitter. The result is stagnation, and what little life there is around you is stunted.

Today, acknowledge what God dreams for you. Remain vigilant and determined to be a glad and willing channel of grace, not a puddle of spiritual residue!

> "At the end of the day, it's not about what you have or even what you've accomplished. It's about what you've done with those accomplishments. It's about who you've lifted up, who you've made better. It is about what you've given back."
> — Denzel Washington

THURSDAY

Be on your guard against all kinds of greed... (Luke 12:15).

Jesus tells a story in Luke 12 about a rich fool who is pleasantly surprised to find his crops have yielded more than he anticipated. He has no idea what to do with his surplus. "I know what I will do," he says. "I will build bigger barns so I can store up all this extra stuff. Then I will say to my soul: 'Soul, now we can eat, drink, and be merry.' But God said to him 'Fool! This day your soul is required of you!'"

In other words, God seems to be saying: "You haven't used your soul, so I want it back!" The implication, according to Jesus, is profound. That part of ourselves that seems most fully us—our soul—is made to be shared. We are meant to interact on a holy level that involves both relationships with others and our relationship with God. Failing that, hoarding this sense of holy and communal connectedness, abuses the very foundation for our existence. The best part of ourselves goes unused.

This day, be a channel of blessing. Don't forfeit God's gift to you. Spread your gifts around.

> "...For one's life does not consist in the abundance of possessions."
> — Jesus, Luke 12:15

FRIDAY

Every generous act of giving, with every perfect gift, is from above... (James 1:17).

In the movie, *White Christmas*, Bing Crosby sings the famous and very insightful song by Irving Berlin, "Count Your Blessings":

> When I'm worried and I can't sleep,
> I count my blessings instead of sheep
> and I fall asleep counting my blessings.
> When my bankroll is getting small,
> I think of when I had none at all,
> and I fall asleep counting my blessings.

Behind Jesus' expectation for our discipleship and the biblical principles of giving is gratitude. Giving makes little sense if it is done with a feeling of resentment.

Today reflect on your own blessings—what you have been given and how you give back. Prepare to offer yourself more freely.

SATURDAY

Rest today. Enjoy the summer world around you. Get some exercise. Practice what you have learned this week and be aware of your blessings and the beauty of generativity, giving, and growing.

AUGUST
Imagination

Originally *Sextillis Mensis*, or Sixth Month, Caesar Augustus (the Roman Emperor when Jesus was born and while he was a boy) continued the reforms in the calendar Julius Caesar began. An extra month was added to the yearly cycle and Augustus named it after himself. The word means impressive, majestic, grand, dignified.

August now serves as a bridge between vacations and the beginning of school. It culminates the time of summer gardens and moves us tentatively toward fall. As both an ending and a beginning, it is a good time to consider what has gone before us and why we do what we do. We will use our imaginations, examine love, consider simplicity, continue to investigate Zacchaeus as a model for transformation, and explore the "Dry Bones" of Ezekiel.

The First Week:
Rome and Living Testimonies

All the saints greet you, especially those of Caesar's household (Philippians 4:2).

When these words of scripture were first recorded, probably around the early 60's A.D., Paul was a prisoner in Rome. Paul had been arrested in Jerusalem,[1] transferred to Caesarea on the coast, appealed for hearing before Caesar in Rome, and, as a Roman citizen, was granted his entitled request.[2]

Roman policy required Paul to rent, at his own expense, a small apartment in that famous, imperial city.[3] It likely stood adjacent to the Palatine Hill, close to the headquarters of the Praetorian Guard, which consisted of the best trained and most trusted of Caesar's private army. They protected the emperor, provided crowd control, and watched over important prisoners.

Apparently, the prisoner policy that applied to Paul was to have a guard in his private apartment watching over him at all times, and perhaps, some say, even chained to him.[4] With each shift, a new soldier would enter the apartment, change places with the former guard, and take their position next to Paul. It was not that Paul was considered dangerous; in fact, he was allowed numerous visitors, though all conversations were probably monitored by the guard.[5] This made for wise Roman policy because it served as implicit censorship of potentially seditious conversations while still demonstrating a measure of benevolence toward the prisoner and his friends.

It also made for a glad paradox. While Paul spoke to friends and foes alike about Jesus, soldiers connected to the Praetorian Guard overheard his testimony. For, according to scripture, his

---

[1] Acts 22:22-25

[2] Acts 25:11-12

[3] Acts 28:30

[4] Acts 28:16; and as for his being chained, see Acts 28:20.

[5] Acts 28:30-31

"imprisonment in the cause of Christ has become well known throughout the entire Praetorian Guard and everyone else."[6] Further, the new faith even infiltrated the confines of Palatine Hill and the residence of Nero himself. Whether carried by these soldiers or by others newly converted to the faith, we still hear the far-reaching implications of these fascinating words: "All the saints greet you, especially those of Caesar's household."

> Lord, allow us to claim glad kinship with those who have gone before. And let us see ourselves equal to the task that lies before us. We are no different than they were. You have saved us equally well, graced us with the same good news, joined us to the same grand company of saints, and strengthened us with the same faith that fortified their lives. Now, Lord, we pray for your power this week to instill in us the same blessed courage to live for your glory and to testify for your kingdom. Amen.

---

[6] Philippians 1:12-13

REFLECTIONS FOR THE WEEK

MONDAY

And this is my prayer, that your love may overflow more and more with knowledge and full insight... (Philippians 1:9).

Use your imagination and go back to this time in history: you are standing in the Forum in Rome. This is where it all took place in those days: fancy shopping, important speakers calling out the latest ideas or announcing the most recent events of the empire. The street you stand on is called the Via Appia, or Appian Way, the most famous street and Roman imperial highway. Notice that paralleling the Via Appia is Palatine Hill, the palatial living space of the emperors and, in those days, home to Nero.[7] Imagine when this marketplace would have been jammed with crowds, orator's calling attention to the relevant causes of the day, senators debating, soldiers marching, shoppers negotiating—all moving through the imperial magnificence of Rome's centerpiece. And imagine also the early Christians, people like you and me, conducting business, paying bills, buying groceries, and carrying on with daily life.

Building on this visualization, spend time thinking about how today's scripture translates from those early Christians' devotion to your own devotion, love, and insight. Live today recognizing that we are continuing the legacy of those early Christian ancestors. The same human struggles they wrestled with remain with us. See yourself as a Christian brother or sister working in tandem with them, connected over the centuries in faithfulness and love. Now, go through the day with renewed strength for what lies ahead.

TUESDAY

And this is my prayer, that your love may overflow more and more with knowledge and full insight to help you to determine what is best... (Philippians 1:9-10).

---

[7] The ruins of those former palaces are still being unearthed and examined, as are the countless other ruins of Rome's former glory lining the Forum.

It is significant that the love hoped for should be overflowing with knowledge and full insight. This just doesn't happen for most of us, at least not often. But it is what we, as God's children, strive for.

Today, imagine yourself growing in wisdom, gaining new insights, adding to your knowledge, expanding your understanding, broadening your perspective. Now consider how you can turn that image into reality. Be bold in learning new things about life and faith. For Paul, it is knowledge and insight that serve as the bedrock of love. And it is this kind of love that will help you to determine what is best for you, for family, for all.

> "When you know better, you do better."
> — Maya Angelou

WEDNESDAY

And this is my prayer, that your love may overflow more and more with knowledge and full insight to help you to determine what is best so that in the day of Christ you may be pure and blameless, having produced a harvest of righteousness... (Philippians 1:9-11).

I love the image "a harvest of righteousness." Imagine your life as a field laid out with beauty, dignity, honor, kindness, humility, courage, wisdom, and love—a *full* harvest, indeed! Live today taking this harvest image with you in all your actions and words. Envision your life as that field. With God's help, think on ways to make this your reality.

> "Wisdom is better than weapons of war..."
> — Ecclesiastes 9:18

THURSDAY

Work out your own salvation with fear and trembling... (Philippians 2:12).

Imagine the "work out" of the above verse to be an exercise routine. We know this to be a good thing that offers physical, mental, and emotional benefits. Good exercise is necessary for a healthy lifestyle.

In the same way, we can exercise our minds and spirits, taking our faith seriously and spending time "working out" our salvation as if we were participating in an exercise class. In such a "class," you would not be in *fear and trembling*. Instead, as your spirit became more "fit," your *awe and wonder* would grow, your understanding would deepen and your inquisitiveness would continue to expand.

For today, consider these spiritual exercises. View the world as a gift from God. Expect small miracles. Look for opportunities to show kindness. Smile. Recognize sacred moments. Notice colors. Feel the breeze. Learn something new. Sit in the shade and watch the world for five minutes without moving. Pray for a friend in need. Give thanks for that friend and for the gift of friendship. Keep on trying.

> "It's hard to beat a person who never gives up." — Babe Ruth

FRIDAY

Work out your own salvation with fear and trembling, for it is God who is at work in you, enabling you both to will and to work for his good pleasure (Philippians 2:12-13).

There was a time when most of uptown Charlotte was under construction. New buildings seemed to rise every other day, and there was positive anticipation about the changes taking place to the skyline. Something good was happening.

God is at work in you. You are under construction. Will you continue to "work out" your spiritual self in valuable ways? This scripture reminds us of a deeper truth: you are not working out your salvation on your own. You are being strengthened "to will," (that is, to make choices), and "to work" for the pleasure of God.

Today, embrace a sense of sacredness in the decisions you make and what you do. Notice, claim, and remember the good that is happening within you.

> "Choose a job you love, and you will never have to work a day in your life."
> — Confucius

SATURDAY

Enjoy this day as a respite from whatever was pushing and pulling you this week. Try getting some good exercise. Work out your body, continue to exercise your spirit, even as you remember that God is "working out" the rest of you!

The Second Week:
Spiritual Love and Physical Life

If I speak in the tongues of mortals and of angels, but do not have love, I am a noisy gong ... If I give away all my possessions, and if I hand over my body so that I may boast, but do not have love, I gain nothing (I Corinthians 13:1-5).

If we asked an astrophysicist about our existence, it is likely the response would involve words about carbon, foundational to all matter in the universe. And it is likely the answer would mention our presence here as a bizarre, remarkable confluence of random occurrences that generated what we are. Humanity exists, they might say, simply because inanimate carbon somehow became animated, infused with some sort of life force or energy that allows us to be. And this is truly a mystery, they might add.

A microbiologist would offer to this definition that existence is predicated upon reproduction. Biologically, our entire system of life, our reason for being, is to continue our species, to make more of ourselves. We, like other living things, have to reproduce or face extinction.

Consequently, we have biological attractions, urges that make procreation attractive and move us in the direction of reproduction. We can feel this and see it as it happens in ourselves, in other humans, and in other species. These urges fit nicely with what our microbiologist would share with us. And while both they as well as the astrophysicist can provide detailed analysis and physical evidence for random, competitive and arbitrary indicators of physical existence alone, there is something significant related to what we know about human existence that is missing in both accounts.

Neither the astrophysicist nor microbiologist can logically and scientifically explain why we have this greatest of all mysteries in the universe: the reason for and the meaning of love. So, let's hear what the Bible has to say about existence in general and love in particular.

Psalm 103, interestingly, begins by agreeing with the scientists about carbon: "God remembers how we were made. From the dust[8] of the earth we are made." But then perspectives diverge as we learn of this mysterious force, this power, this mode of being that the Bible calls *love.*

When life is filled with competition, and survival of the fittest is the primary operational strategy for most social interaction, the biblical understanding of love makes no sense. In fact, from a survival standpoint, one could make the case that self-giving behavior, unselfishness, and love are weaknesses that might well be exploited by emboldened enemies.

But, over the centuries, reality has generally proven this not to be the case. Instead, we have a passage of scripture that declares the seemingly randomness of our creation is made most meaningful by the "steadfast love of the Lord that is from everlasting to everlasting." We are not meaningful beings, nor truly successful beings, without love.

Without love, we are nothing more than a noisy gong or a clanging symbol. Without love, we are nothing but carbon.

> For the world that surrounds us, and for the world that is in us, O God, we give thanks. Let us see, feel and understand more fully the unity you offer us as spiritual and physical people, sharing together in the oneness of your creation. Amen.

---

[8] Dust is made up, primarily, of carbon.

REFLECTIONS FOR THE WEEK

MONDAY

If I speak in the tongues of mortals and of angels, but do not have love, I am a noisy gong... (I Corinthians 13:1).

"The Gong Show" was a comic variety show in the late 1970's. Performers were "gonged" if their performance didn't meet the standards of the panel of judges. The gong was giant, hanging behind the panel, a menacing bronze color with a red center, and the sound carried over all else. We usually wanted that gong to stop the contestant, of course, but yet how terrible that sound was!

Without love, life is like this, Paul says. We can't explain where love comes from scientifically, but we do know that life without it is a terrible thing, regardless of how well you perform.

Today, make a point of enjoying that your life is so much better with love in it. Think of those in your life you are thankful for and consider your feelings for them. You might even want to take a moment and jot them a note, send them a card, or give them a call and let them know of your feelings. At a minimum, pause right now and offer a prayer of thanks for them and what they have meant to your life.

> "Love will make demands on us. It will question us from within. It will disturb us. Sadden us. Play havoc with our feelings. Harass us. Reveal our superficialities. But at last it will bring us to the light."
> — Carlo Carretto

TUESDAY

If I give away all my possessions, and if I hand over my body so that I may boast, but do not have love, I gain nothing (I Corinthians 13:3).

The Teacher of Ecclesiastes drove himself—at least in the parable he constructs in Ecclesiastes 2:4-15.[9] Great dreams and hard work resulted in remarkable success. We can imagine long hours, tireless struggles, gathered savings, clever deals, big risks, and, finally, the remarkable power and incredible wealth he describes.[10] Yet, as he begins to take stock of his life, he concludes all that he worked for, dreamed about, and took pride in was nothing, just "Vanity" (Ecclesiastes 2:15). With all the success he gained, power he accrued, fun he had, pleasure he enjoyed, and beauty he created, he still was missing this key ingredient to living wholly, fully, and beautifully. The lack of love he had in his life was palpable. At least in the parable, it was all about him. The result yielded the rich man's equivalent of a *noisy gong or clanging symbol.*

Make it a point today to learn from the mistakes of others and the warnings of the Bible. Learn how to love freely and well. And don't limit this love to family and close friends. Work in the coming days to expand the boundaries of your love. See how, as you do so, your heart softens and attitude changes.

WEDNESDAY

Love is patient; love is kind... (I Corinthians 13:4).

"I wanna know what love is..." said a 1984 hit song.[11] I Corinthians answers the question with these two words. Patient. Kind.

Sometimes, we treat those we love most with the least patience and kindness. But these words should remain at the forefront and be integrated into all our actions.

---

[9] Jesus uses this parody as his model for the "Rich Fool" of Luke 12. In both cases, self-absorption is so pervasive, the thought never occurs to either of the protagonists to share their excess with others. Nor does either mention the desire for or recognition of the power of love.

[10] Great palaces, vast gardens, plentiful vineyards, servants, wives, swimming pools... the description in this second chapter is impressive in both scope and, likely, cost. And it is, as the teacher says, "vanity."

[11] "I Wanna Know What Love Is" by Foreigner, the British and American group. It was a #1 hit in both the U.S. and Britain.

The Bible is clear on how we are to love. Today, make a point of loving the way the Bible advises: live with patience as much as possible. And be kind as much as you can to those you love. Then use that love beyond just your immediate circle of friends and family today. See how the love you nurture in kindness and patience expands as you share it.

> "All you need is love..." — The Beatles

THURSDAY

Love is not envious or boastful or arrogant or rude
(I Corinthians 13:4b-5).

This famous chapter in I Corinthians can be divided into thirds. Verses one through three are poetic. They set the stage for the larger picture. The final third, verses eight through thirteen, are more cosmic, even eschatological (a fancy word having to do with the end of things). They serve as a kind of bookend to the first three verses. But the middle third, as my father used to say, is "where the rubber hits the road."

Yesterday, we were reminded what love is: *patient and kind*. Today, still as a part of this middle third of the passage, we point out *what love is not—envious, boastful, arrogant, rude...* But such things do slip into life without much warning. Maybe you've had a long day; you're feeling sorry for yourself; you don't feel as successful as the guy across the street; you're irritated with the man sitting next to you in the restaurant. Such behavior teeters on the brink of "non-loving;" but here's the good news: we have a choice as to how we act and react.

Today, *choose* to be loving. Pause; take a deep breath; relax; say yes to patience and kindness—and say no to these other feelings. You and all those around you will benefit.

> "Imagine all the people, living life in peace..." — John Lennon

FRIDAY

Love does not insist on its own way; it is not irritable or resentful; it does not rejoice in wrongdoing but rejoices in the truth ... Love never ends (I Corinthians 13:5-8).

Only two words describe what love is. But three full verses tell us what love is not. Perhaps the situation in the Corinthian church was the cause. As with many other churches, and with any gathering of people anywhere, there will always be problems that arise. Then, like now, there were folks insisting on their own way; they were irritable with those they didn't particularly like, resentful of those who appeared to get preferential treatment, glad when things went wrong or feelings got hurt...

As Christians, especially in a faith community like a church, these kinds of attitudes are out of bounds. They violate God's hopes for us. But it takes great maturity to remain loving in the face of tension and conflict. If we feel threatened in a fellowship, the first thing that begins to suffer is trust. The second is love.

Today, make every effort to follow the advice, admonition, and clear description of a loving person. And do your best to let your love be genuine. "Faking it" will soon get wearisome for you and those around you. But genuine love is contagious. Trust will grow. And love will flourish. Imagine it to be, and then do your best to make it happen.

SATURDAY

Rest. Relax. Reflect on all the love in your life and your experiences of this past week. And do your best to love *all* those around you.

> "With malice toward none, with charity for all, with firmness in the right, as God gives us to see the right, let us strive on to finish the work we are in, to bind up the nation's wounds."
> — Abraham Lincoln

The Third Week:
The Complexity of Simplicity

Be still and know that I am God (Psalm 46:10).

St. Francis never would have wanted it this way. Like Jesus, his life had been devoted to simplicity, chastity, poverty, and service to all of God's creation. Now, however, in his simple village of Assisi, there stands a commanding Gothic structure towering over the quiet countryside. The lovely town bustles with summertime activity; shops and stands sell every imaginable ware and trinket even remotely connected to Italy's famous patron saint. Crowds from all over the world push and pull and sway through the bustling, echoing church.

The structure, with its three separate chapels and the gorgeous surroundings of green, rolling hills dotted with homes and punctuated with tall, straight cedars beckon the visitor to faith, mystery, and a deeper love for God. And yet, in spite of the hopeful creativity that lies behind this sacred place, there remains a strange paradox: somewhere between his life and his death, the beautiful simplicity of St. Francis and his ministry got lost.

Around the year 1200 A.D., Francis, a popular, wealthy, and athletic young aristocrat, became a prisoner of war. While in captivity, and sick with a fever, Francis began to review his life and priorities. Slowly, an inner spiritual transformation began to motivate an outer change in all that he stood for.

After seasons of struggle, a dramatic reorientation in his faith ushered in a lifestyle concerned for the poor and ostracized, centered on the goodness of God, and rejoicing in the beauty of God's creation. He sought to purify a corrupt church, energize a disillusioned people, and personify the life of Jesus on behalf of the poor.

In some ways, the condition of Assisi seems sadly indicative of our human condition: too much noise and too many distractions. Something in us appears incapable of allowing the treasure of calm holiness to simply be. We institutionalize to glorify what St. Francis *and* Jesus sought gently and in simplicity. We make noise even though God intends for us to be reflective and quietly spiritual.

> Calm us down, Lord. Open our eyes to the ever-present glories of your world. Thank you for the simple things: the curious eyes of children, the joy of music, the warmth of a summer evening, the flowers that color your world, the taste, texture, and wonder of summer fruit and vegetables, the gift of companions, the treasure of friendship, and the reassurance of your love for now and forever. Calm us, Lord. Let us be still and know. Amen.

REFLECTIONS FOR THE WEEK

MONDAY

Praised be my Lord, by means of our sister Mother Earth, Which sustains us and keeps us, and brings forth varied fruits with colored flowers and leaves (St. Francis, from "Canticle of Brother Sun").

There is a real healing quality in nature. Following the death of my father, my mother was part of a grief support group that advocated hugging a tree—literally. And, in a small, mysterious way, she acknowledged some sense of healing in doing so. Most of us can attest that interacting in God's natural world offers serenity, perspective, and a valuable connection to the larger world. There is considerable evidence there's something to this.

As St. Francis advises above, make a point today of interacting with God's world. And be renewed to the infinite value of simplicity and the healing qualities of experiencing nature as God intended.

> "One touch of nature makes the whole world kin."
> — William Shakespeare

TUESDAY

The heavens are telling the glory of God; and the firmament proclaims his handiwork (Psalm 19:1).

There are limits, certainly, to seeing God's handiwork in the goodness of nature. There are hurricanes and tornadoes. If we look closely and long enough, we discover a true "survival of the fittest" among the plant and animal species. St. Francis of Assisi was painfully aware of human foibles and how cruel life can appear. Yet still, he, like the psalmist quoted above, recognized in nature God's hand—the quiet, day-to-day rhythms of light and darkness, wind and rain, seasons and sunshine. We see this in another verse from "A Canticle of Brother Sun":

Praised be my Lord, by means of all your creatures, and most especially by Sir Brother Sun, who makes the day and illumines us by his light: For he is beautiful and radiant with great splendor; and is a symbol of you, God most high.

Today, seek the truth and beauty of God's world. Live with assurance that you are an integral part.

> "A little simplification would be the first step toward rational living, I think."
> — Eleanor Roosevelt

WEDNESDAY

There is a boy here who has five barley loaves and two small fish... (John 6:9).

Sometimes, simple gifts are the most profound.

In this sixth chapter of John, Jesus has been preaching to this huge crowd of people. It has been a long day, and Jesus becomes concerned about the crowd and their hunger. He asks the disciples, "Where shall we buy bread so that they may eat?"

Philip replies, "A whole week's pay wouldn't buy enough food for all of these people!"

Then Andrew, Peter's brother, chimes in: "Wait, there is a boy here with five barley loaves and two small fish. But what is that among so many?"

This, of course, is the prelude to John's version of the "Feeding of the Five Thousand," an important story in the other three Gospels, too. But here, it is a simple gift from an unnamed boy that initiates a miracle. I like to imagine what some might call a naïve enthusiasm. That is, he doesn't stop to think: "The crowd is so big and my gift is so small, what difference can I possibly make?" Instead, his quiet offering changes everything.

There are many interpretations of this story. But this one is my favorite because it shows what one person's simple gift and attitude of giving can do to the dynamic of a crowd.

Imagine you are there, hungry, tired, ready to complain about the long trip home and the lack of food, when you see this young man's generous gesture. Perhaps there are others around you who also brought small amounts of food, just for themselves. The boy's witness presents a challenge—and an example. You, and others, too, offer what you have to Jesus. Before long, there's a shift in the attitude of the crowd, now inspired to be like that boy—to give what they have into the wise hands of Jesus.

Let this be your challenge today. Whatever arises, trust your generosity and some simple gift into the wise hands of that sacred Presence beyond our understanding.

> "God became one of us so that we might find a way to become something like Him."
> — J.B. Phillips

THURSDAY

Your steadfast love, O Lord, extends to the heavens, your faithfulness to the clouds (Psalm 36:5).

Sunsets are remarkable things. The waning sun dropping from the sky, casting beams of light through, under, and around cumulus clouds, rays extending up and over, colors profuse—orange and golden—glowing against a backdrop of purple and azure, all highlighting the remaining fluffy white of the clouds. The dark is coming but not until the sun offers a final, simple, glorious farewell. Surely, it was the vibrant sky of an early evening sunset that inspired Psalm 36:5.

God's love and faithfulness is a part of everything—a sunset, a flower, you. There are times in August when the heat and humidity bake the garden's flowers. But there are plants and flowers that thrive despite the obstacles. Crepe Myrtles are good examples. In and around the Charlotte area, we have a plethora of these remarkable plants. The hotter and dryer it is, the better they seem to like it. Whether at the beach in sandy soil or on the edge of mountains in clay and stone, they seem to flourish.

Today, look for the "survivors"—those elements of life and nature that continue to make it regardless. Concentrate on these examples of endurance and see them as embodiments of God's everlasting love—and your potential. Be aware—and thankful.

> "Simplicity and repose are the qualities that measure the true value of any work of art."
> — Frank Lloyd Wright

FRIDAY

They set a net for my steps; my soul was bowed down. They dug a pit in my path, but they have fallen into it themselves. My heart is steadfast, O God, my heart is steadfast (Psalm 57:6-7).

I wrote a short piece a while back that, I think, says all I need to say for today:

SURROUNDED: A WOMAN IN THE WOODS
There is a cabin in the woods near my house.
A woman lives there with her dog.
Developers wanted her to sell.
She was in the way of progress.
But the woman liked her cabin in the woods.
It was her home.
The development proceeded.
They surrounded her
With big houses, manicured yards, sidewalks and paved streets.
They wanted her to leave.
But still she lives there, surrounded.
With a little woods around her, the two acres that is her yard—
Just enough to shield her...
Alone with her dog
Surrounded...
And steadfast.

Today, devote yourself to a worthy purpose. Be faithful in what you stand for. Be steadfast—to yourself and for others.

> "Many persons have a wrong idea of what constitutes true happiness. It is not gained through self-gratification, but through fidelity to a worthy purpose."
> — Helen Keller

SATURDAY

Rest today. Relish the time to relax. Enjoy God's handiwork in nature and reflect on the good things you've done this week. Continue to enjoy the simple things of life. Be grateful.

> "Beauty of style and harmony and grace and good rhythm depend on simplicity."
> — Plato

THE FOURTH WEEK:
Zaccheus and Tough Love

He entered Jericho and was passing through it. A man was there named Zacchaeus; he was a chief tax collector and was rich (Luke 19:1-2).

This week, we return to the story of Zacchaeus. It remains one of the more enduring and enjoyable stories of the Bible—a little man climbs a tree, Jesus calls him down, Jesus invites himself to dine at this man's home, and the man, so influenced by this experience and his time with Jesus, truly changes. Over the next week, we will explore more thoroughly the story we examined briefly last month.

There is far more to these passages than what we might assume. A familiar song from my Sunday School days summarizes at least a part of the encounter. I have no idea who made it up or when it began to be used by children, so I trust it is in the public domain. Here's how it goes:

> Zacchaeus was a wee little man
> and a wee little man was he.
> He climbed way up in a Sycamore tree
> for the Lord he wanted to see.
> And as our savior passed that way,
> he looked up in that tree.
> And he said: "Zacchaeus, you come down!
> For I'm going to your house today.
> Yes, I'm going to your house today.

While it offers the gist, the song vastly simplifies what the scripture actually says. What we shall see should be a familiar theme. For Zacchaeus, the desire for power and the temptations of greed loomed large, as did his apparent lack of concern for others. These same dynamics continue to play a consistent role in everyday life. For us as Christians, how we go about our interactions often is determined by how we view life and faith. This was the case of Zacchaeus, and this is what his encounter with Jesus changed.

As you move through this week, reflect on all that you have calling for your time and energy, and think of this man we will come to know and love from the nineteenth chapter of Luke. Then, like him, be prepared to be confronted by Jesus—and learn something new.

> Lord, let me see myself through your eyes. Allow a new sense of perspective and humility so that what you would have me do is not about me and what I want but about you and your hopes for the world. Allow me to grow into wisdom so that I might love and be loved with no strings nor hidden agendas. Temper my pride with humility. And let it be in the name and with the spirit of Jesus. Amen.

REFLECTIONS FOR THE WEEK

MONDAY

He entered Jericho... (Luke 19:1).

It was a biblical encounter in a town called Jericho. This lovely oasis town located in the desert just north of the Dead Sea is the oldest consistently inhabited town on earth. For ten thousand years, this amazing place has been blessed with a multitude of fresh springs that offer abundant water. Consequently, it has thrived in the middle of hostile surroundings. Palm trees, lemon, orange and all manner of citrus trees, bananas, figs, dates—virtually any vegetable or fruit flourishes because of the rich soil and abundant water. Even today, the markets of Jericho are filled to overflowing with some of the biggest and most beautiful eggplant, peppers, tomatoes, squash, and some of the sweetest bananas I have ever tasted. You name the fruit or vegetable, and Jericho has it, spilling from market stalls out into the streets off the central square—a colorful sign of vitality both for Jericho and for the rest of Palestine and much of Israel.[12]

This was the town of Zacchaeus, and these were likely the same conditions when Jesus walked that way two thousand years ago—abundant food and colorful surroundings, but also oppressive policies that stunted spiritual growth, stifled the heart, and created disillusionment. Hidden within this biblical story is the daily reality of oppression, injustice, and greed—along with the fear and small-mindedness necessary for such policies to remain. It also, ultimately, has to do with *tough love*.

Today, think of areas in the world where ordinary people like you and me, through no fault of their own, live under unjust laws and in difficult circumstances they cannot control. Imagine what it would be like—how it would feel to live under an authority with little regard for you or your family's well-being.

---

[12] The Israelis have a special agreement with Jericho, which is part of the Occupied West Bank. Because of the abundant produce that comes from there, they allow the Palestinians to trade with Israel. Every day, Israeli trucks leave there loaded with fresh fruit and vegetables. This is not true with other Palestinian areas.

Make this day about gentleness, compassion, and imagination. What would it be like to live in the situations many find themselves in today. Pray for those you do not know in places you may never visit but who are suffering under oppressive policies and harsh conditions. They share your humanity—and are connected as brothers and sisters to our common source of life.

TUESDAY

He was trying to see who Jesus was, but he could not, because he was short in stature. So he ran ahead and climbed a sycamore tree to see him... (Luke 19:3-4).

Jesus' interaction with this tax collector always intrigued me, partly because of the cute song we grew up singing and because it was the only story in the Bible I knew of where somebody climbed a tree. For a little kid who loved to do just that, I felt a special connection to the story. But now I have a much deeper appreciation. As I've mentioned, there is a play on words in this passage. The word used to describe Zacchaeus is one that can be literally interpreted as "short of stature" and also refer to someone of "stunted character"—one whose spiritual and emotional nature is shriveled and seriously lacking. Obviously, Zacchaeus is physically short since he has to climb a tree to see Jesus. He is also spiritually stunted and needs what Jesus has to offer. Perhaps he is aware of his own insufficiencies. Or maybe he is simply curious. But Jesus calls attention to his spiritual shortcomings. Either way, we discover a clue to what lies ahead.

Today, be aware and look at your life situation in terms of what motivates you to do what you do, whether in work, play, or relationships. Ask yourself if your motivations are sincere and how they coincide with Jesus' calling.

> An eastern perspective on the Seven Deadly Sins: "Wealth without work; pleasure without conscience; science without humanity; knowledge without character; politics without principle; commerce without morality; worship without sacrifice." — Mahatma Gandhi

WEDNESDAY

When Jesus came to the place, he looked up and said to him, "Zacchaeus, hurry and come down; for I must stay at your house today" (Luke 19:5).

As pointed out previously, Zacchaeus was a *chief* tax collector. As such, he took money from his fellow citizens—the people he grew up with, his neighbors. That money funded what most in those days considered the occupation of Jewish land by a foreign invasion force. The Romans paid for their building projects like roads, palaces, fortresses, aqueducts, and fountains largely through local sources. In many places, these policies were generally tolerated because of the benefits that came along with them.

But in this land, resentment ran deep. The undercurrents of hostility against any who cooperated or collaborated with Rome ran strong. So, the story of Zacchaeus emerges immediately as the story of a man assisting the enemy for his own advantages. He is wealthy and powerful because he plays a double game without rules; he cares not for those around him but only for himself and increasing his own wealth.

Unlike those under him, Zacchaeus had private security at his disposal. He had the power and political authority to use force to take what he believed was owed.[13] Apparently, he used it in spite of the fact that the Law and tradition explicitly declared that one's home was a sanctuary where no political authority should have the right to invade. Zacchaeus seemed not to care. He increased his own wealth at the expense of others' resources and dignity.

Today, imagine being in a place where you have complete power over others, where you could requisition possessions or resources at will. What would it feel like? What would you do? How would others feel about you? Now, make an effort to listen and learn from this story—and what Jesus does in response to what he knows is going on with this man.

---

[13] Rome and the overarching local authorities expected their percentages, and they also allowed for certain financial gains to be accrued by their collecting agents.

THURSDAY

So he hurried down and was happy to welcome him. All who saw it began to grumble and said, "he has gone to be the guest of one who is a sinner" (Luke 19:6-7).

Growing up, I used to get "called down" a lot: "You need to come down off that high horse, young man," Mom often said in a less than calm voice. Her same words reoccurred even a few times during my college years.

What she meant, of course, was that I was thinking too highly of myself: I was too self-absorbed, unconcerned about others, unaware of my selfishness, and unjustifiably proud. What occurs during Jesus' encounter with Zacchaeus echoes my mother's confrontations with me.

We have already established that Jesus recognized Zacchaeus' *stunted character.* For here was a man who had turned his back on friends, family, culture, heritage; he wantonly disobeyed biblical mores in the name of profit and wealth; he overlooked the needs of fellow citizens for the benefits of quick financial gains; and he likely flaunted his wealth in dress and housing. Jesus looks up in the tree and sees all this.

Coming from Jesus, "Zacchaeus, you come down," becomes a statement about misplaced priorities, dysfunctional relationships, unwarranted wealth, and unhealthy pride, in addition to his emotional and spiritual stuntedness. Consider again your own spiritual inventory and think of actions and inactions this week that might deserve a critique, or a "calling down" from Jesus.

FRIDAY

I must stay at your house today (Luke 19:5b).

Jesus now turns the tables on this chief tax collector. Zacchaeus had invaded the homes of others to get what he wanted; now Jesus "invades" his home.

Jesus' encounter with Zacchaeus ultimately results in salvation. First comes repentance, a confession of and a turning from what he has done. Next comes penance, a making right what had been wrong, unjust, and unethical. And, finally, comes the joy of salvation—a deep, heartfelt understanding that what had been no longer needs to be. The separation from community and alienation from God is made right. Thanks to Jesus' initiative, Zacchaeus is a changed man. And not only he but the entire community becomes transformed. He goes beyond the Torah's specifics for payback—his offering to those he wronged demonstrates not only apology and penance but generosity, restoration, and redemption.

Today, contemplate possible things in your life that might have become spiritually stunted. What in your current life needs to be brought into new focus and transformed? Consider today any ways that Jesus might need to "call you down" or compassionately "invade your home" to make things right. Like Zacchaeus, make the necessary changes. Be generous. Restore what has been lost. And embrace the redemptive joy evident in God's salvation.

SATURDAY

Today, reflect on this past week's learnings. Rest, relax, and humbly seek the company of those you love. Prepare your heart and mind for worship and gathering with a community of faith somewhere tomorrow.

The Fifth Week:
Remembering the Future

Our bones are dried up, and our hope is lost; we are cut off completely (Ezekiel 37:11).

We were on a medical mission trip to an isolated village in Honduras. The little concrete block structure that was to serve as our clinic was a Spartan place. One large room with a concrete floor, it was divided into cubicles by shower curtains hanging from wire strung from the walls. Four doctors, five nurses, and a few others of us arrived in this area that had no access to medical care.

It was stiflingly hot. We began to unload our crates, boxes, and bags of all we would need that week. A long line of expectant people patiently waited in the sun, some having walked miles. As we unloaded and prepared the space, one of our group suddenly collapsed onto the concrete floor. He was unconscious. A quick examination revealed he was suffering from severe dehydration. (He had taken two laxatives the day before, thinking the first had been ineffective.)[14] The heat, combined with the two laxatives, pulled virtually all the moisture from his body. When he finally regained consciousness, he was still unable to move. There was nothing to do but make him comfortable, so we got a roll of toilet paper and placed it under his head. Then we let the people come.

They filed into our little clinic and, as they stepped over our prostrate, still dehydrated medical team member, he looked up at each and said, "Buenos Dias."

What had been a frightening experience became a hopeful opportunity.

In Ezekiel 37, the people of Israel have lost all hope. They are exiled in a foreign land called Babylon. The temple has been destroyed, Jerusalem lies in ruins, and the important members of Judean society, those who have not been killed, have been abducted and taken to this foreign capital of a hostile empire.

---

[14] This is rarely a good idea.

Their refrain, the summary of their situation becomes, "Our bones are dried up, and our hope is lost; we are cut off completely."

Consider this biblical scenario this week. And, as we progress through this passage, envision the resiliency of hope and the power of God.

> In those times, O God, when our hope is lost, when we are frightened for the future and anxious in the present, enliven our spirits. Lift us again for the new morning that awaits. And help us to march boldly through this week with the assurance of your presence. Amen.

REFLECTIONS FOR THE WEEK

MONDAY

Our bones are dried up, and our hope is lost; we are cut off completely (Ezekiel 37:11).

This idea of dried bones graphically illustrates those times in life when there seems little reason to continue. Whatever has led to such a state presents an overpowering sense of despair. In this case, the body of Israel had collapsed. The life of the community was gone. Hope had evaporated. There was nothing left but dried bones. And then God presented a vision to Ezekiel.

The spirit of the Lord "set me down in the middle of a valley; it was full of bones ... and they were very dry" (37:1-2).

"Mortal, can these bones live?" God asks.

"O Lord God, you know" (37:3).

The graphic image is one of a vast, forgotten battlefield strewn with the remains of the unburied dead. This is the House of Israel. Defeated. Left abandoned. Bones bleached by the sun. Then comes a strange thing: God tells Ezekiel to preach to the bones. What good will that do?

Have you ever had a season in your life when nothing you did seemed to turn out right—your hope was gone and frustration had replaced possibility? Even temporary feelings of difficult days, troubles on the job, difficulties at home, these are hard enough.

Today, think on those moments and remember how you felt. Contemplate what God's message might have meant then and what it means for you now. God is still in the business of resurrecting the hopes of discouraged people.

> "A cheerful heart is good medicine, but a downcast spirit dries up the bones." — Proverbs 17:22

TUESDAY

I will cause breath to enter you, and you shall live (Ezekiel 37:5).

Then the spirit of the Lord begins to blow across the valley. The same spirit that readied creation for God to speak life into being now blows across and into the bones. Just as God's breath created the first man,[15] so it is that God's breath—this wind that brings life—now gives animation to the bones that had been lifeless, hopeless, alone.

Today, whatever state you find yourself in, remember that you participate in life with God. Your breath brings you into constant communion with the one who brings you life. Like the spirit blowing over the valley of dried bones, let the simple act of breathing renew your spirit, open your heart, bring you back to yourself, and rejoin you in community with God.

> "All the great things are simple, and many can be expressed in a single word: freedom, justice, honor, duty, mercy, hope."
> — Winston Churchill

WEDNESDAY

...and the breath came into them, and they lived, and stood on their feet, a vast multitude (Ezekiel 37:10).

"Dem bones, dem bones, dem dry bones..." These are the opening words to a favorite spiritual for many. Emerging out of a slave culture where hardship knew few bounds, these men and women still had the audacity to sing about hope. It was a time in which human beings from Africa had been ripped from their homes, confined to the living hell of a slave ship, sold like chattel, conscripted to servitude, exposed to indignities, punished arbitrarily, sold unscrupulously, taken from mothers strategically. There is no way to fully imagine the horrors of American slavery

---

[15] The same word in Hebrew, *ruach*, means wind, breath, and spirit. The same part of creation that allows humans to live (breathe) is part of God's very nature. That which blows across the face of the waters in Genesis 1 and what brings life back to the bones is also the very thing that makes you and me who we are and how we function. We breathe, and in doing so, we remain participants in the ongoing drama of life with God.

in today's world. Yet the reality of this torturous and sinful institution was endemic in our culture and poisonous to all.

And yet, the victims of this slave culture rose beyond an existence rife with indignities—to sing, to proclaim with passion a story of redemption, of resurrection, of hope.

Make today one of animation, of hope. Breathe in the spirit, the breath of God, feel rejuvenated by the presence of God, and reconnect to the hope of God.

> "Hope is a waking dream."
> — Aristotle

THURSDAY

I will cause breath to enter you, and you shall live (Ezekiel 37:5).

We all have days when things are less than we hope them to be. One of the many blessings of participating in a mission trip is seeing and experiencing situations beyond our own. Many of you have had such experiences; you understand the incredible hardship in many mission destinations but also recognize the redemptive work that transpires. It is a great feeling to offer hope and, in return, gain faith, insight, and gratitude.

If you have not been on a mission trip, consider one. And if your participation is not possible, do what you can to support one. Learn what you can about where the group is going and what they will be doing. Research that area and work to understand what that culture may be experiencing and need. And pray. Lift those in that place, remember them, and ask that their hope be enlivened by being connected to caring people who are attempting to understand the ongoing difficulties they live with.

> "Hold fast to dreams, / For if dreams die / Life is a broken-winged bird, / That cannot fly."
> — Langston Hughes

FRIDAY

And the Spirit of God blew across the face of the waters (Genesis 1:2).

It is too easy to feel sorry for ourselves. That is one reason watching carefully for God's work in creation and in our surroundings is a valuable antidote to self-pity. It also is the reason why doing something for another is good medicine. Sometimes, God's movement in our lives occurs in tandem with our own acts of compassion. The movement of God's spirit blowing across the face of the waters of our own chaos and confusion is ongoing, and can, if we are aware and sensitive, activate actions of grace and reactions of hope.

A man in our church near Washington, D.C. was in his eighties. He was good at woodworking and loved to make things for others. He had committed himself to make a small chest for a young couple in our congregation soon to be married. He collected the wood he needed, drew up the plans—and then proceeded to have terrible problems with his legs. His workshop was in his basement, down a steep flight of hard, wooden stairs. But he was determined to make this chest for this couple.

I found out later from his wife that, every day, despite terrible pain, he limped down the hall then, on hands and knees, crawled slowly down steep, wooden, basement stairs and to his workbench. He rigged up ways to sit or lie while he spent hours cutting, shaping, sanding, painting, and finishing what became an exquisite thing of beauty. He never told the couple what he had to do to finish the job—but I did after his wife told me.

He could have felt sorry for himself. He could have given up. Instead, he sacrificed on behalf of others he cared for. And for him—and them—that made all the difference.

Today, search for a way to give yourself to others—to make a difference, no matter how small, in someone else's life. In doing so, take notice of any spiritual awakening in you, remember God's faithfulness, and recognize the hopeful future in God's persistent dream.

> It is in our lives and not from our words that our religion must be judged.
> — Thomas Jefferson

SATURDAY

Relax and think on what you have learned this past week and how your actions have changed Make this a day of beauty. Regardless of the weather, let the hope of God's resurrecting spirit lift you—and give you new life.

SEPTEMBER
Wisdom

Originally considered the seventh month in the Roman calendar prior to the reforms of Julius Caesar, today September stands for new beginnings—at least of the church and school year. It is the beginning of fall and the ending of summer.

For our work, it serves as the start of new insight, broader perspectives, and better wisdom.

THE FIRST WEEK:
Philip, a Eunuch, and Choices

Then the angel of the Lord said to Philip, "Get up and go toward the south to the road that goes down from Jerusalem to Gaza" (Acts 8:26).

The biblical setting for this beautiful encounter is now considered by some to be the world's largest refugee camp. We know it today as the Gaza Strip and hear about it often in the news as a place of hopelessness, rancor, and militancy.[1] But the Bible offers in this passage a refreshing narrative of liberation and surprising openness. There is a loosing of restrictive bonds that, in other days, would have bound the stranger in the story, this Ethiopian eunuch, to a station outside the family of God.[2]

Luke, the author of Acts, describes the situation as though God has this planned. It appears to be a complete overturning of the Levitical law of the previous age. And, as will see next week in a continued exploration of this theme, Isaiah, too, seemed to have a profound sense of God's broader, less restrictive vision.

Philip, the other character in the story, is called to be in the right place, at the right time, and to do the right thing. I look back on certain times in my life amazed at how I ended up in a certain place at a certain time. On some occasions, I am on the receiving end of the blessing. At other times, I seem to be somehow used by God to touch the life of another in a way I never could have planned. And, sometimes, I miss the opportunity and overlook the needs.

---

[1] More than one million Palestinians live in a narrow strip twenty-five miles long and six miles wide. With no natural resources, no natural harbor, and no international connections other than Egypt to the south, it is restricted on three sides from free trade and legitimate sovereignty because of forced displacement, Israeli blockades, dysfunctional government, and angry militants reacting to what they might rightly perceive as an unsympathetic world.

[2] Or "the assembly of the Lord," as the covenant people are called in Deuteronomy: "No one whose testicles are crushed or whose penis is cut off shall be admitted to the assembly of the Lord" (23:1).

I got a call not long ago from a young man I had known years ago in Washington, D.C. The conversation reminded me of Philip and the Ethiopian eunuch. His life had been changed, he said, because of the ways our little congregation had responded to him in his time of great need. We had been there at the right time and place, and, thankfully, had done the right thing. As we move through these next two weeks, this story of Philip and the Ethiopian eunuch will guide our reflections on the same kinds of opportunities that come our way more often than we imagine.

> Lord, let me listen to the gentle urgings of your spirit. There is so much I do not understand. But let me respond faithfully with what I do understand and stay open to your guidance in what I don't. You call me to compassion, grace, and responsiveness. Give me the wisdom I need to be ready, so that I, like Philip, might also be in the right place at the right time to do the right thing. Amen.

REFLECTIONS FOR THE WEEK

MONDAY

So let us not grow weary in doing what is right ... whenever we have an opportunity, let us work for the good of all... (Galatians 6:9-10).

I remembered the young man who contacted me recently well, and I vividly recalled the events he described. But I had no idea the impact we would have on his life. At several points in assisting him and the subsequent African Congolese congregation he helped to start in Silver Spring, Maryland, we could easily have been unavailable, distracted, or declined to be involved. The story went like this.

We had gathered at the airport late in the evening to meet and pick up a young family of five from Sudan. They were refugees from the civil war there and, in conjunction with Church World Service, our congregation would be serving as their hosts. As we met them and introduced ourselves, we noticed the young gentleman standing alone nearby. He kept looking around, checking his watch, clearly waiting for someone, but it was late and the airport was about to close down for the most part. He spoke only French. He was a refugee from Zaire (today, The Democratic Republic of Congo). He had nowhere to go, nothing with him but the clothes on his back and no money. We were a small church with limited resources. We were already committed to this family from Sudan. We only had so much room, people, money, and time. But there was no one else. In this moment, had God provided an opportunity to "work for the good of all?"

As you contemplate this question today, consider the moments in your own life when things seemed to mysteriously come together and you were called to action in God's service. How did you respond? Think about needs you might be made aware of this week. Be open to what you hear and discover. And consider any resources or contacts you might have at your disposal to help. Could there be any indication of God at work in what you have and what is needed?

> "This sense of cooperation with God in the little things is what astonishes me..."
> — Frank Laubach

TUESDAY

...lead a life worthy of the calling to which you have been called... (Ephesians 4:1).

Was our initial encounter and subsequent relationship with this young man from Zaire a coincidence? Or had this encounter been divinely arranged? These are the same questions that arise from the story Luke shares with us in Acts 8. (We will revisit this text in more depth but, for today, it is enough to view this text through the initial experience of Philip.) Why did Philip go where he did? What if he had been too preoccupied with other issues?

Consider today how God might be gently communicating *where* you should be going. Reflect on this as you meditate, keeping in mind *your* opportunities to "work for the good of all" and to "lead a life worthy" of what God has dreamed for you and called you to.

> "Here and now comprise the coordinates of your daily life."
> — Sarah Young

WEDNESDAY

...lead a life worthy of the calling to which you have been called with all humility and gentleness, with patience, bearing with one another in love... (Ephesians 4:1-2)

We invited the young man from Zaire to come with us. The next day, I called Church World Service and discovered that, indeed, there had been a mix-up. They wanted to know if we could assist him a while longer. The rest of the story was simple. We came to appreciate the time we shared as a gift from God. As I remember it, all these years later, we did a few things to help him get settled. We were a support system, a home base, a place he knew and felt accepted and appreciated. But to him? Years later, in what I believe to be another providential moment, he reconnected with me and spoke passionately about what the timing of our relationship had done in his life—and what he believed God had done *through us.*

Over the years, remembering his first few weeks in this country, he passed forward what we had done and blessed the lives of countless others in the process. He ended up being instrumental in beginning that new Congolese congregation in Silver Spring, Maryland.

What about you, today? Recognize your calling to be used by God in what lies ahead—a little thing, a small kindness, an offer of gentle support. Be attentive to God's presence, the timing, the need, and your potential.

> "The pliability of an obedient heart must be complete from the set of our wills right on through to our actions."
> — Catherine Marshall

THURSDAY

Then the angel of the Lord said to Philip, "Get up and go toward the south to the road that goes down from Jerusalem to Gaza" (Acts 8:26).

Opportunities for holy encounters, times when you and I have the chance to be used by God in profound ways, avail themselves every day. Each morning becomes a new chance to be used by God, just as Philip was used in Acts 8. The key we can see from the text: Philip responded to the Spirit's urging. I am sure many of you have similar stories. So take a moment and reflect on the following.

(1) When have you been surprised to discover you were used by God to touch someone else in a significant way?
(2) Remember that specific time: what happened?
(3) Reflect on *how* God used you, perhaps even in spite of yourself.
(4) Jot down some of your feelings related to your story and the events surrounding it.
(5) What is God teaching you from this memory?

That night at the airport, we saw the need and said yes—reluctantly perhaps, confused about what would lie ahead, not knowing why or how—and responded with what little understanding we had in that moment. It was years later before any of us realized the impact of our simple acts of hospitality and kindness. We discovered, like Philip, a beautiful but unexpected blessing—to be used by God to touch the life of another. And the ripple effect of that blessing continues today.

Open yourself today to God's holy miracles of context and timing.

> "Jesus is taking students in the master class of life."
> — Dallas Willard

FRIDAY

So let us not grow weary in doing what is right ... whenever we have an opportunity, let us work for the good of all... (Galatians 6:9-10).

A good friend once shared with me this wisdom: "We need to do less more deeply." This week's passage from Acts 8 is a good example of why such advice makes sense. For there is far more to Philip and the man from Ethiopia than we have touched upon yet.

Consequently, next week we will examine the same passage from Acts 8 using the text as our guide to further understanding. As we do so, we will find that what arose in the life of this early church would become quite controversial. Even today, the echo of hostility and misunderstanding resound both inside and outside the walls of our congregations. So, our examination of these words from scripture over the coming days will be vitally important.

For now, consider the things God is trying to teach you through scripture and its connection with everyday life. Think specifically about today—your setting and the people in it.

> "The more our being in God is embraced, the more our doing will reflect the image of God."
> — Tilden Edwards

SATURDAY

There were several Orthodox Jewish communities around our neighborhood outside of Washington, D.C. On Friday afternoons, I used to love watching them rush to and fro from the local markets, preparing for their Sabbath celebrations. The men, women, and children anticipated the evening with joy, for with the setting sun came their day of rest, a focused time to be with God, and a blessed time of renewal.

Today, enjoy your day. Don't rush; there is time. Just relax, breathe deeply, and relish a calm sense of God's presence in your life as you prepare yourself for worship tomorrow.

> "As we carry on the business of the day, inwardly we keep pressing on toward the Divine Center ... We gain power, not deplete resources."
> — Richard Foster

The Second Week:
Philip, a Eunuch, and Change

"Look, here is water! What is to prevent me from being baptized?" (Acts 8:36b).

This enthusiastic question explodes in the midst of one of the Bible's most poignant conversion experiences. The content pulsates with the joy of this man's newfound vision for life. He wants to be a part of this experience, this new relationship that Philip describes. He desires a new perspective, he longs for a new family, and he feels called to follow and to worship this new Jesus that Philip has related to him.

Last week, we focused on Philip, his availability, and the resulting encounter that occurred. This week, we focus on this stranger, this unnamed man traveling on the road from Jerusalem down to Gaza, and then on to his home far to the south in Ethiopia.

Though his identity is somewhat mysterious, Luke tells us he is a significant official in the court of the Ethiopian queen. He is "in charge of her entire treasury" (8:27). He is also a eunuch.

Whether in official capacity on a diplomatic mission or traveling to worship at the temple of Jerusalem, we are left to wonder. But Luke makes clear this man has intense spiritual curiosity. He has somehow secured a scroll that is a copy of the prophet Isaiah. This would not have been cheap or easy. In those days, scrolls were not the kinds of things just anyone could walk off with and read on their own. So, he is a man of means, he is spiritually curious, and he has a good education. Few people could read in those days. In fact, perhaps only three to five percent of the Roman Empire in the first century would have been literate.[3]

What we witness in Acts 8 is the very first conversion experience of a non-Jewish, non-Samaritan person. In other words, this

---

[3] There was little reason for those involved in agriculture to read, and this would have been the vast majority during that time. The hard work and ongoing responsibilities prevented farmers and laborers the luxury of the long hours needed to move out of illiteracy. And to what end? What was there for them to read?

Ethiopian eunuch is the *first gentile convert* to the Christian faith. Surely, there were plenty of other stories of people who were not Jewish whose stories Luke could have related. What is it about this man and his conversation that, for Luke, is so vital?

Luke chooses an Ethiopian, a black man from Africa whose country in those days was virtually hanging off the map. Why him? Was it his skin color? His country? His profession?

Now, we enter into what I like to call the "unspoken narrative" of the story—a narrative centered around this controversial fact: he was a eunuch.

> Give us wisdom, Lord. There is much we do not understand. There are controversies that concern us and issues that confound us. There are people whose lifestyles are vastly different from our own. We have difficulty relating to what they do and why, how they think and what they are about. And yet, remind us this week of your purposes for each of us.
> Give us wisdom as we seek your way. Amen.

REFLECTIONS FOR THE WEEK

MONDAY

"Look, here is water! What is to prevent me from being baptized?" (Acts 8:36-37).

In the Torah, Deuteronomy 23:1 stated that a person like this man, a eunuch, "shall not be admitted to the assembly of God." Those instructions are *pretty clear.* Yet, as Philip interprets Isaiah 53, and as he speaks to the man about Jesus, this Ethiopian eunuch now desires very much to be a part of "the assembly of God." So, he asks Philip the question above that, in my opinion, is one of the most controversial questions in the Bible: "...what is to prevent me from being baptized?"

Deuteronomy 23:1 for starters.

If Philip played by the traditional rules and related the *law*, he would have, perhaps apologetically, replied, "I'm glad you are interested in joining, but all the spots are full right now. And we've got this little problem with your application process. See, you don't quite fit the criteria we're looking for."

In other words, Luke assumes that we are acquainted with scripture and understand that, while Deuteronomy excluded people like this from being a part of God's family, the prophet Isaiah overturns these ancient strictures. The inspiration of the prophet's veto, ironically enough, comes only three chapters (Isaiah 56:3-5)[4] after the material Philip relayed just moments before (Isaiah 53:1-9).

Consider today what the Bible's purpose is in recording these different perspectives over time. How do you interpret, learn, grow through the various biblical contexts? How do you expand your own perspective on the Bible's teachings?

---

[4] For thus says the Lord: "To the eunuchs who keep my Sabbaths, who choose the things that please me and hold fast my covenant, I will give, in my house and within my walls, a monument and a name better than sons and daughters; I will give them an everlasting name that shall not be cut off" (Isaiah 56:3-5).

TUESDAY

He commanded the chariot to stop, and both of them, Philip and the eunuch, went down into the water, and Philip baptized him (Acts 8:38).

Likely, this eunuch spoken of in Acts was aware of the Torah's exclusion of eunuchs from the family of faith. So, his question carries with it an expected response. But Philip says nothing in answer to the eunuch's question. Rather, the next thing Luke records is these two men in the water and the eunuch has just been welcomed into the family of faith, the assembly of God. How did this happen? By what authority was Philip welcoming him?

Throughout Acts, Luke recognizes the sacred work of what he calls "the Holy Spirit." The *ruach (breath)* of God mentioned in Genesis is now depicted by Luke, and with the same understanding. This is the Bible's way of describing, simply, that God, the creator of the universe, is active in the affairs of people like Philip and this man from Ethiopia. When feeling the presence of God at work in our lives, the Bible can and does refer to this as "the Spirit of God"—the Holy Spirit.

It is this same movement of God's presence, the inspiration of God's spirit, that seems to motivate Philip's radical break from traditional, Levitical norms. Though Luke doesn't cite Isaiah 56:3-5, it seems clear that this serves as the backdrop for what God wants—an inclusive, not exclusive, kingdom.

Today, think about who, in your life, represents the Ethiopian eunuch. That is, who appears to be expressly excluded? How can you work to *include* this person or persons? What new insight does this text offer you?

> "God, of your goodness give me your self, for you are enough for me. And only in you do I have everything. Amen."
> — Lady Julian of Norwich

WEDNESDAY

The eunuch saw him no more, and went on his way rejoicing (Acts 8:39).

Ralph Waldo Emerson once said: "A foolish consistency is the hobgoblin of little minds." Perhaps Isaiah—and Philip's graceful interpretation of Isaiah's words—demonstrates God's overturning of the "hobgoblin" of small minds.

We simply do not know what caused Isaiah's word of the Lord to be different from Deuteronomy's. But it is clear that the story Luke relates exemplifies the New Testament vision that the church of Jesus Christ can and must continue.[5]

And we do know one other thing for certain: the eunuch "went on his way rejoicing." Such is the clear affirmation of Philip's action and full affirmation of this man who once had been an outcast.

The eunuch's haunting question: "What is to prevent me from being baptized?" ought to echo in every sanctuary and boardroom of every church in God's kingdom. May our answers be imbued with the wise openness of Philip and the subsequent joy of the man from Ethiopia.

Today, take care in your interpretation of others and events. Don't miss the opportunity to see how the spirit of the Gospel transforms your understanding of today's world.

> "The people cannot be all, and always well informed. The part which is wrong will be discontented in proportion to the importance of the facts they misconceive."
> — Thomas Jefferson

---

[5] Eunuchs were considered less than whole in those days because, in many but by no means all cases, they were without testicles. Therefore, they were believed to fail in the expectations God had of them for procreation, especially the production of sons. In many clearly recorded cases, eunuchs could procreate but chose not to because they were not attracted to the opposite sex. Many also were seen as effeminate. Historical documentation from a number of sources considered eunuchs the ancient equivalent of today's gays and lesbians. This makes Isaiah's pronouncement and Philip's decision all the more profound. For more on this topic: see *Thesis: Eunuchs are Gay Men* by Faris Malik or Google "Eunuchs and Homosexuality" to find a variety of sources.

THURSDAY

Look, here is water! What is to prevent me from being baptized? (Acts 8:36-37).

When attempting to study the Bible, we generally need to work with the passage looking for two things: What it *meant* and what it *means*.

There are several reasons why Luke might have included this story for his times. Remember, he had at his disposal countless stories to spread the good news of Jesus' teachings around the Roman Empire. He chose this one. Why? The obvious reason might be that this man represented the general audience Luke wished to reach. Today, we can see that this man represents the vast flexibility of God's inclusive family.

Jeremiah 38:7 records another Ethiopian, also a eunuch (in the King's house here as opposed to the Queen's house in Acts), who saves Jeremiah's life. Does Luke see Ebed-melech, the Ethiopian in Jeremiah, as a valuable precursor to the unnamed man in Acts 8? Or does Luke simply recognize in this eunuch of Acts a man who epitomizes the ultimate outsider whom God was welcoming with open arms: foreign, alien, different—racially, sexually, religiously? Or could it be a combination of both?

Today, take a good look at how you *see* and treat people different from yourself. What could you do to make your worldview more inclusive? What do you need to see and understand differently today?

FRIDAY

I am about to do a new thing; now it springs forth, do you not perceive it? I will make a way in the wilderness and rivers in the desert... (Isaiah 43:19b).

The encounter between Philip and the Ethiopian takes place in the wilderness (Luke even specifies: "This is a wilderness road"). Notice the language of this text: "I am about to do a new thing; I will make a way in the wilderness..." Luke obviously knew his Old Testament, especially Isaiah. I suspect Luke's choice of story, setting, and the inclusion of this particular conversion experience was very intentional and *fully inspired*.

God is making a way in the wilderness, then and now. Regardless of how you feel, whatever your difficulties are, whoever has made you feel less than worthy, God wants you to know you are not alone. Remember, always, God is at work!

Today, examine a moment in your life when you felt "lost in the wilderness." Did you seek God's comfort? Consider how you may keep God's presence close to you, even in difficult or challenging times.

> "For I, the Lord your God, hold your right hand; it is I who say to you, 'Do not fear, I will help you.'"
> — Isaiah 41:13

SATURDAY

Today, relax, reflect on the positive things you experienced this past week and the challenges you faced. And reconnect with your family and friends.

THE THIRD WEEK:
The World Is Round

Does not wisdom call, and does not understanding raise her voice ... Take my instruction instead of silver, and knowledge rather than choice gold; for wisdom is better than jewels, and all that you desire may not compare with her (Proverbs 8:1; 10).

Living between 276 and 194 B.C., Eratosthenes was the chief librarian of Alexandria. This was definitely the place to be if you were searching for knowledge. It was the storehouse of virtually all the documents, manuscripts, and letters that were of any importance in the ancient world. And it was Eratosthenes who oversaw this vast collection of wisdom, insight, and understanding.

We make a lot of assumptions about what people of that time believed. One of our worst misconceptions is that all people of that day believed the world was flat. But a careful reading of the Bible reveals that they knew the earth was round.

Have you not known? Have you not heard? Has it not been told you from the beginning? Have you not understood from the foundations of the earth? It is he who sits above the circle of the earth... (Isaiah 40:21-22).

And Eratosthenes not only knew the earth was round; he figured out almost exactly how big around it was. Here is how he did it.

He had heard of a special well in his native Egypt near a town called Syene. He knew that, at noon on June 21—the day of the year when the sun would have been straight overhead for the Summer Solstice—the sun's rays shone directly to the bottom of the well. Alexandria was due north. So, he knew if the sun was directly overhead in Syene, its rays would hit Alexandria at an angle. He imagined the shaft of the well continuing all the way to the center of the earth and a similar line going to the center of the earth from Alexandria.

He understood that the angle formed by these lines could be calculated by the angle of the shadow cast in Alexandria.[6] Then, imagining the world as a circle, and having the angle of two points on the circle already measured, Eratosthenes needed only one more piece of information to figure out the circumference of the earth.

He hired a pacer, a professional who was specially trained to walk in measured steps so as to gauge distances. This man walked and measured the precise distance from Alexandria to Syene. Once Eratosthenes knew this number, he could, from the angle of the sun's shadow he had determined in Alexandria, extrapolate the size of the circle by figuring the fraction of the circle's circumference that distance represented. The answer he found was one-fiftieth—that is, if you walked back and forth from those two cities fifty times, you would have the distance around the circle of the earth.

Using this method, Eratosthenes estimated the circumference of the world to be 24,700 miles. Today, using the same measuring principles with modern instruments, we believe the distance to be 24,902 miles. Not a bad calculation for a guy working *two thousand* years ago. Brilliant, we might say.

But brilliance is not necessary to be wise. One doesn't have to be a genius to keep heart, mind, and eyes open for ways to be better at what we do and how we do it. We can work for better understanding in our community, deepen our knowledge of the world, and broaden our perspectives of other cultures and other people. Throughout history, people like Eratosthenes have experienced great joy at nurturing their intelligence and using it to benefit others. May it be so for you this week. Let us learn something new, good, and exciting. And let that newfound knowledge help us to be better people on behalf of others.

> Help us, O God. We understand too little and have fallen short of the wisdom and knowledge you call us to. Lift us this week and allow us to learn, love, and enjoy with gusto! Amen.

---

[6] From the Greek mathematician Pythagoras (570-490 B.C.).

REFLECTIONS FOR THE WEEK

MONDAY

A certain woman named Lydia, a worshiper of God, was listening to us; she was from the city of Thyatira and a dealer in purple cloth. The Lord opened her heart... (Acts 16:14).

My father once told me, "If you ever wonder what you should pray for, pray for discernment." The compliment to discernment is "keenly selective judgment," and, I would add, very good listening skills. It is using wisdom to make important decisions. Discernment integrates knowledge and facilitates wise judgment.

As we saw from studying the Ethiopian eunuch and Philip, both were faced with momentous decisions—ones that they considered fully before choosing well. Today, let us consider another figure Luke presents in Acts—Lydia.

She was already a worshiper of God, so she was on the right track. But she needed to know more, to live more fully and believe more thoroughly. She "was listening," Luke tells us.

Since childhood, I've been told: "You have two ears and one mouth for a reason—listening is more important than speaking!" Obviously, Lydia understood this well.

For today, concentrate on listening and make note of what you hear—the good and the bad. This is not to say that you should eavesdrop. Just be quiet and see what comes to your attention. And make this listening a part of your prayer life for the day. What devotional wisdom arises from your silence and the chatter around you?

> "Govern everything by your wisdom, O Lord, so that my soul may always be serving you in the way you will." — Teresa of Avila

TUESDAY

The Lord opened her heart... (Acts 16:14).

Lydia was wealthy. She was a trader and businesswoman. She interacted with the aristocracy of the day. She owned a home large enough to serve as the first Christian church on European soil. She had no husband.

These subtle pieces of information allow us to put together a probable back-story to the beginnings of our expanding church heritage that Luke relates in the text (Acts 16:14-15 and 16:40). She had done well for herself. She had to have been savvy and intelligent to compete with the largely male-dominated Greco-Roman world. But what occurs in this story has little to do with intelligence and much to do with her wisdom to honor the movement of God in her life. She was listening to what was being said. Then, "The Lord opened her heart" (Acts 16:14).

As the Lord wishes, open your heart today. Are you ready? Can you be honest with yourself, with what you need, and with how God can help?

> "Honesty is the first chapter in the book of wisdom."
> — Thomas Jefferson

WEDNESDAY

The Lord opened her heart to listen eagerly... (Acts 16:14).

I like the wording here: "to listen *eagerly*..." At first, she was overhearing what was being said. But what she heard intrigued her. She "was listening" but it wasn't until "the Lord opened her heart" that she began "to listen eagerly." She could have simply been interested in what was being said and gone on with her routine. She was successful and busy and likely had a schedule to keep. But her mere listening was transformed into eager listening by God's intervention.

Sometimes, maintaining a routine and keeping a schedule is the one thing that keeps us sane. With the many demands on us and the pushes and pulls from a variety of directions, maintaining consistency often is a survival strategy. But it can also squelch the movement of God in our hearts. Lydia was able to put aside her schedule so she could listen with passion and earnestness. This signals to us her excitement and her awakening to God's call. As a result, her life and the lives of many others were changed.

Make it your mission today to listen more deeply to others. Be eager to learn from them, to discern your own motivations and actions, to experience something new of God's desire for you.

> "It is not that I'm so smart. But I stay with the questions much longer."
> — Albert Einstein

THURSDAY

If you have judged me to be faithful, come and stay at my home (Acts 16:15).

Interestingly, in this simple conditional statement Lydia poses to Paul, Luke, Timothy, and Silas, we witness the beginning of an entirely new era in the life of the church. In this moment, according to Luke's telling, the church moves from Asia to the continent of Europe. Lydia's home, then, becomes the site of the first Christian church on European soil. "And she prevailed upon us," Luke says. She was, after all, a trader and salesperson accustomed to making deals and "prevailing" upon her customers. The eagerness with which she heard the gospel preached, she now begins to live. She offers hospitality to strangers. But more, she opens her home to be used by God as a sanctuary, a place of worship, a refuge, a hospice, a place of recovery.

Did you hear of a need this week with which you could assist? If so, consider how you acted. If not, concentrate on listening for such an opportunity.

FRIDAY

After leaving the prison they went to Lydia's home; and when they had seen and encouraged the brothers and sisters there, they departed (Acts 16:40).

Paul and Silas staggered back to Lydia's home for refuge. They had just been released from prison after being flogged. Imagine their being welcomed by their fellow believers all gathered in her house. How long were they there? How often did they come? What was her role as hostess and owner of the house that doubled as the church? We don't know. But we can speculate. Her home was large enough to accommodate many. Her hospitality was warm enough to keep the faithful returning. And her house was safe enough that, following an arrest, Paul and Silas, nor the others, would be harassed by authorities.

How hospitable are we in our circles of friends? How willing are you to offer hospitality in the name of Jesus? Today, think of some ways you might be hospitable on behalf of a significant cause. See if, by your thoughts on Lydia and prayers for discernment, God might be calling you to offer hospitality in some way.

> "There is no hospitality like understanding."
> — Vanna Bonta

SATURDAY

Relax. Rest. Consider what you have learned this week and continue to practice listening. Look forward to worship and being with friends tomorrow.

The Fourth Week:
The World Is Flat

(You) have clothed yourselves with the new self, which is being renewed in knowledge according to the image of its creator. In that renewal there is no longer Greek and Jew, circumcised and uncircumcised, barbarian, Scythian, slave and free; but Christ is all and in all (Colossians 3:10-11).

In 2005, Thomas Friedman published his book *The World Is Flat*, with subsequent revisions and additions by 2007. Though written before the 2008 Great Recession, his premise still stands: the developed world, the developing world, and the less-developed world—along with people across boundaries and languages—are becoming increasingly intertwined, competitive, and similar. California's Silicon Valley, Brazil's Sao Paolo, and India's Bangalore have much in common.

Other people and cultures no longer simply hope and strive to be like the developed Western world as might have been the case following the dissolution of the Soviet Union. Now, diverse places across the globe add creativity, insights, and new technology to the fascinating mix of twenty-first century innovation.

The current president of Brazil, Dilma Rousseff, declared, "Brazil ... will become the world's fourth largest economy by 2030, behind China, America and India ... In the past eight years, we have lifted over forty million Brazilians ... out of poverty and into the middle classes with access to health, education, credit, and formal employment" (*The Economist*, "The Brazilian Model," December, 2011, p. 60).

Meanwhile, the largest human migration in history moves forward in China, as literally tens of millions of people move from the countryside into new cities that did not exist three or four years ago. Today, these cities are filled to overflowing with millions of residents. This is unprecedented.

This is not in any way meant to overlook the tragedies of the countless millions living in grinding urban poverty, existing on starvation rations in unimaginable conditions. Yet, never before have so many had access to so much so quickly. Along with the urbanization of the lands across the globe, technological advancements spread exponentially.

The changes occurring in our world boggle the mind. And so it was for the early Christians. Those first believers experienced similar shifts in reality—some for the better, some for the worse. There were plenty of negative responses to Paul's assertions. This new world order of equality and inclusiveness made many uncomfortable and created further tensions in a number of congregations and gatherings (the Corinthian church, for example).

What is our response today? How might God assist us in adjusting, accommodating and, finally, celebrating the reality of God's vision in the world?

> Give us wisdom this week, Lord. Allow our decisions to flow from a discernment not ours alone, but filled with your insight beyond our own. Help us to investigate more deeply, understand more fully, learn more thoroughly, and share more considerately. Amen.

REFLECTIONS FOR THE WEEK

MONDAY

(You) have clothed yourselves with the new self, which is being renewed in knowledge according to the image of its creator (Colossians 3:10).

Biblically speaking, we live in an era that offers unprecedented opportunities for the vision of Colossians to become the fulfillment of God's hopes. Notice the wording of this first part of our passage for the week. They were in the process of having what we know to be true "renewed" by the "creator."

In other words, God's vision for the world was reflected in the new reality the Colossians were discovering and that Paul was affirming. Therefore, they (and we) are justified in putting on the "new clothes" of the "new self." The imagery here is valuable. We wouldn't consider wearing the same out-of-style or threadbare clothes of our earlier years. In the same way, Paul affirms the dreams of God to progress to an entirely new era of action and interaction.

Today, allow your knowledge to be renewed. Embrace the expanding vision of God's call in your life.

> "...We might as well require a man to wear still the coat which fitted him when a boy as civilized society to remain ever under the regimen of their barbarous ancestors."
> — Thomas Jefferson

TUESDAY

In that renewal there is no longer Greek and Jew, circumcised and uncircumcised, barbarian, Scythian, slave and free... (Colossians 3:11).

Paul's words have a particular ring when placed beside the realities we see unfolding before us. In his book *The Gifts of the Jews*, Thomas Cahill explains the precursor to the vision Paul articulates in Colossians above. It was the Jews—this ragtag, often contentious group called to be covenant people of God—who first caught the vision God cast before them. It was that all people had worth, everyone was important, individual opinions mattered, and people should be respected, fed, housed, clothed, and cared for—even enemies (Proverbs 24:29; 25:21; Matthew 5:43-45; Romans 12:20-21). Aliens should be loved: "...love the alien as you love yourself, for you were aliens in the land of Egypt..." (Leviticus 19:34). Justice, kindness, and humility should prevail over tithing and donations to the temple: "He has told you, O mortal, what is good; and what does the Lord require of you but to do justice, to love kindness and to walk humbly with your God" (Micah 6:8).[7]

Meditate today on what needs realignment in your life. What new things should you be noticing about the world around you?

> "Change your thoughts and you change your world."
> — Norman Vincent Peale

WEDNESDAY

...Christ is all and in all (Colossians 3:11).

There will continue to be territorial disputes, hunger, famine, economic hardships, terrorism, and other threats to our safety and livelihoods. But this has always been so. It was certainly so in Paul's day, and still his vision of an equitable, peaceful coexistence with others continued. Paul understood that Christ was *in* the everyday *and* beyond the moment, steadfast with love.

Today, search for what God needs you to see. Realize how much you need others—in your office, down the street, in the class next door, in a city in China, on a farm in Brazil. Regardless of who or where, *Christ is all and in all.* Discover this for yourself and make it so for others today!

---

[7] It is Cahill's contention in *The Gifts of the Jews*, and with good evidence, I think, that true democracy came from these biblical, early Jewish ideals.

> "This world of ours ... must avoid becoming a community of dreadful fear and hate, and be, instead, a proud confederation of mutual trust and respect."
> — Dwight D. Eisenhower

THURSDAY

Clothe yourselves with compassion, kindness, humility, meekness, and patience (Colossians 3:12b).

It is one thing to appreciate the increasing pluralism of our world. It is another to understand the same of our "own backyard." In our own country, the previous majority of white Americans has, as of this writing, just dipped below fifty percent. This new statistic supports the description of the United States as a *tossed salad* of colors and creeds in which we must be increasingly cognizant of one another's needs, outlooks, and heritages.

Our passage today offers this formula: compassion and kindness are essential for proper and decent interaction. Together, they contribute a sense of warmth to the community and a desire to reciprocate. Compassion and kindness allow disparate groups to get along, support one another, and thrive as a larger unit.

However, compassion and kindness eventually wear thin when manipulated or used as leverage. That's what makes humility, meekness, and patience such valuable partners in the facilitation of community. Early church members wrestled with issues not so different from our own widely eclectic neighborhoods and strove to be good Christians in the process.

Today, as you interact with the community you are a part of, *dress for success* as you "clothe yourself" in this way. Let your compassion and kindness show through patience and understanding of others. Be humble in your offerings.

FRIDAY

And whatever you do, in word or deed do everything in the name of the Lord Jesus, giving thanks to God the Father through him (Colossians 3:17).

How we live represents more than just ourselves. The imperative of this verse reminds us that we are representing Jesus and the whole movement of the church that follows him. I remember as a teenager being so thankful for the church family I was part of where my father was pastor. Many people in that fellowship profoundly influenced my life. I wanted to honor them by what I did and how I acted. The thought of embarrassing my church, or making anyone there concerned about bad decisions I might have made always helped me in choosing more wisely.

What we say and how we act impacts the way others see Jesus, for good or ill. On the other hand, what an honor it is to represent Jesus, to live and work and interact in his name. And, just like with my church growing up, as we live in honor of and in the name of Jesus, we can be thankful. To give thanks to God "in Jesus' name" is not some magic formula required so that our prayers might be heard. Rather, it is a personal reminder, a memory device *for us* so that what we are *thankful for* and *inspired in* all that we do. May it be so for you today.

> "May your constant, brooding love bring forth in us more love and all the graces and works of love."
> — Evelyn Underhill

SATURDAY

Rest. Reflect on this past week and revisit what you've learned about yourself and others. Relax.

> "You have given me all that I have, all that I am, and I surrender all to Your Divine will."
> — Ignatius of Loyola

OCTOBER
Staying Power

Originally the eighth month of the Roman calendar (and thus the prefix "Oct" for eight in Latin), it moved to number ten in the calendar after Julius Caesar and Caesar Augustus inserted months named after themselves (July and August). We also know this to be the prime month of fall, that time when the leaves begin to turn.

Depending on where you may live, this can be a spectacular time. But it also represents change—and the eventual movement toward winter. As we move through this month, our themes will reflect the transitions that come, sometimes swiftly, other times slowly—and the "Staying Power" so vital to getting through them.

THE FIRST WEEK:
Retreat is Not Defeat

When some Midianite traders passed by, they drew Joseph up, lifting him out of the pit, and sold him to the Ishmaelites for twenty pieces of silver (Genesis 37:25-27).

I remember back in seminary, a great Baptist preacher from Detroit, Fred Sampson, came to address our student body in chapel. He spoke honestly of genuine struggles—of growing up poor, an African-American originally from the south and the target of much hatred. Part of a strong family and with mentors who maintained dignity, withstood discrimination, and overcame poverty, his story reflected a nurturing community filled with courage and deep roots of faith. This, along with his profound biblical interpretations, poetic cadences, and deep baritone, all held me spellbound and on the edge of my seat. Then came the culminating, rising crescendo:

Retreat is not defeat; failure is not final and death with Jesus is not dying, it's just a departure to a better place.

It would not be accurate to call this escapist theology. Coming out of the African-American experience, this "better place" is both a state of mind and an improved condition, not just off in heaven later on but here in this time and in this place. It is a determined word that tragedy will not overcome the human spirit. This is a truth we can claim today, tomorrow, forever.

This same truth so movingly conveyed in Fred Sampson's sermon is illustrated in the Genesis story of Joseph. There, we hear of a brash youngster, enamored with himself, transformed through hardship into a courageous, willful, determined young adult of high morals and deep faith. But there is also the foreground story, the Christian story of Jesus. With a subtly the Bible often employs, these two stories are juxtaposed by an economic element: Joseph is sold by his brothers into slavery for twenty pieces of silver; Jesus is sold into the hands of the religious authorities for thirty pieces of silver. Joseph, in spite of and out of his bondage, saves his people from physical hunger and famine; Jesus, in spite of and out of and through his death, saves all of us, his people, from spiritual hunger and sin.

For Fred Sampson's sermon, and for our own daily stories, giving our lives over to follow Jesus, to be his disciples, to be learners of his way, merges seamlessly with the faith of Joseph, the faith of the early church, and the faith of today. Somehow, in ways we cannot fully fathom, our God of history, the God of Joseph, the God seen most fully and perfectly in Jesus, guides us still, inspires us fully, and leads us on so that our better place—whatever blessing or goodness or opportunity that might come our way—may be used to lift the lives of others along with our own.

It is good to know that humility has its distinct and biblical advantages; it is valuable to remember that good news is a matter of perspective; and it is essential to claim: whatever circumstance you find yourself in this week, tragedy will not have the last word. You are in the hands of God.

> Open our hearts, O God, to the truth of your surrounding presence and the inspired staying power those who have preceded us felt, understood, and acting upon. This week, make us brave in our actions and interactions. Allow others to see in us some inspiring act of courage that offers them a glimpse of the eternal hope found only in you. Amen.

REFLECTIONS FOR THE WEEK

MONDAY

Do not fear what they fear, and do not be intimidated...
(I Peter 3:14).

I love this verse from I Peter. "Do not be intimidated..." What a good word for this week as we consider the theme of "Staying Power." For the next few days, we will hear a little history about a couple of individuals who demonstrated great courage and remarkable staying power: Anne Hutchinson and Roger Williams.

In 1634, Anne Hutchinson left England for the Massachusetts Bay Colony after the birth of her fourteenth child. She and her family settled in the growing city of Boston. A midwife who gradually gained a reputation for profound biblical literacy and great religious insight, she hosted large numbers of women who became increasingly swayed by her perspectives. Men, too, liked what she said, and her reputation spread.

Like her father, a pastor in England, she was increasingly concerned about ill-prepared preachers whose sermons reflected not the Bible or the teachings of Jesus but their own personal prejudices and biased perspectives. But, by confronting some, she got herself into trouble.

Anne Hutchinson is one example of the many who stood up for their beliefs, regardless of the consequences. Such courage is what our faith, and the early history of our country, was founded on. For today, consider what kind of courage you need to display, when, and with whom. Think about the "staying power" that has been in others, and still can be in you!

TUESDAY

...in your hearts, sanctify Christ as Lord (I Peter 3:15).

Anne Hutchinson was America's first feminist and female minister. She stood against the Puritan leaders of the Massachusetts Bay Colony as an early advocate for religious freedom.

Freedom of thought, speech, and worship are gifts we enjoy thanks to her and many others who courageously stood up to the intimidating majority of pious religious and political authorities. In her case, these male leaders were convinced of their righteousness and her foolishness. At her trial in 1637, her prosecutors were well-spoken preachers and political leaders who ridiculed her, laughed at her, belittled her ideas of grace, religious freedom, and God's desire to speak to all people. They scoffed at the notion that a woman could teach, or preach, or lead in worship.

Using only the Bible to defend herself, she stood before these men, forty-nine in all, and did *not fear.* She was *not intimidated.* And she continued to *sanctify Christ as Lord.*

Today, imagine what it would have been like in that courtroom—the taunting, belittling, patronizing treatment. In your heart, reclaim "Christ as Lord." Now, consider your own situation anew. It may be that you have a new perspective for whatever it is that you are experiencing right now. Be strong in your convictions, stand for what you believe in, and, in doing so, offer others an example to do the same. You will find that you are not alone.

> "Success is not final, failure is not fatal: it is the courage to continue that counts."
> — Winston Churchill

WEDNESDAY

These things I have spoken unto you, that in me, you might have peace; in the world, you shall have tribulation; but be of good cheer, for I have overcome the world (John 16:33).

There were numerous times in Roger Williams' life when he could have given up. Trained as a minister in London, he came to these shores in 1630 as a refugee, fleeing religious persecution from the Church of England. He discovered the Puritans of Massachusetts to be no more hospitable. The *heresies* that got him into trouble were religious toleration, advocacy of church and state separation, respect for Native American rights, and respect for all people regardless of background.

Williams was horrified to see the way the Puritan leaders treated the Native Americans. Already, the colonists acted with foolish haughtiness. The Puritans and Pilgrims strutted about these new colonies with a self-perceived entitlement to land that had been lived on, cultivated, and loved for centuries by Native Americans. Roger Williams fought this attitude and the pervasive fixation of white superiority. He befriended the Native Americans, learned several of their languages, and attempted to ally with them against the other colonist's abuses—until he was forced to flee from Massachusetts. Those he was attempting to protect then protected him. The Narragansett Indians welcomed him as one of their own, into a place that would later become known as *Providence*.

He could have quit, but the "staying power" of his faith was strong. Today, consider the strength of your own beliefs. How far would you go to stand up for what you believe in? Cultivate a sense of your own staying power, and see what can happen when you hang in there.

> "Defeat is simply a signal to press onward."
> — Helen Keller

THURSDAY

Do not fear what they fear, and do not be intimidated, but in your hearts, sanctify Christ as Lord (I Peter 3:14-15).

When forced to flee a second time, Roger Williams, founded what became known as Rhode Island. In 1636, he established a new city on Narragansett Bay he called Providence. And to this new place he welcomed other exiles, like Anne Hutchinson from Massachusetts and many Baptists, Quakers, Jews, Native Americans, and even what he called "Turks" (Muslims). Williams was a man ahead of his time.

He was the first Baptist on American soil and began what is still known today as "The First Baptist Church in America" in Providence, Rhode Island. Thanks to his courageous, progressive, spirit-filled staying power, our country now attempts to embody everything he stood for.

Today, whatever obstacles come your way, remember those who have come before—Roger Williams and Anne Hutchinson could have limped off into the sunset and sulked. Instead, they helped to transition history into a new era of respect, understanding, and multiculturalism that serves as the moral, ethical, and spiritual foundation for our nation. So hang in there. Whatever your difficulties, allow them to make you stronger, and to make a difference.

FRIDAY

Always be ready to make your defense to anyone who demands from you an accounting for the hope that is in you; yet do so with gentleness and reverence
(I Peter 3:14-15).

Following on the heels of our previous verse from I Peter, these words offer a valuable conclusion to our thoughts on "Staying Power." Notice the wording "an accounting for the hope that is in you." Implicit in that statement is that you live in a way demonstrating a particular kind of perspective to others—a "hope that is in you." As a Christian, we can live every day knowing that, in the famous words of Julian of Norwich, "all is well, and all shall be well." God is in control, and truth offers great resilience. Hope, then, can and should be evident in the way we conduct ourselves, the ways that we act and interact.

But when you are asked about this hope, the second part of the biblical equation remains equally vital: share with "gentleness and reverence." The hope that is in us is not something to be flaunted. Rather, it is a gracious gift to be gently lived out and reverently passed on.

Consider, today, how you exhibit hope to others. Ask yourself who, in your life, needs a little staying power and reach out to them.

SATURDAY

Rest. Relax. Remember your heritage today. Give thanks and be glad for your inspirations this past week. Treat yourself to a nap.

THE SECOND WEEK:
On Dying and Living

God himself will be with them; he will wipe every tear from their eyes. Death will be no more, mourning and crying and pain will be no more... (Revelation 21:3-4).

I was asked this question not long ago: "What will happen after we die? Specifically, does the Bible say anything about recognizing each other after we die?"

There are many speculations but no definitive answers to this, as far as I can tell. Like with much in life, we go on faith. Circumstantial evidence seems to point to recognition of an afterlife, as when some have died, been resuscitated, and then recount what they saw and felt. These kinds of experiences and descriptions have been recorded as far back as ancient Greece and Egypt.[1] Of course, some would explain such occurrences as simply adrenaline just before or after death that momentarily heightens imagination and memory. No one really knows.

The Bible is understandably circumspect. Though describing a "new heaven and new earth" where there will be no more tears, these are human attempts at describing the indescribable—eternity with God and with each other. Thus, we must be careful when interpreting the Bible, particularly the New Testament book of Revelation, which is highly symbolic in its language and intent.

In Luke 10:25-28, Jesus responds to a question regarding eternal life and how to *inherit it.* "What do the scriptures say?" Jesus asks. The man quotes Deuteronomy 6:5 and Leviticus 19:18: "Love the Lord your God with all your heart, soul, strength, and mind; and love your neighbor as you love yourself" (Luke 10:27). And Jesus' response is: "You have given the right answer; do this and you will live" (10:28).

Notice, the question was about eternal life, implying a future after death. But Jesus changes this, the tense he uses no longer

---

[1] Interestingly, in this country, often "life after death" experiences recount moving toward some kind of light. In Japan, however, the experience most often described is tending a garden.

implies future but literal present. This is very important on several levels, but specifically related to a legitimate concern of the afterlife. I take it to mean we should be careful not to get too caught up in scenarios we can't fully understand or adequately describe; instead, we can and are called to recognize that God's grace and purpose are available to us here and now; we are to embrace this grace and purpose and live accordingly—and fully—in the present.

So, live like we will recognize each other and believe that we will be eternally joyful; focus on the now and what needs to be done; enjoy each other and God's good creation; be thankful, humble, resourceful, responsible, and strive to be good and do good; love God with all that you are and all that you have; love your neighbor as you love yourself, and everything else will take care of itself—God will provide.

> Help us this week, O God. Allow us to focus on your callings to each of us in the here and now. Give us the wisdom to live in hope and eternal expectation while simultaneously embracing the goodness and wonder of our daily experiences, our everyday relationships, our casual encounters, good food, and the creative loveliness that surrounds us always. This week, make us keenly aware of our current participation in your eternal and abundant life. Amen.

REFLECTIONS FOR THE WEEK

MONDAY

...take hold of the life that really is life (I Timothy 6:19).

I have been a part of several funerals over the years that incorporated bagpipes. Either you love them and are moved by them, or you hate them. A colleague and friend of mine once commented on his grandfather's perspective: "They's two kinds of music I cain't stand, and bagpipes is both of 'em."

But, for some of us, bagpipes convey a mystical message that only this odd combination of sound can produce. It is strangely, almost impossibly, whimsical and sacred at the same time. And part of the tradition from the rough Scottish highlands is the valuable message the music of bagpipes implies: that life is *both* whimsical and sacred.

The pipes were often used when marching, so the idea of a journey is woven into their purpose. And life is a journey. So much of what we know and do, and who we are, is bound up in the odd complexities of being alive, balancing relationships and responsibilities, hopes and dreams, defeats and small victories.

As you move through this day, imagine the sound of a bagpipe accompanying your *march*. Step boldly in cadence to the kind of life the Bible envisions. Imagine each step as both sacred and whimsical, holy and light-hearted, elegantly eternal and solidly present. And, finally, allow those bagpipes to make you smile.

> "Though the road's been rocky, it sure feels good to me."
> — Bob Marley

TUESDAY

See to it that no one fails to obtain the grace of God; that no root of bitterness springs up and cause trouble... (Hebrews 12:15).

Staying power requires numerous components. We have discussed courage and discipline; vision and perspective and faith. Now, we hear again of the need for purpose. The temptation to quit and to give in to whatever is pushing us diminishes considerably when we have a clear purpose and focused calling. The variety of gifts and various interests we cultivate over the years adds a vast diversity to what we offer to others as Christians. The author of Hebrews, however, follows the imperatives of both Old and New Testaments and provides bright clarity in our focus for today: "See that no one fails to obtain the grace of God."

So, let us make that our goal. Live today with grace in mind—God's grace for others, through us.

Like the great cloud of witnesses[2] that precedes us in faith and enfolds us in support, you are more than the change that is; you are not alone, and never will be. And God's grace makes it so.

Imagine today unfolding before you in this way:

>Lifted by grace
>Sustained by love
>Emboldened by faith
>Encouraged by hope
>Enriched by joy
>Embraced by eternity
>In the arms of God
>And offered to the world—
>As a beautiful gift—you.
>By grace, with grace, for grace
>To others—today.

WEDNESDAY

Death will be no more, mourning and crying and pain will be no more... (Revelation 21:4).

In 1755, in the midst of the Enlightenment, when great thinkers were certain that life's purpose and meaning were

---

[2] See Hebrews 12:1.

entwined in the perfection of God's well-planned universe, a devastating earthquake virtually destroyed the ancient and beautiful city of Lisbon, Portugal. Thousands were injured, crushed, killed in the most horrible natural disaster that the newly modern world had ever experienced. The famous French philosopher, Voltaire, wrote a poem expressing his horror at the loss and revulsion at the attempts of religious justifications for the earthquake. Next week, we will see Voltaire's words. But more appropriate for our theme this week is Jean-Jacques Rousseau's response to Voltaire on the Lisbon earthquake of 1755.[3] Notice Rousseau's redemptive perspective:

> I cannot prevent myself, Monsieur, from noting ... a strange contrast between you and me as regards the subject of this letter. Satiated with glory ... you live free in the midst of affluence. Certain of your immortality, you peacefully philosophize on the nature of the soul ... I, an obscure and poor man tormented with an incurable illness, meditate with pleasure in my seclusion and find that all is well. What is the source of this apparent contradiction? ... I hope, and hope beautifies everything ... I have suffered too much in this life not to look forward to another. No metaphysical subtleties cause me to doubt a time of immortality for the soul and a beneficent providence. I sense it, I believe it, I wish it, I hope for it, I will uphold it until my last gasp...
> I am, with respect, Monsieur,
> Jean-Jacques Rousseau

Today, meditate on Rousseau's words. In spite of his struggles and difficult condition, he declares, "I hope, and hope beautifies everything."

Do you agree? Disagree? Ask yourself why. Contemplate how you would respond in the face of such tragedy. And think today on what it is that gives you hope—and what difference that makes.

---

[3] Rousseau's books, *On the Social Contract* and *Discourse on the Origin of Inequality*, strongly influenced American thinkers like Thomas Jefferson, Thomas Payne, and Benjamin Franklin.

THURSDAY

I thank my God every time I remember you, constantly praying with joy in every one of my prayers for all of you because of your sharing in the gospel from the first day until now (Philippians 1:3-5).

At Providence Baptist Church where I have the honor to serve as a minister, there is a columbarium situated in the courtyard between our sanctuary and part of our educational wing. This is significant. First, *columbarium* is simply a fancy Latin word that comes from the word *columba*, or dove, and refers back to the recesses or slots made for doves to nest in. Now, it refers to a sacred space where family can place the ashes or the remains of their loved ones after death.

This is the intention at our congregation; however there also are other roles that this and other, more traditional cemeteries can play in our lives as Christians. They can:

- remind us of those who have gone before us (the great cloud of witnesses).
- remind us of our mortality (we won't live forever and should be prepared).
- remind us to consider our immortality (additional preparation).
- remind us to treasure the now (the eternal present).
- remind us to treasure those who are *with* us in the now (things change so quickly).

Today, think on each of the above statements. Remember someone specific who has gone before you, part of your great cloud of witnesses. Honor them for a few moments with gratitude and fond memories. Give thanks for their life and for the impact they had on you. And, finally, spend a few moments considering how it is you might be remembered. What impact do you or have you had on others? Consider the legacy you will leave behind someday. Now, live today with renewed purpose.

> "The purpose of life is a life of purpose." — Robert Byrne

FRIDAY

...take hold of the life that really is life (I Timothy 6:19).

When the great French scientist, philosopher, inventor, and mathematician Blaise Pascal died, the following note was found stitched into his jacket. It described his conversion experience on Monday, November 23, 1654, from about half past ten in the evening until about half past twelve:

> Fire.
> God of Abraham, God of Isaac, God of Jacob, not of the philosophers and scholars.
> Certitude. Feeling. Joy. Peace. God of Jesus Christ.
> Forgetfulness of the world and of everything, except God.
> Greatness of the human Soul.
> Joy, joy, joy, tears of joy.

This day, find a quiet moment and reflect on your own sacred experience(s), that moment or moments, perhaps infrequent, probably fleeting, but times of reassurance, of affirmation, of grace and joy. Be reassured again of life's eternal connection, of your sacred heritage—and of the mystery, holiness, and wonder that is God's gift to us and the essence of life.

> "Don't cry because it's over; smile because it happened."
> — Dr. Suess

SATURDAY

Embrace this day even as you prepare for the next. Think of good moments in your past, smiles in your present, experiences you look forward to in the future. Rest and enjoy.

> "The most wasted of all days is one without laughter."
> — e.e. cummings

THE THIRD WEEK:
Bad Things Do Happen

We know that all things work together for good for those who love God... (Romans 8:28).

I find Job appropriate to include in the month of October since Halloween represents an attempt begun by our Celtic ancestors to inject meaning into the fear of suffering and death. The book of Job wrestles with the same issues and troubling questions. And, if read carefully, the book actually pokes fun at some of the attempts by Job's friends to explain his *inexplicable* suffering.

The book of Job presents thoughtful deliberations regarding how life works, why there is suffering, and who or what, if anything, is in control. Though he directs his grief, dismay, and anger at God, ultimately, Job is rewarded for his faithfulness and is told to pray for his knuckleheaded friends and their misplaced piousness. And, though he never arrives at an adequate answer—there *is* no answer—he does understand that God is still in control of the universe; God has created all of life; and sometimes things occur which we do not comprehend, which appear horribly unfair and for which we have no viable explanation.

This week, we will explore various biblical perspectives from Job and beyond. We want to be hopeful, and yet honest. We want to be biblical. And in doing so, we shall discover that the Bible is truthful about suffering—and helpful in the midst of it.

> We give you thanks, O God, that we can be honest about our feelings, our questions, and our doubts. There is so much we do not understand. And still we give thanks. For, in the midst of our questions, discomfort, and even heartache, we can tell the truth about our pain. We also have gifts that we cannot count, friends we cannot repay, and family we sometimes take for granted. This week, Lord, remind us again what surrounds us. And calm us even in our restlessness. Amen.

REFLECTIONS FOR THE WEEK

MONDAY

My God, my God, why have you forsaken me? Why are you so far from helping me? (Psalm 22:1).

You may recognize these words as the ones Jesus spoke from the cross (Mark 15:34). But the Psalm has more to tell us. There are days in every life when we are faced with more questions than answers. We know that, on those days when nothing seems to go our way, whether because of tragedy, loss, illness, or deep anxiety, we also know that we are not alone. We are in good company. Over the centuries, people just like us have struggled with issues just like ours.

Today, strive to maintain your balance and perspective, no matter what you face. Remember those who have gone before—facing just the same or similar issues—and triumphed.

> "...the real growth in the life of the Spirit comes in the darkness of faith and the living of a life of Christian love."
> — Kenneth Leech

TUESDAY

If you will seek God and make supplication to the Almighty, if you are pure and upright, surely then he will rouse himself for you and restore to you your rightful place (Job 8:5-6).

The part of the Bible where we find the book of Job is called "Wisdom Literature." It is a collection of books in scripture that attempts to explain why bad things happen (as sometimes in Proverbs), to lament when bad things happen (like Psalm 22 and Lamentations) to ask the deeper questions about life and meaning (as in Ecclesiastes), and to acknowledge that, sometimes, there are no answers (as in Job).

Job is an innocent man suffering for no reason. Yet, his friends try to make there be a reason. Neither they nor Job know what has transpired. And their arguments, intentionally portrayed as deeply serious, are realistically silly. They reflect real attempts by usually well-intending people to explain the inexplicable. Job's later response is tellingly and sarcastic: "No doubt you are the people, and wisdom will die with you..." (Job 12:2). In other words: "You think you are such hot stuff... Leave me alone!"

Today, be there for someone who needs your support. But keep in mind that the fewer words you use, the better friend you will be. Listening is enough.

> "The Christian hope which inspires me is not a thing but a Person."
> — Paul Tournier

WEDNESDAY

Why did I not die at birth, come forth from the womb and expire? (Job 3:11).

Do you ever have days when you feel like Job in this third chapter? I hope not. But if you ever do, know that what you read in Job, and what the Bible acknowledges consistently throughout scripture, is that, sometimes, life is just plain hard. There is no way around it. Suffering happens. Questions arise. Troubles come. And no matter how hard we try, explanations elude us.

There are other times, of course, when our own actions or inactions are to blame for whatever situation we find ourselves in. One of the first key insights into our human condition that the Bible shares comes from Genesis, chapter 3. The man and woman have tasted of the fruit from the tree of the knowledge of good and evil, their eyes are opened, and they suddenly realize that they are naked—that is, they are vulnerable to all kinds of bad possibilities and exposed to things they cannot control.

God questions them: "Who told you that you were naked? Have you eaten from the tree...?" (Genesis 3:11).

The man said: "It was the woman!" and the woman said: "It was the serpent!"

In other words, the wisdom of the Bible declares, with a touch of humor, that we too often fail to take responsibility for our own actions and inactions. We blame others for our problems and, in doing so, our discipleship is diminished and our learning is curtailed.

Today, make it a point to stand tall, to accept responsibility, and to receive whatever consequences there might be. You will be better for it.

> "The greatest challenge of the day is how to bring about a revolution of the heart, a revolution which has to start with each one of us."
> — Dorothy Day

THURSDAY

The Lisbon Earthquake of 1755 awakened the world to a disaster unprecedented in that period of Enlightenment and Scientific Revolution. All the new knowledge and great insights could not explain the awful tragedy that was Lisbon. Some, like the friends of Job, attempted to explain it in theological terms: God willed this destruction because of sin or the need to teach people a lesson. The great French philosopher, Voltaire, would have none of it:

> Will you say, "It is the effect of everlasting laws
> Which necessitates this choice by a free and good God?"
> Will you say, seeing this heap of victims:
> "God is avenged, their death is the payment of their crimes?"
> What crimes, what bad things have been committed by
>   these children,
> Lying on the breasts of their mothers, flattened and bloody?
> Lisbon, which is a city no longer, had it more vices
> Than London, than Paris, given to doubtful delights?

This sounds very much like Job's response to his own unjust suffering. But, in last week's meditations, Jean-Jacques Rousseau offered a poignant and far more redemptive reply. Still, Voltaire was fully justified in shaking a philosophical fist at the conventional wisdom of that day. Then, as now, questions remain, suffering exists, and in the midst of these difficulties, we are called to support one another and remain faithful.

Today, mark how you respond to the small issues—those most might call "annoyances." Keep them in perspective. There may be broader, deeper troubles you are aware of. In these cases, consider Job's struggle, his response, and his ultimate discovery. Finally, is there anything you might do to help alleviate suffering somewhere (i.e. contribute to a reputable hunger fund, give blood, donate food or clothing, raise awareness, offer your time, pray...)? Consider doing what you can and do it!

> "If this yawning emptiness was the enlargement of my inner capacity for God, then I would welcome these desert experiences."
> — Joyce Hugget

FRIDAY

We know that all things work together for good for those who love God... (Romans 8:28).

As we conclude our week, considering the theme "Bad Things Happen," it is also important to recall the scripture that began our week. Particularly in the face of "All Hallows Eve" or Halloween, no other verse so aptly concludes our considerations of suffering, sadness, and difficulties. Children will be donning masks and costumes evoking superheroes and princesses, goblins and villains, witches and devils. They will portray in fantasy what we too often experience in reality: life can be a vast drama of very good and very bad. And we exist in the tension between the two—wanting to thrive but too often just hoping to survive.

Romans 8:28 is not saying that God causes bad things to happen but that, in those bad things, good can arise. "All things"—the good and the bad—can be leveraged for the better, can be transformed in community and with friends, for the good of the community and for the benefit of the kingdom. We do not always understand, much like Job, so there will be much we will ask God. But, in the meantime, we contend with what is:

love, beauty, goodness, compassion—along with poverty, sadness, loss, suffering, discontent. There is much we will never know. But we are not alone; we are all in this together; God is in control of our present and future; and in the power of God's love, ultimately, *all things work together for good.*

Reflect on your own history. Can you remember a time when you were confronted with something that caused you to question God, to wonder about faith, to fear for your future? How did that work out? How do you feel about that period of time now?

I can think of numerous times in my own pilgrimage when these dynamics were very much at work. But I also now recognize the changes that occurred in me, both during and after. Questions of faith prompted new understandings and broader perspective; recognition of vulnerability triggered deeper relationships; and new appreciation of church life opened more significant friendships, a maturing faith, and new insights for the next phase of my journey.

I'll bet the same is true for you.

> "It is the times of greatest trial that arouse the greatest courage."
> — Paul Tournier

SATURDAY

Today, consider the ultimate goodness of life and of God's creation—and visualize your positive place in both! Relax. Enjoy.

> "If we don't know where we're going, any road will get us there. But if we have a destination—in this case a life lived to the glory of God—there is a well-marked way, the Jesus-revealed Way."
> — Eugene H. Peterson

THE FOURTH WEEK:
Go and Do; Sit and Listen

...a woman named Martha welcomed him into her home. She had a sister named Mary, who sat at the Lord's feet and listened to what he was saying (Luke 10:38-39).

Around 1655, the great Dutch Renaissance artist Johannes Vermeer painted a famous portrayal of this story of Jesus with Mary and Martha.[4] In the painting, Mary sits at Jesus' feet listening carefully to what he has to say. Martha stands behind Jesus, peering over his shoulder. She is holding a basket of bread and has an expression that appears only mildly puzzled. Many suspect this was Vermeer's first major work and that, in focusing on technique, he missed the fascinating dynamics of this biblical scene. In fact, the text reveals significant tension—far more than Vermeer conveys. From the way Luke shares the story, there is confusion, frustration, weariness, and bitterness from Martha. And she has her reasons.

But Mary is listening intently to Jesus. From Luke's artistic, pithy description, we can imagine her mental state: awe, devotion, hope, deep interest, and growing excitement. Vermeer's portrayal misses all this and, in just a cursory reading of the passage, so do we. But, before we continue with the exploration of this story and its value for our time, let us remind ourselves again of the value of biblical context.

Within the flow of Luke's Gospel, this story appears intentionally placed: this passage is told directly after one of the most famous and important stories in the New Testament: The Good Samaritan (Luke 10:25-37). As we will see in November with Nicodemus and the Woman at the Well, the Gospel writers often placed passages next to each other in order to provide comparison and contrast among stories and characters. This allowed them to make broader points about Jesus, his ministry,

---

[4] *Christ in the House of Martha and Mary*, 1655, now housed at the National Gallery of Scotland in Edinburgh.

and the larger picture of God's hopes beyond what the individual stories themselves conveyed.

Over the next few days, we shall look more closely at Martha, a busy woman searching for answers within the context of her time and culture. And we'll compare this story with the parable of the Good Samaritan about a man also searching for purpose and clarity. Mary, too, offers us valuable insights into what Jesus thought about women, work, learning, and discipleship. For each, we gain new insights into our own time and place, and the delicate balancing act necessary for us to fully access the abundant life available in the here and now.

> Lord, we thank you for biblical examples of people just like us. Allow us to move through this week knowing that, like these we are learning about, we also struggle with busyness, expectations, responsibilities, faith questions, resentment, misplaced priorities, confusion, and unresolved frustrations with people we love. Give us patience as we learn, insight as we grow, and enthusiasm as we discover new things. And may all of these contribute to the staying power we so badly need for our time. Amen.

REFLECTIONS FOR THE WEEK

MONDAY

Just then, a lawyer stood up to test Jesus. "Teacher, what must I do to inherit eternal life?" (Luke 10:25).

"Lord, do you not care that my sister has left me to do all the work by myself? Tell her to come in here and help me" (Luke 10:40).

As we covered yesterday, this tenth chapter of Luke juxtaposes two stories that, on the surface, appear to contradict each other. They have significant similarities, but the conclusions drawn appear to teach the opposite ideals. In 10:25, Jesus encounters an *intelligent man* who is searching for his purpose in life, but he tries to *test* Jesus. As we shared earlier, the man's question to Jesus about inheriting eternal life prompts Jesus' answer about loving God and neighbor. The man's follow-up question prompts Jesus to tell the parable of the Good Samaritan.

In the very next passage, a *busy woman*, Martha, is also searching. Instead of "testing" Jesus like the man did, she *scolds* Jesus. She wonders why her sister can sit and listen to Jesus, foregoing all conformity to tradition while she, Martha, is left with all the work to make the home comfortable and welcome guests, especially Jesus. Placing these two stories side by side, we can recognize the apparent contradiction, yet also the subtle wisdom of the technique—and the teaching.

The *intelligent man*, while testing, asks Jesus about *eternal life and himself* (Luke 10:25). The *busy woman*, while scolding, asks Jesus about *work and her sister* (10:40). To the intelligent man, Jesus says "go and do" (10:37). To the busy woman, Jesus says "sit and listen" (10:42).[5] So which is it? Should we go and do or sit and listen? These clearly are not the same life stances.

---

[5] His actual words are: "Mary has chosen the better portion, which shall not be taken away from her," referring to her desire to listen, learn, and become a disciple, which is what sitting at the feet of rabbi meant.

As we consider more deeply the story of Mary and Martha over the next few days, I hope the richness of this scripture will offer new depth to our discipleship and how we should view life, work, and learning for our everyday experience.

Today, consider both of these stories from Luke 10. Ask what purpose it serves to have them side by side. What issues related to "going and doing" or "sitting and listening" might be a part of your questions? Would your posture be one of "testing" or "scolding?" Whether working outside the home, laboring among house and children, or desperately trying to balance the many demands of each day, open yourself today to the perspective Jesus brings to your situation through the characters in these passages. Trust the biblical wisdom that is to come.

TUESDAY

Martha, you are worried and distracted by many things; there is need of only one thing (Luke 10:41-42).

So, are we to go and do or sit and listen? The *Staying Power* we are exploring as the theme for October is part of the dynamic of this story of Mary and Martha. And discovering the answer to this question, this life stance, offers significant assistance in our ability to cope with what confronts us each week. Going and doing versus sitting and listening sound like two different personality types. But let us move more closely to the details found with these two sisters and their relationship to Jesus.

First of all, there's a detail that often gets overlooked: Martha apparently owned her home. Like Lydia, the business woman who hosted the Corinthian church in her home from Acts 16, Martha appears to be a progressive woman, in a social sense. She is in control of her property. This was rare, particularly given that, in those days, women themselves were often considered property. Martha has somehow defied this societal norm and appears physically in control of her surroundings. We can surmise she is also strong and confident. How else would she have the gumption to confront and even make demands of Jesus: "...do you not care that my sister has left me to do all the work by myself? *Tell her* then to help me!"

Can you think of anywhere else in scripture where a follower of Jesus talks to him like this? She wants things ordered and proper, and Mary is upsetting the balance. Whatever harmony in the room there had been is no more. So, Martha represents a strong, courageous, progressive woman determined to make things work the way she feels proper.

For today, think about boundaries that are being stretched in our own society. Consider areas of life that appear increasingly uncomfortable for anyone who happens to be a traditionalist. As we move more deeply into this story, think about what Jesus says and how he handles these two sisters. They were his friends and followers, and they were non-conformists in their own ways. (We'll discuss Mary's break from tradition tomorrow.) What might you surmise about the nature of Jesus' view of certain social traditions, given his interaction with these two?

Let your mind be opened today to what other areas of social, even religious tradition, might be less essential than we thought.

WEDNESDAY

"Mary has chosen the better part, which will not be taken from her" (Luke 10:42).

Mary, too, is a progressive woman. Like Martha, she is vastly stretching the boundaries of conformity. For that day and time, any person sitting at the feet of a rabbi had only one reason—they were offering themselves as a disciple. It is clear from Luke's description, this is Mary's intention. Jesus' reaction is that Mary *should* be taught, *should* learn, and *should* increase in her disciplined understanding of Jesus' teachings.

Not only does Jesus go along with Mary's desire; he affirms it and uses it as an example for Martha to follow: "Mary has chosen the better part" (10:42).

Does this diminish Martha's position as the host, the "responsible one," the one concerned about hospitality and cleanliness and order? There are some who would rightly say, "If I don't do these basic necessities of keeping our home in order, no one will and all will be chaos!" This, apparently, is not Mary.

Martha is the one who expects things to be done properly and responsibly, and Jesus never condemns Martha for her work. He never calls on her not to be concerned about making others feel welcome or attempting to maintain a disciplined home. He simply counsels her for the state of her emotions: "Martha, Martha, you are worried and distracted by many things..." (10:41).

Worry and distraction were serious issues then, and they are today. Jesus clearly affirms Mary's actions. Discipleship is good. But so is work. And so is caring and expressing hospitality. It is *worry and distraction* that are the problems; it is this Jesus pinpoints as issues of concern.

Today, think about distractions in your life that keep your focus on less important things and issues. What are you overly concerned about? Look for ways you can diminish your worry. See if you can compartmentalize those issues and items distracting you from better discipleship, spiritual depth, and emotional calm.

We have no record of how Martha responded to Jesus' critique of her perspective, and thus the message. *We* have the opportunity to change—to offer ourselves as better prepared, less stressed, and more focused people.

> "When we are unable to find tranquility within ourselves, it is useless to seek it elsewhere."
> — Francois de La Rochefoucauld

THURSDAY

Jesus said to him, "Go and do likewise" (Luke 10:37).

While Martha is concerned about adequate hospitality but detoured by unwarranted or misplaced priorities, the lawyer in the preceding story is interested in what he must do to inherit eternal life but, simultaneously, does not trust. When Jesus turns the man's question back on him, the lawyer correctly responds with two scriptures: "Love the Lord with all your heart, mind, soul, and strength" (Deuteronomy 6:5) and "Love your neighbor as you love yourself" (Leviticus 19:18). And

Jesus replies, "You have given the right answer. Do this and you will live" (Luke 10:28).

Remember, though, that this account begins with the man testing Jesus. Apparently, sensing his lack of success in putting Jesus in an uncomfortable spot to this point, the lawyer continues: "And who is my neighbor" (10:29).

As pointed out previously, the real lesson lies in Jesus' parable of the Good Samaritan. The "Good Samaritan" is the hero of the story, despite his status as an enemy. And the lawyer who confronts Jesus, though reluctant, must admit to understanding this truth because it is undeniable that the Good Samaritan demonstrates tremendous compassion and great courage.

This smart, probably well-connected, religious scholar might have felt knowing *what* to do was enough to fulfill all the right requirements for God. So, for him, to be called to "sit and listen" would have been too easy. But *showing* compassion becomes the necessary remedy for *his soul*. He needed to *get to work* on feeling—and caring—and see with new eyes the world that Jesus was envisioning.

In what ways might you need to re-envision your surroundings and the societal norms you take for granted? Think about the boundaries in these consecutive stories—race, ethnic tensions, gender roles, control—and notice that, in each case, Jesus either pushes those boundaries himself (as in the case of race and ethnic issues) or affirms the changes being pushed (by Mary's discipleship and Martha's ownership and authority). Think on this, and then share with a friend on how these perspectives from Jesus might translate into our day and with issues that continue to breed controversy.

FRIDAY

Draw near to God, and God will draw near to you (James 4:8).

From Mary and Martha and from the lawyer confronting Jesus in the crowd, we have seen Luke's clever use of these two stories to open our perspectives. We have heard from Jesus as he taught the man about the need to make a difference by doing the unexpected, going the second mile, and demonstrating compassion through clear, even risky, action. Now, let us hear from a humble and unassuming man who, in Christian history, offers a good role model for accomplishing this delicate spiritual balance Jesus seems to advocate.

Brother Lawrence wasn't sophisticated enough to be a priest; he wasn't educated enough to be a monk; but he was devoted enough to become a helper in the Discalced Carmelite Monastery in Paris. Previously a soldier, a conversion experience and growing faith motivated him to do what he could to support the work of the church. At the monastery, he worked in the kitchen, washed dishes, and cleaned the monks' sandals. Over time, his humility grew from his service to others. Both the monks and community began to recognize his guiding wisdom and gentle spirituality. He never recorded his advice for publication. It was not until after his death in 1691 that others compiled and finally shared his words. The collection from his letters became known as *The Practice of the Presence of God* and has served as inspiration and guidance for countless Christians over the ensuing centuries. In this book and from his life, we are reminded of what Jesus hoped for in both Mary and Martha as well as the lawyer trying to test him. With gentle spirits, we can work and learn, we can relax within our busyness, we can listen carefully, wash dishes thankfully, or clean sandals thoroughly—and we can give God glory as we do so.

Today, practice God's presence. Be aware in all things—in the office, at home, exercising, watching over small children, disciplining older children, cleaning the house, working in the yard, visiting with a person in need, reading a book, or learning something new. Whether you are "going and doing," or "sitting and listening," there is a place and a time for both.

And in both, in all, God *is*.

> "Is it not quicker and easier to do our common business wholly for the love of God?"
> — Brother Lawrence

SATURDAY

Relax today and practice the presence of God. Smile.

The Fifth Week:
Vesuvius and the End of the World

...and there came hail and fire ... hurled to the earth; and a third of the earth was burned up and a third of the trees were burned up, and all the green grass was burned up ... and something like a great mountain, burning with fire was thrown into the sea ... and a third of the living creatures in the sea died, and a third of the ships were destroyed" (Revelation 8:7-9).

Romans luxuriated in this fertile paradise. The rich volcanic soil surrounding the mysterious Mt. Vesuvius overlooked the beautiful Bay of Naples. The land grew almost anything: lemons, oranges, pomegranates, olives, grapes, a host of vegetables and grains. The attractive climate, lovely scenery, and abundance of natural hot and mineral springs brought visitors from all over the Empire to this spectacular spot. The picturesque towns of Pompeii, Herculaneum, and Stabiae—along with the island of Capri in sight just off the coast, had evolved into a resort playground for the rich and famous. Palatial villas with spectacular views dotted the landscape on the hills and islands around the bay while the Roman Emperors utilized Capri as a summer escape from the crowds and heat of Rome.

All that would change on the morning of August 24, 79 A.D. For several days, there had been strange signs all was not well—odd rumblings in the earth; wells inexplicably dry; aqueducts no longer running; dead fish in the hatcheries of seaside villas; the smell of sulfur wafting through newly opened vents in the earth. And then it happened.

From the Roman naval base of Misenuem, due west of Vesuvius, the famous botanists and author of the world's first encyclopedia, Pliny the Elder, looked out over the Bay of Naples. A thick, rising plume of smoke erupted across the iridescent blue of the Italian sky. Distant rumbling punctuated the calm August air. His unquenchable curiosity piqued, Pliny, as admiral of Rome's fleet based in the Bay of Naples, ordered ships to sail at once in the direction of the billowing cloud. His intention was to study the phenomenon and to evacuate those in need.[6]

But Vesuvius had other ideas. The power of the mountain overwhelmed the study and rescue effort. Pliny the Elder died on the beach of asphyxiation. Many of his sailors were killed by falling debris and choking ash. And any who remained in or around Pompeii were burned alive the next day by what most viewed as a force from hell: a superheated cloud of fire that ripped along at ground level, sucked up all surrounding air to feed its fiery appetite, and incinerated everything in its path.

This eruption shook that part of the world, both literally and figuratively. Even John the Elder, author of Revelation, appears to reference this cataclysmic event in his apocalyptic vision described in the passage above.

As Halloween comes, it is appropriate we consider what our faith might or might not expect regarding the end of the world. Contemplate your own feelings concerning Revelation.

> Lord, give me the wisdom I need to be the kind of person you would have me be. Regardless of time, you are the same always. You touch hearts and inspire lives today just as you did in the days of the early church. Allow me the courage to stand firm in my convictions. May I discover in myself this week a new perspective on your eternal work in and through ordinary people. Amen.

---

[6] We have a detailed account of this horror from Pliny the Elder's nephew, Pliny the Younger. He accompanied his uncle, survived, and recorded the details of the eruption. For his first-hand account, see the May/June 2001 issue of *Archeology Odyssey*, p. 37: "The Day the Earth Shook." Another excellent historical novel on the topic is *Pompeii: A Novel*, by Robert Harris.

REFLECTIONS FOR THE WEEK

MONDAY

...and there came hail and fire... (Revelation 8:7-9).

Vesuvius' eruption was felt hundreds of miles in all directions. Most assumed the end of the world was at hand. Very likely, John alludes to this event in his vision so vividly portrayed in Revelation. Like many, he would have seen the ash, experienced the darkness, felt the climate change—and wondered what it meant.

Worrying about the "end of the world" is still a focus. It has been for some preachers for more than a century. Sadly, this kind of preaching is often manipulative, fear-based, and misleading.[7]

Too much concern in the "end times" impedes our call to God's mission in the present. Remember, Jesus said not to worry about when or how the end would come: "It is not for you to know the time or the season... (Acts 1:7). Recall, too, the Torah forbids foretelling the future: "If any turn to mediums and wizards (to tell the future/communicate with the dead) ... I will cut them off from the people" (Leviticus 20:6).

For good reason, the people on and around Vesuvius were certain the world was coming to an end. But, once the smoke had cleared, they found life returned to normal.

Today, take care not to get distracted by unhelpful and unbiblical "prophecies." Consider your call to compassion and find more constructive, biblical ways to spend your time.

> "Stand at the bottom of the great marketplace of Pompeii and look up at the silent streets ... the broken houses with their inmost sanctuaries open to the day, away to Mount Vesuvius, brighter and snowy in the peaceful distance; and lose all count of time ... in the strange and melancholy sensation of seeing the Destroyed and the Destroyer."
> — Charles Dickens

---

[7] An excellent resource on the phenomenon of Revelation's popularity stemming from the likes of Darby and Schofield is *Revelation for Today*, by James Efird, a professor at Duke Divinity School.

TUESDAY

They cried out in a loud voice, saying, "Salvation belongs to our God..." (Revelation 7:10).

Pompeii, Herculaneum, and Stabiae were buried under thick layers of ash and volcanic mud that hardened with each rainfall and passing season. At first, soldiers, government officials, and local surviving citizens attempted to salvage what they could by digging in the ruined remains, but these efforts lasted only a few months. Interest gradually waned. The Empire moved on to other things. And the resting places of these three cities passed out of memory for roughly 1600 years. Then, by chance, the ruins of Pompeii were rediscovered in the 1700's. Slowly but surely, what can be viewed today has been unearthed by careful removal and preservation of one of the greatest archeological finds in history. What the visitor sees is astounding[8]—perfectly preserved remains of life as it was in 79 A.D.

Pompeii was not an unusual town. There were illicit activities, to be sure; there were also people trying to do the right thing, caring for their families, contributing to the community.[9] For us today, what will visitors to the remains of our homes and cities find of interest? What evidence of our faithfulness will we leave? What legacy will follow us when, centuries from now, archeologists find the remains of our lives. What will they discern were our priorities?

Today, reflect on your legacy to the future. What will *you* leave behind for others to remember and appreciate? What are you contributing to the present?

And remember, "Salvation belongs to our God..."

---

[8] The casted figures of people going about their daily tasks, only to be trapped in ash and stones and then asphyxiated, if not incinerated in the final firestorm, a pyroclastic flow of superheated gas and rock traveling at 450 miles per hour at ground level and reaching temperatures of 1830 degrees Fahrenheit.

[9] There were Jews and, likely, Christians in Pompeii. Paul landed very close to the city on his Fourth Missionary Journey on his way to Rome, some twenty years before the eruption of 79 A.D.

WEDNESDAY

Holy, holy, holy, the Lord God the Almighty, who was and is and is to come (Revelation 4:8).

Things are not always as they seem. Within this lovely, peaceful setting of southern Italy lives a telling parable. In the distance stands the graceful form of Vesuvius, gentle slopes descending into thick foliage and cultivated crops of lush, fertile land. Unseen is the unpredictable power of this great mountain. Climbing it a few years ago, a friend and I were able to peer down into the cinder cone.[10] Steam rises from dark vents inside the crater and the smell of sulfur is ever present. It is easy to understand Roman fascination with Vulcan, god of the underworld.[11]

One of the purposes of Revelation was to dramatically present the ways of God in contrast to the Roman world of skewed power, principles, and priorities. Previously, Christians had appreciated the laws, highways, trade, and successful global economy of the Roman Empire. Under Emperor Domitian, however, corruption and abuse of power became endemic. Christians, in particular, were targeted for their refusal to speak the phrase *dominus et deus* (Lord and God) in reference to Domitian. This served much the same purpose as our present-day "pledge of allegiance," a demonstration of loyalty to the empire, but it became a test to uncover suspected subversives and insubordinates. Remember this today as you give thanks and consider the multitude of good in your life, including a free country where you practice your Christian faith without fear of abuse. Remember those who have gone before.

> "I have cherished the ideal of a democratic and free society in which all persons live together in harmony and with equal opportunities. It is an ideal which I hope to live for and to achieve. But if needs be, it is an ideal for which I am prepared to die." — Nelson Mandela

---

[10] It was early November and snowing as we made our way to the top. The temperature in nearby Naples and Pompeii was in the upper 50's.

[11] Later, there evolved among Christians a feeling that Hell surely must be "down there in a place of fire and sulfur." One visit to a volcano will demonstrate why, and how the thought gives pause.

THURSDAY

You are worthy, our Lord and God, to receive glory and honor and power... (Revelation 1:11a).

A great deal of John's concern in the way he presents the unfolding drama of Revelation is to uncover the lie that the surrounding culture was trying to portray: that the power of Rome was invincible. Loyalty to the culture and the empire was essential, *don't question* the status quo. Everyone was doing it, so be like everybody else. Does this sound familiar?

In response, the primary point of Revelation was to reveal the truth and to expose the lie. It was never a message for later generations to decode. Rather, it used a form of standard and understood writing of the day known as *Apocalyptic Literature*. Through this interesting but often confusing book, then, the basic and ultimate message is that God is in control. The power of Rome or any overly dominant culture can become corrupt, temporal, and misguided. Only God holds true and eternal power. This was a hopeful yet subversive message then, just as it still is. Only God is worthy of glory, honor, and power.

Consider today what John might address about our own culture. What concerns should we have regarding the Christian perspective? Today, make these words an echo in your heart and mind: *Holy, holy, holy, the Lord God the Almighty, who was and is and is to come.*

FRIDAY

...for you created all things, and by your will they existed and were created (Revelation 4:11b).

Daniel, the second half of Zechariah, portions of Ezekiel and Isaiah, and Revelation were all considered part of this literary genre called *Apocalyptic Literature*. The reason authors like John chose such an unusual, bizarre, form of expression was understandable for that day and age. There was crisis. The people were losing their livelihoods and their hope and fidelity to faith and what the church stood for. John was inspired to construct the masterful drama that we know as Revelation[12] because he must have felt the traditional pleas for fidelity were insufficient in the face of the severe struggles the church was going to endure during Domitian's reign.

The pressures and difficulties those early Christians often faced are hard to imagine in our society. But there are people and places still very much in the midst of such difficulties.

For instance, our church has become increasingly aware of the plight of the Chin and Karen people of Burma. The language and angst of Revelation is not so far removed from these people struggling under oppressive rulers and frightening power wielded harshly against even the slightest opposition. And this is just one place. There are many scattered across the globe wishing for safety and security, peace and hope, but living every day with fear and oppression, hunger and thirst.

Make this a point of prayer and concern today. You might want to research some of the troubled areas of the world so that your prayers are more focused. Your church should have helpful information to guide you. As you go through your day, be thankful for the incredible gifts you have. And use them for good and for the benefit of others less fortunate.

SATURDAY

Rejoice today for your life, your family, your friends. Relax and consider this present moment—this day—as a gift.

> "My life is an instant, an hour which passes by. My life is a moment which I have no power to stay. You know, O my God, that to love you here on earth—I have only today." — Therese of Lisieux

---

[12] It is seven acts with seven scenes in each act. Utilizing numbers, colors, and wild occurrences, they are deftly woven together with Old Testament scenes and images. Virtually half of Revelation is lifted either directly or implicitly out of the Old Testament. Many of the images are recast slightly to fit into the scenes and scenarios of Revelation.

NOVEMBER
Gratitude and Giving

Though "Nov" means nine in Latin (and "Dec" means ten), November and December—like September and October—were bumped in the line-up to the eleventh and twelfth months.

November is an interesting bridge between the often-glorious colors of autumn and the duller days of December and winter. And November is the month we in the United States celebrate that most American of holidays, Thanksgiving.

So, it is to that progression of seasons, to the dynamic of humble gratitude, and to the giving of thanks that we will devote much of our focus this month. And, since the emotional partner of gratitude is compassion, we will share time on that as well.

The First Week:
Unheralded Devotion

Present your bodies as a living sacrifice, holy and acceptable to God (Romans 12:1).

As you walk through St. Peter's Basilica and the nearby Sistine Chapel in Rome, one thing certainly stands out—the incredible artwork. Michelangelo's *Pieta* and the amazing dome in St, Peter's, as well as the frescoed ceiling of the Sistine Chapel, present astounding examples of a world-famous Renaissance man at his best. Many rightly wonder how one individual could possess such renowned talent, while most people exist in relative obscurity.

But let us view this from a different angle. The vastness of St. Peter's is humbling. The artwork is magnificent. The scope and shape and detailed perfection are breathtaking. And yet, the very size of St. Peter's lends itself to another truth: working under and alongside the famous masters were literally thousands of valuable workers contributing their own hard work, creativity, ingenuity, sweat equity, and considerable talent in faithful devotion to a cause larger than themselves. Though many never even saw the finished product, St. Peter's today remains a thankful reminder of them.

Each day, workers carried bricks, shaped marble, created vast mosaics from tiny tiles, raised columns to the sky, and, in many cases, risked their lives. We do not know their names, but we do experience the magnificence of their combined efforts and their anonymous contributions to the larger grandeur of St. Peter's. In each detail, in every corner high and low, their devoted labors live on. This is another kind of testimony: a spiritual worship, a quiet, humble witness to the glory of God. These are ongoing offerings with no fanfare, little recognition. But the lasting contributions to the larger beauty of St. Peter's have brought wonder to visitors throughout the centuries.

In the same way, let us faithfully present our lives "as living sacrifices, holy and acceptable to God..." In doing so, may future generations be blessed for the contributions we make, however humble or unrecognized.

This week, we will share ways to give ourselves as "living sacrifices." Through others' examples, may you find inspiration and clarity for yourself in God's world.

> Use my life this week, O God. Allow whatever efforts I offer in these coming days to be lasting contributions to a larger cause. Give me the vision to see beyond my own circumstances and envision, like the creators of St. Peter's, the beauty of what lies ahead in the future of your goodness. Amen.

REFLECTIONS FOR THE WEEK

MONDAY

So, if anyone is in Christ, there is a new creation: everything old has passed away; see, everything has become new! (II Corinthians 5:17).

Painting a room can be transformative. The same old room—one you've lived in for years—can become a different place that feels renovated, ready for a new start. This is how Paul describes the Christian experience—as a new creation. And such transformation need not be a one-time change. If we are serious about living every day as new and being disciples of Jesus in this lifelong journey, we also understand the newness each morning.

Today, ask yourself what you want this new day to look like and do at least one new thing, whether planning a trip, eating something you've never tried, or just tying your shoes differently. Imagine that *you* are a new creation, created to do and be more. This is good news indeed. Now live it with gladness.

> "While I know myself as a creation of God, I am also obligated to realize and remember that everyone else and everything else are also God's creation."
> — Maya Angelou

TUESDAY

All this is from God, who reconciled us to himself through Christ, and has given us the ministry of reconciliation ... and entrusted the ministry of reconciliation to us (II Corinthians 5:18-19).

A few years ago, several of our staff were standing in the Rotunda, the welcome area of our church, when the door opened and a woman came in carrying a huge tray filled with all kinds of Asian food—fancy, beautiful, and very tasty. She was from Viet

Nam, and she put the tray on the counter as she spoke in halting English, "This is for your church from our family. My husband is in a wheelchair, and I could never get him out of our house because of our front steps. Two weeks ago, some men from your church came to our house and built a ramp. Last week, our house caught fire. My husband would have died if you had not built the ramp for us. The people in this church saved his life."

The ministry of reconciliation, of serving as living sacrifices, doesn't have to be a huge endeavor, but it does mean offering ourselves in the service of something bigger than ourselves. *All this is from God*, and we have the awesome opportunity to be a part of it. Today, think of some way God wants to use you to do something special.

> "If you add a little to a little, and then do it again, soon that little will be much."
> — Hesiod

WEDNESDAY

So we are ambassadors for Christ, since God is making his appeal through us... (II Corinthians 5:20).

I love this wording: *You are ambassadors for Christ.* You have the honor to represent the holy, the sacred, the hope and presence of Jesus in the lives of people in need. There was a man in the church where I served in Washington, D.C. who had been a U.S. Ambassador to another country. I always appreciated his positive spirit, big smile, genuine support, and love of God and country. He seemed to me the perfect ambassador, a person who represented our country well and of whom we could be proud.

You and I have this same kind of sacred responsibility as disciples of Jesus. Every day, we represent a cause, a movement, a history. We are a great cloud of witnesses, and the ultimate and beautiful dream of God. We are all ambassadors of Jesus.

Today, remember you represent something far larger than just you and be thoughtful in your interactions with others. Represent well today!

> "Our works of charity are nothing but the overflow of our love of God from within."
> — Mother Teresa

THURSDAY

...we are ambassadors for Christ... (II Corinthians 5:20).

There are folks I know personally who, every week, are ambassadors for Christ. Beginning in November on through March, men and women in our church host a ministry program called "Room in the Inn." Many volunteers welcome friends in our Mission Center who have nowhere else to live.[1] These people in need receive a filling dinner, an excellent breakfast, good fellowship, and a place to call home for the night.

Not long ago, our church office received a call from one of our local hospitals telling us a member of our congregation had just been admitted and was asking for a visit. His name didn't appear on our membership lists or even in our visitor records. Nevertheless, the minister on staff whose day it was to visit went down to see him. The minister recognized the man as part of our "Room in the Inn" ministry, one of the gentlemen who came to our church Saturday nights in the winter because he had no other home. But he considered Providence Baptist his home church, a place where he had connections—because folks had served as *ambassadors for Christ*, representing the gospel through action, presence, and purpose.

Today, consider what helping ministry you can join or, if you are already involved, consider asking someone to join you.

FRIDAY

...God is making his appeal through us... (II Corinthians 5:20).

Every week, on Tuesdays and Thursdays during the school year, we have another group of volunteers who serve as mentors

---

[1] We do this in glad partnership with Urban Ministries and other congregations throughout our area. Like us, each congregation has volunteers who feed and shelter those in need.

and tutors in our Rama Road Elementary School program. They help Hispanic children with schoolwork and, sometimes, even with family and financial issues. There are countless inspiring stories of achievement from these children because someone cared and was willing to spend time acclimating them to language, and place, and a faith that could make all the difference.

And every Wednesday night we have adults and youth who work together to teach "English as a Second Language." It is thrilling to hear stories from our youth about what interesting things they learn, how much fun they have, and how good they feel when working with their new friends in the program.

It is not only feeling good about the work we do and the connections we make; it is remembering that God is working through us, "making his appeal through us," potentially using us to make a difference in someone else's life. This thought is humbling—and exhilarating.

There are so many needs and so many ways to help. Today, plan to ask your pastor or other church leaders about ways you can be involved, or more involved. Remember, too, you can be an ambassador for Christ anywhere. And this is the message, really—this moveable feast of the Gospel, anytime, anywhere, for all. May you fulfill your calling today with joy.

> "The creation of a thousand forests is in one acorn."
> — Ralph Waldo Emerson

SATURDAY

Rest. Consider your personal involvement in compassionate endeavors. And, as you prepare yourself for worship tomorrow, reflect on how God might be calling you to move more deeply into sharing yourself and your resources for the benefit of others.

> "Come! Spirit of Love! Transform us by the action of your purifying life."
> — Evelyn Underhill

THE SECOND WEEK:
A Man's Ambition

Now there was a Pharisee named Nicodemus, a leader of the Jews. He came to Jesus by night and said to him, "Rabbi, we know that you are a teacher who has come from God; for no one can do these signs that you do apart from the presence of God" (John 3:1-2).

Have you ever gotten what you thought you always wanted, only to find there was still something missing? Our considerations for this week revolve around the quest for these issues so prevalent in our society—ambition and meaning. We are taught from an early age to "reach for the stars," to "be the best we can be," and "to go for the gusto." While all these phrases fit well into our cultural surroundings, they can also leave us with unrealistic expectations and, potentially, a higher degree of disappointment.

The Gospel of John is keenly aware of these dynamics in our lives. In a variety of ways, and through a diverse array of characters, John offers both insights to our human condition and subtle solutions for our difficulties. Over the next week, we shall focus on one example in the third chapter, a man by the name of Nicodemus. Like a multitude of other characters throughout scripture, he is not just a man who has an encounter with Jesus or experiences a dilemma that needs resolution.

He represents all of us. In other words, Nicodemus—and Zacchaeus, Peter, Martha, Mary, Sampson, Jacob, Leah, and all the biblical characters—represent *our* idiosyncrasies, failures, foibles, and successes.

Nicodemus appears to have everything. Yet he seeks more.

As we move through the next several days examining how John presents him and what we can learn from his life and spiritual journey, be prepared to take seriously the reflections of your own experience. Move along with the story in this part of the Bible and see if there are any connections you can make through this fascinating, mysterious man and what John shares.

His story will continue once we leave chapter three. Though he appears to fall off the radar screen after verse ten, we hear from him again—twice. And, each time, his journey of faith and commitment moves to a different place. Be aware of the movement. See if there might be echoes of your own journey that relate. Think about what you consider your current ambition. Would you say you have found true meaning in what you stand for and have accomplished so far? Reflect on this as you move through your week and as we move more deeply into John 3.

> Let me learn from Nicodemus this week, O God. Allow his story and the way that John tells it to speak to my heart and to my own story. Clarify for me my motivations and help me to listen to your urgings in my spirit more closely. And, in the same way you inspired Nicodemus, increase my courage, expand my understanding, and broaden my curiosity so that, when this week concludes, I will be a better, braver, and more conscientious follower of you. Amen.

REFLECTIONS FOR THE WEEK

MONDAY

Now there was a Pharisee named Nicodemus, a leader of the Jews (John 3:1).

The Gospel of John utilizes a fascinating array of techniques to help us, the audience, engage with this story. In just one sentence, we learn *three* very important details about this man and his situation: *his affiliation, his name, and his social status.* All combined, we recognize telltale signs of hearty ambition.

For today, let's focus on his affiliation and name.

Nicodemus was a Pharisee, a religious and semi-political party connected to regular people. They were generally good and concerned men committed to facilitating righteousness in everyday life. They were *from* the people and *of* the people; generally, they were viewed favorably. But, as we well know, some of Jesus' most vehement antagonists came from this group. Ironically, this was because they were closest in proximity and in theology. They had much in common, though what they disagreed on tended to be very emotional. Thus, as a Pharisee, Nicodemus could be viewed as closely affiliated yet possibly opposed to Jesus.

Interestingly, John does not share the names of many of his characters; rather he refers to "a Samaritan woman" (4:7), or "one man" (John 5:5), or "a boy" (6:9), or "a woman who had been caught in adultery" (8:3), or "a man blind from birth" (9:1).

But John tells us this man's name: Nicodemus. Likely, in John's agenda, we are given an exact name because Nicodemus comes from a family of means and has a reputation that precedes him.[2] Thus, John would be relaying much to his audience without having to spell out details.

Today, ask yourself what role you play in your circle of influence. What would people know about your name or your

---

[2] There does seem to be evidence of a Nicodemus in the previous generation serving as a delegate to Rome among a group of prominent Jews sent with a request of Caesar.

reputation? Consider where John might be taking us through this encounter with Jesus and why it might be important for you. Finally, think about your own ambition. What are you hoping to accomplish? Why? And for what purpose? These are questions that quietly echo over time—and that we will attempt to explore over the coming days.

> "Trust in the Lord with all your heart, and do not rely on your own understanding..."
> — Proverbs 3:5

TUESDAY

...a leader of the Jews. He came to Jesus by night... (John 3:1-2).

Following our line of thought from yesterday, remember that the information John so concisely offered provides key insights into who Nicodemus has been and where his ambitions have led him so far. Now, let's concentrate on his social status.

John calls Nicodemus a "leader of the Jews," or a member of the Sanhedrin, the ruling council comprised of the most important members of Jewish society in that day.[3] They were responsible for religious, social, and political decisions.

From these first three pieces of information we've learned, we can begin to see how John subtly lets us know that this is a man who is well-off, well-connected, well known, and well-bred. He has most everything a man of that day and time could want. He is and has been ambitious and successful.

Then, John offers a glimpse of this man's reality—his spiritual state. *He came to Jesus by night.* For John, such a description is not merely referring to a time of day. Throughout his Gospel, John consistently uses light and dark to symbolize spiritual realities. Thus, we have a clue to this man's *state of being*.

It is not just that Nicodemus is curious about Jesus and embarrassed to come to him during the day. If this were so, he could have easily sent an emissary to ask Jesus questions and

---

[3] Usually seventy members from the two largest groups of Jewish leaders, the Pharisees and the Saducees.

bring back answers. Rather, John offers us an example of an ambitious man, a successful man, a man at the top of his game and the pinnacle of status—and yet he is in the *dark*. He is missing something. Or, in the words of a woman in one of my classes when I asked about Nicodemus' condition, she shouted out: "He's lost!"

Today, think about the phrase "in the dark." What does that mean to you? What might Nicodemus have been feeling? What was the woman in our class suggesting when she called him lost? Now, ponder the words ambition and meaning.

> "In all your ways acknowledge him, and he will direct your paths."
> — Proverbs 3:6

WEDNESDAY

Now there was a Pharisee named Nicodemus, a leader of the Jews. He came to Jesus by night... (John 3:1-2).

You've probably experienced the feeling of being lost. Before GPS, did you ever find yourself wandering aimlessly on a country road, fairly sure where you wanted to go, or you knew where you needed to be, but weren't sure where you were or how to proceed?

You were lost. So was Nicodemus. He was aware that all was not as it should be. Given his success and accomplishments, he should have lacked nothing: his journey should have been fulfilled, his destination achieved, his goals accomplished, his ambition completed. His life should have had meaning. My friend declared he was lost. John says it only a bit differently—he was in the dark. Something is not right. *He came to Jesus by night.*

Today, think about a time you could relate to Nicodemus' plight. What was *not* right in your life? What could or should you have done to make it right? Did you? How would you react today if the same situation presented itself?

> "Life is just a mirror, and what you see out there, you must first see inside of you."
> — Wally "Famous" Amos

THURSDAY

"Rabbi, we know you are a teacher who has come from God..." (John 3:2).

This second half of verse two offers a clear indication that Nicodemus is not just curious. He is searching. His comment is complimentary, but Jesus discerns a deeper meaning and, through John's telling, moves immediately to what is called, in pastoral care, "the presenting problem." Jesus knows there is something missing in this important man's life when he says: "...no one can see the kingdom of God without being born from above."

Throughout his Gospel, John utilizes not only darkness and light but also above and below, heaven and earth, death and life. Jesus' wording of "born from above" is often translated from Greek to English as "born again." While the wordings are slightly nuanced, the idea is the same: God is not finished with Nicodemus, and Nicodemus, too, knows that his fulfillment—his completion as a spiritual person in search of God's presence, peace, contentment—is yet undone. Regardless of his accomplishments, this important, successful man still *needs* something deeper, more purposeful. He is still looking for *meaning*.

But the ensuing conversation is confusing to this important Pharisee: "Nicodemus said to him, 'How can these things be?'" (John 3:9). John leaves this conversation, and Nicodemus' spiritual quest, dangling for the moment. And, given John's sophistication in the way he weaves his story of Jesus, this is no accident.

What about you? Much in our own spiritual journeys too often dangle unresolved. Is there anything about Nicodemus that feels familiar to your own questions and restlessness? Has your own ambition left you wondering? Spend time today reflecting on what is "missing" in your own life—and what you could do to give your experience more meaning.

> "God, you have made us for yourself. And our hearts are restless until they find rest in you."
> — St. Augustine of Hippo

David Jordan

FRIDAY

Nicodemus, who had gone to Jesus before, and who was one of them, asked, "Our law does not judge people without first giving them a hearing to find out what they are doing, does it?" They replied, "Surely you are not also from Galilee?" (John 7:50-52).

Here is a good example of a spiritual journey that took thought, courage, and time. The encounter Nicodemus had with Jesus in the third chapter had no resolution. John artfully reintroduces him in this seventh chapter. Having been exposed to Jesus, we get the impression his initial encounter impacted him significantly. Though still not clear on his spiritual status (like many of us), Nicodemus speaks out courageously on behalf of fairness. Charges are being manufactured, an arrest is pending, and Nicodemus is rightly concerned. Justice, a key principle of Judaism, is about to be violated. More importantly, the violation involves Jesus.

"Surely you are not also from Galilee?" the religious leaders shout. In other words, "Are you one of his followers, too?" A troublesome charge—and one to which Nicodemus gives no response—is he or isn't he? We are left to wonder—and to admire his mental, emotional, and spiritual process. He is taking this seriously, for there are serious consequences, regardless of his ultimate decision and final loyalty.

It is not until chapter nineteen, through a simple reference following the request by Joseph of Arimathea[4] to Pilate for the body of Jesus, that the final mention of this fascinating and courageous Pharisee is addressed: "Nicodemus, who had at first come to Jesus by night, also came, bringing a mixture of myrrh and aloes, weighing about a hundred pounds..." (John 19:39).

Is he a disciple or not? Did he respond to Jesus spiritually or did he simply respect him socially, ethically, politically, and religiously? We don't know because John doesn't say. But we can infer that he does risk controversy, alienation, and ultimate

---

[4] Joseph is described as "a disciple of Jesus, though a secret one because of his fear..." (19:38). No such description is offered regarding Nicodemus.

danger by carrying the very heavy and very expensive spices and lotion to Jesus' tomb.[5]

This is but one of many subtle ways John lets us in on the ongoing process of change and transformation happening in the lives of a diverse spectrum of people.

What kind of process is going on in your life and spiritual journey? What kinds of questions have been at work in your spirit? Today, consider how, like Nicodemus, you are called to be courageous, to take a risk on behalf of another. Finally, consider the *ambition* that has motivated your life—and the *meaning* that ambition has (or has not) generated. Are there any dangling questions?

> "Honor the Lord with your substance and with the first fruits of your produce."
> — Proverbs 3:9

SATURDAY

Relax and reflect today. Where are you on your spiritual journey? What remains for you to take seriously in your life's journey?

> "Do not forget the value and interest of life is not so much to do conspicuous things ... as to do ordinary things with the perception of their enormous value."
> — Pierre Teilhard de Chardin

---

[5] Every ten years, the Oberammergau Passion Play in southern Germany reenacts the final chapters of the Gospel of John and final earthly days of Jesus. In 2010, I witnessed their portrayal of these passages in John. They took considerable liberties with the text, but their rendition of Nicodemus was superb. In this play, he spoke passionately and defended Jesus vociferously. There was no question in this version that Nicodemus was an ardent follower and disciple. In fact, in this play, he was ultimately banned from the Sanhedrin and kicked out of the influential circles of religious power.

THE THIRD WEEK:
We're All in This Together

Jesus was about thirty years old when he began his work. He was the son of Joseph son of Heli, son of Matthat, son of Levi ... son of Seth, son of Adam, son of God (Luke 4:23-38).

I know this appears to be an odd text to begin our week, but it has considerable significance. Luke and Matthew, though similar in many ways, have different names, orders, and perspectives in the genealogy regarding Jesus' birth. They also have different audiences. Luke's Gospel was intended initially for non-Jews (Gentiles). Matthew's was directed primarily to Jews. As such, Matthew's objective throughout the Gospel is to demonstrate that Jesus is the Messiah of the Jews and, ultimately, God's gift to all the world—but to and through the Jews first. And Matthew traces the lineage beginning with Abraham (including five women)[6] and ending with Jesus. This was to demonstrate that Jesus was the culmination of loyal and important Jewish patriarchs.

Luke, on the other hand, begins with Jesus and traces his lineage all the way back to Adam in order to underline Jesus' connection not only to the Jews but to all the people of the earth, all children of Adam.

Muslims, Christians, Jews—all three religious traditions—trace our roots back to Abraham as our first forefather. We begin as one family, but there is tension. Abraham has two sons and loves them both dearly, though at first it appears that Ishmael, the oldest, is his favorite. Sarah is jealous because Isaac, her son, is younger and appears to be losing ground to the older (there are many levels and interpretations to this). Remember, Sarah at first was barren and gave Abraham her slave, Hagar, to serve as the surrogate mother for the founding of their tribe. Ishmael is her son.

---

[6] Tamar (Mt. 1:3), Rahab (1:5), Ruth (1:5), "the wife of Uriah" or Bathsheba (1:6), and Mary (1:16). Interestingly, each of these have issues—Tamar, Rahab, Bathsheba, and Mary due to actual or possibly inappropriate sexual relations, and Ruth, a foreigner and childless widow, was a hated Moabite.

In general, Muslims trace their lineage back to Abraham through Ishmael. Jews and Christians do it through Isaac. This, too, creates tension regarding interpretation. But it also adds to the richness of the Bible's wisdom since it so realistically reflects the real world and the many ways, often sad, that we tend to deal with our differences. More important is the text of the Bible itself, unashamed to convey reality and honest in its portrayal of the key biblical "heroes" who turn out to have clay feet and significant personal issues. Like them, all of us fall short. None of us have all the answers. And all of us need others to help us be the people God ultimately wants us to be. This week, work again to recognize in your co-worker, neighbor, or passerby on the street, a partner in God's creation and a fellow traveler in the journey of life—and a joint struggler in the efforts of being human.

> Soften my heart this week, O God. Sensitize me to the lives and needs around me, different from me, but still related, connected, and similar. Let me hear with new ears, see with new eyes and respond with a renewed commitment to other partners in your creation. Allow me to strengthen my discipleship by opening myself to others. Amen.

REFLECTIONS FOR THE WEEK

MONDAY

A friend of mine from the Middle East once commented, "The Bible always seems so honest when talking about its heroes. Like David and his affair with Bathsheba and the way he ended his life a broken man, or Abraham? You know, if you really read the Bible carefully and listen to the way he is portrayed, he makes a lot of mistakes and treats Sarah terribly—and he doesn't come across to be all that intelligent, either."

She continued, "As a Muslim, this is quite shocking. In the Koran, everyone is portrayed as strong, wise, pure, and larger-than-life. We don't hear about all these human traits like you do in the Bible."

It's true. The Bible is brutally honest—because life can be brutally hard. Few of us make headway without mistakes and missteps along the way, including these biblical heroes. This is because life is made up of choices, freedom, and a host of varying possibilities—some good, some bad. Without this continuum of potential, there would be no opportunity to choose. This is what makes life interesting, challenging, beautiful—and difficult. And that is why the Bible tends to be so honest.

We are partners in creation—fellow journeyers on this fascinating and unpredictable road of life. Contemplate, today, what difference that makes for you. How might you view others with this knowledge of our all being equally human—all with the potential for wisdom or foolishness?

> "Gratitude flows from the fullness of a heart informed by an open mind and appreciative of the minuscule and majestic miracles of life."
> — Jeanie Miley

TUESDAY

Recently, on a plane from Istanbul to Amman, I talked with a Jordanian man in the seat next to me. Our discussion soon centered around religion. He is Muslim. I am Christian. We asked each other questions, corrected false impressions, offered commentary on the Bible and the Koran, shared insights into our own faith journey. Finally, he shared his belief that only Muslims would make it to paradise, that Christians and Jews were called "people of the book" in the Koran, a respectful designation but not good enough to attain paradise.

I shared that many Christians felt this same way about Muslims. We both chuckled a bit, and then I shared what has been a helpful way of seeing things for me over the years. It comes from Karl Barth, a famous and probably the most influential Christian theologian of the twentieth century.

Barth offers an illustration of a large circle. In the middle of that circle he situates what he would call the focus and goal of every human being. We could call it "the sacred" or the "holy." Around the circle equidistant from the center is lined every human being of every religion and race. Each strives to reach that sacred space in the middle. We all have different ideas of how to do that; we all attempt our own versions of worship and service and learning and growing. But we are all, in the long run, attempting to move toward the same center.

For today, consider the implications of this picture of life and faith. What might you discern from Barth's suggestion? How and what moves you closer to the center?

> "Peace is generosity. It is a right and it is a duty."
> — Oscar Romero

WEDNESDAY

God desires that all people be saved... (I Timothy 2:4)

The great thing about the circular model of faith Barth proposes is that, as each of us moves in the direction of the middle of the circle, we also move closer to one another. Whatever our tradition, if we are doing the best we can with what we know, we are moving in the right direction both socially and spiritually. My Jordanian seatmate was fascinated by this idea. With a look of genuine enthusiasm at this new way of looking at life and faith, he exclaimed, "I love that! I love that!" We were, at that moment, closer to the center and each other.

There remains much we do not and will likely never understand. But we need not worry. "Who is in" and "who is out" is not the call any of us will ever make. God will. And this is good news. What we can do is live our lives with compassion, joy, concern, and as much love for as many as possible.

Today, find just one way you can exhibit this positive living to others who cross your path.

> "Friendship with oneself is all important because, without it, one cannot be friends with anyone else in the world."
> — Eleanor Roosevelt

THURSDAY

*When Jesus saw **their** faith, he said to the paralytic, "Son, your sins are forgiven." (Mark 2:4-5).*

I remember hearing this story as a little boy and being fascinated that these friends got to tear up somebody's roof. I remember thinking, *If I did that, I would get in so much trouble!*

Further, at least according to the way Mark describes the scene, the roof they mess up was *Jesus' house*. Wow. Yet, the real mystery here lies in what Jesus concludes because of the mess they make and the trouble they go to on behalf of their friend who was unable to walk or to do for himself.

The man is healed and his sins forgiven, not because of anything he does or believes or repents of. Instead, it is because of *their faith*, that is, his friends—what *they* believed and what they *did* with what they believed.

Today, recognize the power you have and the influence you might convey in the life of another *because of your faith and how you act on it.* These are possibilities of eternal significance and become the essence of lasting community. Also, when considering what other people might or might not believe, recognize here the other mystery of this passage. Jesus seems completely unconcerned about the man's belief system—only that he had friends who cared and a community to be a part of. Think about that!

FRIDAY

Today, try reading *Love Wins* by Rob Bell. It is short, easy to read, and both controversial and compelling. It is a must when considering what God's love does to and for the world and our role as part of that love. In preparation, consider God's creation of all people in the image of God. Every person is created by God, loved by God, blessed by God: "For God so loved the world..." (John 3:16). Does love really win in the end? Think about this today as you interact with those around you.

SATURDAY

Rest. Relax. Take time to be calm and meditate on what new you have learned about yourself this past week. Breathe deeply. Feel content. Be thankful.

THE FOURTH WEEK:
A Woman's Thanksgiving

...with thanksgiving let your requests be made known to God... (Philippians 4:6).

For this week of Thanksgiving, our focus is gratitude. Whether it be country, family, heritage, health, material abundance, inner peace, or general prosperity, most of us have far more to be thankful for than we usually contemplate. Remind yourself of someone in your life who had very little materially or who suffered with physical ailments and yet was still able to be positive and thankful. I have had several people like this in my life. And I am eternally grateful to them for their influence and living testimony to the value of gratitude, even in the face of difficulty.

I remember John, a camp counselor on crutches and with cerebral palsy, always had a smile and an encouraging word for us campers struggling to find our way. And Mrs. Nash—blind, feeble, and way up in years—was always with Mr. Nash on Sunday mornings preparing her room, playing music, smiling, and welcoming the second graders into her class for the morning Sunday School lesson. And my father, though an introvert and stressed by crowds, worked and served mightily. He was called to make a difference in people's lives, honored to represent the Gospel in everyday life, extraordinarily compassionate and caring, and thankful for the chance to serve God in whatever capacity needed—regardless of the toll it took on his health and energy. These, and many more, were and are thankful people overcoming difficult circumstances—and expressing gratitude through their actions.

For these next few days, we will examine a story in the Gospel of John that illustrates this dynamic of thanksgiving in spite of trouble. The primary character had little to be thankful for and much to be upset about. Yet her encounter with Jesus changed everything. She and her story serve as both a counterpoint and a compliment to the story of Nicodemus. And it is this long-suffering woman, this troubled and ostracized figure, who ultimately and gladly exudes a sense of thanksgiving. She discovers a great gift—and her contagious enthusiasm and overt gratitude evangelizes her entire village. In fact, according to the Gospel of John, she is the first evangelist—not just the first woman preacher but the first preacher of any kind to talk about Jesus and to invite others to experience him.

Before there was gladness and preaching, though, there was sadness, rejection, exclusion, infamy, and loneliness. So, let us move together through John's telling of the bookend to Nicodemus: The Woman at the Well of Samaria.

> Help me this week, Lord, to learn from this Woman at the Well. Remind me of the many people like her who live near me, walk past me and work beside me who are thankful in spite of their circumstances. Teach me a new and deeper gratitude. And with a thankful heart, and like this Samaritan Woman, lead me to share your good news authentically and joyfully. Amen.

REFLECTIONS FOR THE WEEK

MONDAY

It was about noon. A Samaritan woman came to draw water... (John 4:6-7).

This unnamed woman works in an unfamiliar place in the middle of the day. Reading carefully, we notice a clear connection to our story of Nicodemus in the previous chapter of John. Here, however, John presents a character from the opposite end of the social spectrum, and with an opposite outcome.

Nicodemus had valuable affiliation, a name, reputation, social standing, leadership, and wealth; this person of chapter four has none of that. And she is a woman. With no name given, where she lived and what she was apparently coincided with her reputation. She was a Samaritan. Samaria was enemy territory to most Jews, and any Samaritan caused observant Jews visceral anger at their alleged cultural transgressions and *half-breed* natures.[7] There had even been acts of terrorism on both sides followed by the broad residue of suspicion and distrust. Often, a Jew would spit when the word "Samaritan" was spoken, so hated were these people. Thus, we deduce that John, as with Nicodemus, is stating this woman's reputation and social status by inference. We will work with this further tomorrow.

Today, consider the various aspects of your life that are less than what you would like. What is lacking? What might be something that makes you sad or lonely? Then remember ways God touched your life before, ways that allowed new perspective, new growth, new opportunity. And, finally, listen carefully over the next few days about what occurs to and with this unnamed woman from Samaria.

> "Authentic gratitude flows from conscious awareness that the giver of life is extravagant and generous beyond imagination."
> — Jeanie Miley

---

[7] See my book, *Subversive Words: Biblical Counterpoints to Conventional Wisdom*, pages 115-116; 124-125, for details on the deep anger and distrust between these neighboring people.

TUESDAY

It was about noon... (John 4:6-7).

There is a subtle anomaly here: *it was about noon.* Typically, women got the water for their families by gathering either early in the morning or later in the evening when it was cooler. Her noontime appearance hints at alienation—an outcast woman even among her own outcast people. Her alienation seems confirmed moments later when Jesus says, "...you have had five husbands, and the one you have now is not your husband..." (4:17-18). This stands in further contrast to Nicodemus, who was solid, his life in order, his family in place, and his reputation impeccable. Where might John be taking us?

Today, spend some time thinking about who you know that may be an "outcast" in your community. What would it feel like to be one of them? How do you interact with this person? How could you act better or differently?

WEDNESDAY

Take a look at John's careful contrast of these two—both of whom needed Jesus, interacted with him, learned something new, and were left with an offer in need of response:

Nicodemus (Ch. 3)	The Samaritan Woman (Ch. 4)
A Man	A Woman
He came to Jesus.	Jesus came to her.
At night	In the middle of the day
Name	No name
Good reputation	Bad reputation
Important	Unimportant
Well-connected	Rejected
Wealthy	Poor
No resolution w/ Jesus	Immediate resolution w/ Jesus
Responds Eventually	Responds Immediately
Had much	Had nothing
Finally gets what he needed	Immediately gets what she needed

Faced criticism *Faced criticism*
Gives expensive spices *Gives her testimony;*
  evangelizes village

As you can see, it is no coincidence that these two figures have their stories told in consecutive chapters. John wants us to know something. Today, think on what might you discern from this dichotomy. What might this woman's story say to you now as you anticipate a day of giving thanks?

> "We are not human beings having a spiritual experience. We are spiritual beings having a human experience."
> — Pierre Teilhard de Chardin

THURSDAY

Many Samaritans from that city believed in him because of the woman's testimony (John 4:39).

A woman rejected is now accepted and thankful. Not only is she a woman, hard enough in those days; not only is she a Samaritan, difficult even in the best of circumstances; not only is she shunned by her own people, the very ones who should have offered her support; she has been rejected by five consecutive men in five consecutive marriages. I grew up hearing she was a "loose woman" since she'd had so many relationships. But remember, a woman in those days had no power to divorce. She was at the mercy of each of these men, and each one, in turn, rejected her, abandoned her, left her to fend for herself.[8]

You can see the extreme contrast to the well-connected and ambitious Nicodemus. What is the point to all this? Why

---

[8] One reason for multiple marriages was caring for a widow following the death of the husband. With no insurance or social security, family income ceased, and women, especially younger ones, were left with no alternative but to turn to prostitution. The Bible attempted to offer ethical alternatives by requiring the brother or closest relative to marry the widow and care for her and her family. The story of Ruth hinges on this requirement as the "next-of-kin" refuses to care for Ruth and allows Boaz to marry her instead (Ruth 4:1-12).

the trouble? We will attempt to resolve this tomorrow. For now, enjoy your day today. May it be with family and good friends. And may your appreciation for what you have, who you are, and who you are with expand the boundaries of your heart and broaden your compassion even more for those without. Give thanks with gusto. And resolve to put your gratitude to work!

> If possible, attend a community Thanksgiving service. In Mecklenburg County, we are blessed to have a grand tradition of an interfaith service usually attended by two thousand people or more. This yearly gathering (usually on Tuesdays before Thanksgiving and sponsored by Mecklenburg Ministries) is a valuable model for interfaith cooperation and celebration. May your community work for a similar blessed experience.

FRIDAY

Look around you, and see how the fields are ripe for harvesting ... Many Samaritans from that city believed because of the woman's testimony (John 4:35; 39).

Finally, we come to the end. This woman who had nothing now has all she needs. The man who had all he wanted finally discovers what he needs—and, we think, becomes a follower. The two stories, though involving opposite characters and conditions, have the same resolution. Regardless of our status in life, no matter our social standing or emotional condition, we need what Jesus offers. And discovering the spiritual power available in this discipleship turns our lives around. Whether it be from rich and famous to courageous and risk-taking, or from down and out to respected, accepted, and listened to, both stories offer us valuable insights for this Thanksgiving weekend.

> "Give your riches away if you want to live richly."— Joy Jordan-Lake

Today, continue your holiday in thanksgiving and strive for deeper meaning, better friendships, and higher callings.

> "I know God will not give me anything I can't handle. I just wish that He didn't trust me so much."
> — Mother Teresa

SATURDAY

Continue to enjoy your long weekend. Rest today. Reflect. Prepare for a good morning of worship tomorrow.

DECEMBER
Advent

Originally the Roman tenth month (with the Latin preface "d-e-c" for ten), our current twelfth month serves as the ending of the year, the beginning of winter, the month with the longest amount of darkness in a twenty-four hour period, and the time for the Christian season of Advent and celebration of Jesus' birth.

It can be cold and dark; it can also be colorful and festive. It is often poignant, filled with nostalgic memories of Christmases past, made all the more sentimental by familiar music, old-fashioned Christmas carols and classic movies.

This month, we will focus primarily on the four themes of Advent, with a fifth week serving as a bridge into the New Year. This is our traditional order: Hope, Love, Joy, Peace, and Faith.

THE FIRST WEEK:
Hope

I like what Herm Albright once said: "A positive attitude may not solve all your problems, but it will annoy enough people to make it worth the effort." We all understand the humor in this quote; however, as we shall see, hope is far more than a positive attitude. Notice the words of Emily Dickinson:

> Hope is the thing with feathers
> That perches in the soul,
> And sings the tune—without the words,
> And never stops at all,
> And sweetest in the gale is heard;
> And sore must be the storm
> That could abash the little bird
> That kept so many warm.
> I've heard it in the chilliest land,
> And on the strangest sea;
> Yet, never, in extremity,
> It asked a crumb of me.

Dickinson captures the depth and breadth of this fascinating emotion. In her assessment, hope is hard and steady, as she says, "sweetest in the gale..." Storms are not the place for mere optimism or positive attitudes. This is the place for hope.

To live with biblical hope, to stand with the prophets of old speaking truth to power, weeping over lack of justice and corruption in the land, extolling ordinary people to be extraordinary citizens of the kingdom—this is the power and steadfast nature of hope.

The challenges of difficult times call us beyond positive thinking. Biblical hope moves with a depth of emotion that appraises the world with stark realism and, in the face of difficult circumstances, knows that the last word is not yet spoken. In the face of hostile empires, against the prevailing winds, and as counterpoints to conventional wisdom, biblical hope can be as gentle as a lamb on Christmas Eve. It can also be as harsh as a pointed finger at an unjust king. One does not speak out against injustice if there is no hope.

So, it is not a passive stance that simply wishes current circumstances would improve. Biblical hope rises with initiative and offers alternatives to present realities and new perspectives on current problems. It takes an active voice and positive role so that justice need not be ephemeral or peace be unknowable.

The prophets saw in Israel a hope for humanity, God's dream offered in new ways with fresh possibilities of unshackled blessings and widened community. Incarnated in Jesus, that hope of old breathed new life into the disillusioned past of his day just as it now can enliven the embers of a darkened present.

Hope, this grand word we claim in Advent's first week, necessitates a response. Like its other three partners in the Advent progression, hope calls us not only to do what can be but to accomplish what *should* be. It summons love into the equation of sacred interaction; it invokes peace as the partner confronting all that is and all that might be; it stands with justice, entices joy, enhances vision, strengthens commitment, broadens fortitude, deepens courage, and enlivens faith.

The hope of Advent offers change to circumstances otherwise mired in complexity, derailed by ignorance, or stymied by anger. This biblical hope—the hope Jesus brings through word, deed, and transformation—allows the insufficiencies of my life and your life to be joined in a broadened force of glad assurance: we are not alone; we are not without. For there is hope, and it:

> perches in the soul,
> And sings the tune—without the words,
> And never stops at all...

May if be so for you. And may this Advent and Christmas season be one that fills you to overflowing with hope. Make it a point, this week, to see the world through new eyes and an enhanced, hopeful vision for all you encounter.

> Surprise me with hope this week, O God. Help me to see beyond whatever circumstances confront me. Encourage me with a renewed sense of possibility. Regardless of the data and in spite of the obstacles, let my hope continue and grow. Amen.

REFLECTIONS FOR THE WEEK

MONDAY

The Lord is my shepherd, I shall not want; he maketh me lie down in green pastures; he leadeth me beside still waters; he restoreth my soul (Psalm 23:1-2).

Hope exists in the world—in spite of... Hope recognizes all is not as it should be but believes and is willing to work to make what is hoped for a reality. Hope is realistic and knows well how difficult life can be.

In his book *The Message of the Psalms*, theologian and Old Testament Scholar Walter Breuggemann divides this biblical collection of songs, poems, and sayings into three types: Psalms of (1) Orientation, (2) Disorientation, and (3) New Orientation. The famous Twenty-third Psalm above exemplifies a "Psalm of Orientation"—all appears to be well with the world. The verse describes a time of quiet goodness and rejuvenating serenity. But then something happens. In scripture, just like in our lives, ease of living too often gives way to complications and complexity. The Bible offers words from another time and place as the psalmist experiences similar difficulties in *Psalms of Disorientation*.

We will explore these tomorrow. But for today, consider this: the possibility of hope in these times of change or confusion seems increasingly fragile, if not absent. It's likely you have experienced a season of life that felt this way. If so, think about the Bible's honest appraisal of how, too often, life seems to spin out of control. And in your consideration, notice how things are in your life now. Be aware of the dynamics surrounding you in family, job, and friendships. Where is hope? What role does it play for you this week? And what do the Psalms say to you?

In preparation for tomorrow, *read all of Psalm 23.*

> "Our hope as committed Christians lies not in what we have or in who we are, but in whose we are."
> — Elton Trueblood

TUESDAY

My God, my God, why have you forsaken me? (Psalm 22:1).

Psalms of Disorientation: Where is hope now? From the relative ease of "all-is-well" to the increased discomfort of "what-do-we-do-now?" rumble the Psalms of Disorientation. They represent a clear shift in perspective. In these passages, there emerges a mood and condition that tends to be unpleasant to read. But they can be extraordinarily therapeutic when one is caught in the web of unsettled emotions and complicated relationships. Overwhelmed by confusion, sadness, anger, frustration, loneliness, even depression—these can be the bitter fruits of disorientation. God seems silent. There is an absence of presence or, as Martin Marty once called it, a "winter of the heart." Listen to Psalm 22:

> *My God, my God, why have you forsaken me? Why are you so far from helping me, from the words of my groaning? O my God, I cry by day, but you do not answer; and by night, but find no rest* (22:1-2).

We recognize this, too, as the cry Jesus makes from the cross (Mark 15:34; Matthew 27:46). Having learned it as a boy, no doubt, taught it by parents or teachers, reciting it as a loyal and studious Jew, Jesus remembered well the suffering of those who had gone before him. Disorienting tragedies played out in previous human journeys were relayed through the pathos of psalmist poetry. And Jesus calls forth this Psalm of Disorientation in his time of *deepest* disorientation. As he does so, he demonstrates the continuing truth: life, on occasion, presents us with times of potential despair and confusion. Yet, a deeper mystery exists—there still is and always will be hope:

> *Yea, though I walk through the valley of the shadow of death, I fear no evil, for thou art with me, thy rod and thy staff, they comfort me* (Psalm 23:4).

Hope lives. Our personal ability to hope may have temporarily been curtailed. But the truth of God's presence remains. Therefore, hope continues—even in the darkness and despite our inability.

Today, center yourself. That is, take a deep breath and focus your thoughts on what is going on in your life, the good and the bad. Now, find your center, that place of existence that you can rely on, a trusted focal point that offers you a sense of comfort and strength. As a child, this might have been your home or parents or a trusted friend. Today, think about what it is that offers you solace and strength. What is it that gives you hope?

> "The only requirement is that we place our confidence entirely in God."
> — Brother Lawrence

WEDNESDAY

Yea, though I walk through the valley of the shadow of death, I fear no evil, for thou art with me, thy rod and thy staff, they comfort me (Psalm 23:4).

The other side of *disorientation—New Orientation—*offers further insight to hope and a new way of viewing the world. We have new empathy, broader perspective, deeper understanding. We have a new orientation to who we are, how the world works, the presence of God, and what we might need to do next. Hope lives. As with the case of Jacob in Genesis, we may walk with a limp, but we have a new name—Israel: "One who wrestled with God yet survived" (Genesis 32:28). Psalm 139 is a Psalm of New Orientation. Notice here, a new maturity birthed from the experience of life and a new hope rising with the memory of it:

Where can I go from your spirit? Or where can I flee from your presence? If I ascend to heaven, you are there; if I make my bed in Sheol, you are there. If I take to the wings of the morning and settle in the farthest limits of the sea, even there your hand shall lead me, and your right hand shall hold me fast... (Psalm 139:7-10).

Like Jesus' cry from the cross of Psalm 22, the writer of this psalm knows the stark reality of darkness, distance, absence—and light, comfort, and eternal presence. The psalmist *hopes*.

Today, you may find yourself somewhere on this spectrum of faith and emotion. Whether calm, despairing, or newly matured, move forward in expectant and hopeful anticipation. God is with you and guiding you into something new. It will be beneficial. May you have the patience, perspective, and ongoing hope necessary for the journey.

> "A journey is like marriage. The certain way to be wrong is to think you control it."
> — John Steinbeck

THURSDAY

May the God of hope fill you with all joy and peace in believing so that, by the power of the Holy Spirit you may abound in hope (Romans 15:13).

FROM DIANE:

Life is uncertain, fragile, sometimes tragic, but the promises of God hold firm. "I am with you always," says Jesus. And he is. As you read the following from my daughter, David's sister, let God's hope fill you.

> *This hope we claim means there will someday be a family reunion the likes of which we've never seen. There will be music, I'm certain—folk music first, bluegrass and country and blues, and then, who knows, rap, where the lyrics are wildly, outrageously hopeful. The place will be thick in streamers and golden balloons, families and friends parted by that spoiler death will be throwing themselves into full-bodied, flying-leap hugs. Karl Marx famously labeled faith "the opiate of the people," promising an afterlife in which things will be better. Maybe.*
>
> *Or maybe it's more like a spine. Maybe it's hope that draws its strength from having stood toe-to-toe with despair and come out on top. Because Jesus promises not only a tomorrow of celebration, the party to end all*

parties, but also hope in the storm-ravaged now. Hope
that will not forsake us...

> Not in the Valley of the Shadow of Death
> Not in a life shipwrecked by drugs and abuse.
> Not in the face of a criminal record and a past mangled by pain.
> Hope ... lived out, passed hand to hand and voice to voice.
> Hope, the only answer to death.
> Hope, the only lifeline to tomorrow.
> Hope, the impertinent. The beautiful-bold.
> Hope, the fist in the face of despair.
>   — Joy Jordan-Lake

Make today a day that your hope is strong, tough, thorough, unbending, far-seeing, and joyful! And pass it on to others!

FRIDAY

After Jesus was born in Bethlehem in Judea ... Magi from the east came to Jerusalem and asked, "'Where is the one who has been born king of the Jews? We saw his star in the east and have come to worship him" (Matthew 2:1-2).

Matthew probably intended us to understand them to be from Persia or, in those days, *Parthia*.[1] They were called *magi*. We call them "Wise Men." They were likely spiritual advisors—in some traditions, even "kingmaker" advisors and overseers in the Parthian royal court. We don't know how many there were, what they looked like, or exactly where they originated. We do know: (1) they were not Jewish, (2) they were not Greek, (3) they were not Roman. In other words, they were the consummate outsiders.

The hopeful word of the magi quietly woven into Matthew's birth story tells its own story. God is doing something beyond our own agendas and circumstances. Far outside of our little communities, God is at work in other lives, other cultures, other agendas, bringing about healing, hope, and redemption. Through unknown actors from a distant place, God offers new

---

[1] Modern-day Iran. Parthia was the only empire close to the Roman Empire the Romans had been unable to conquer. By telling the story in this way, Matthew was likely sending a not-so-subtle message to Rome: "Your enemies know the true king—so should you!"

ways of seeing, thinking, and being. If God can inspire Persian astrologers and astronomers to see beyond their own surroundings and into God's providence for being birthed in Bethlehem, surely the obstacles within the circumstances of our lives are less large than we imagine them to be.

This is not to say that our issues, problems, and difficulties don't matter. But, in the broader scheme of things—and considering the depth and breadth and scope of history—seeing with insight a new star on the dark horizon, living with perspective in the difficult present, recognizing touches of the eternal in the ordinary moments, glimpsing God's light within and beyond our current circumstance—all this and more offers a new way of viewing the world and our situation in it. Just as Jesus entered a world of difficulty and complex troubles, so also into our world, God offers the same source of redemption, transformation, and hope. Claim that hope today—breathe hope into others and live it for yourself.

> "Hope is the only thing stronger than fear."
> — Suzanne Collins, *The Hunger Games*

SATURDAY

For God so loved the world... (John 3:16).

During this time of year, it is inevitable that shopping will be part of your weekly routine. For some this is fun. For many, it becomes stressful and distracts from what should be gentle reflections on the meaning of Christmas. So, if you shop, especially today, do your best to keep things in perspective. Remember the hopeful nature of the season, take particular notice of the colors and decorations adorning shops and homes—and recognize in all the ongoing message of light in the darkness, color in the blandness, and God's gift of hope to a world still struggling. Live into hope today, even as you shop!

> "The word 'hope' in the Bible is a virile, strong, dynamic, soldierly word."
> — Leslie Weatherhead

The Second Week:
Love

For God so loved the world... (John 3:16).

Both Frank Sinatra and the Four Aces sang and made famous the song "Love Is a Many Splendored Thing."[2] In the first verse, we hear:

> Love is nature's way of giving
> A reason to be living...

And, while Sinatra croons of love between a man and woman, the meaning of these words from a secular song speak deeply about this emotion we celebrate this time of year. There is, indeed, something about love that gives us *a reason to be living*. The love of friendship, romance, or the deep and abiding commitment to and with others that motivates sacrificial stances, is the love we hear about in the Bible. It is all those things and much more.

In biblical love, the love of God in Jesus, the love we celebrate this week of Advent, we see this mysterious, majestic, indescribable movement of the heart and spirit that is response, not initiative. The love we feel and we share comes not from within but from without. We do not initiate it; we respond to it. We participate in it and are called to it from a source beyond ourselves and outside of our own self-seeking and personal desires.

It is God's love that makes possible our ability to love and to be loved. As recipients of God's loving initiative, we love because God first loved us. From the blessing of creation, to the calling and blessing of Abraham and Sarah, to the protection and guidance of the Hebrews in times of trouble, to the prophetic calls for compassion, justice, kindness, humility—each of these is motivated by and culminates in love: the love of God, neighbor, alien, self. And all of these are finally lived out best and most fully in Jesus.

Throughout the troubled and tumultuous history of those who have gone before us, the love of God remains that "many

---

[2] There was also a movie by the same name inspired by Han Suyin's novel. The lyrics to the song were written by Paul Francis Webster. The music was composed by Sammy Fain.

splendored thing," that golden thread of grace and truth that binds us together, joins us with our past, roots us in our present, and calls us to our future—God's people, blessed to be a blessing—and loved so we might love others, even as God has loved us.

Though Sinatra expressed the love of romance, these words could just as well describe what God is doing in us:

> Your fingers touched
> My silent heart, and taught it how to sing;
> Yes, true love's a many splendored thing.

For this Advent season, may your heart, too, be touched, taught how to sing, and filled with true love—the one true love that God gives to us. Remember, today, those you love and do some small act to show them your love. This ultimate love of God in Jesus is indeed a many splendored thing. May it come alive—in you!

This week, O God, inspire my responses to your love so abundant in my life. Grant me the wisdom and focus to pass along this priceless gift to others. May my blessings be a blessing—all in the name of Jesus. Amen.

REFLECTIONS FOR THE WEEK

MONDAY

For God so loved the world, that he gave... (John 3:16).

The Christmas season can be such a festive time of year. There have been seasons when our family gets overwhelmed with events to attend, parties to go to, and festivities to participate in. And, whether busy or not, the backdrop for this second week of the Advent season remains this mysterious and powerful emotion, this many splendored thing, this gift from God—given to us, flowing through us, renewing us, and ripe for giving to others. In his musical *The Children of Eden*, Stephen Schwartz captures well this remarkable gift to be both received and given. Specifically about the love of a parent to a child, notice the flowing, growing, and vulnerable nature of this gift:

The Hardest Part of Love
As a child, I found a sparrow that had fallen from its nest,
And I nursed it back to health till it was stronger than the rest.
But when I tried to hold it then, it pecked and scratched my chest
Till I let it go.
And I watched it fly away from me with its bright and selfish song.
And a part of me was cursing that I had helped it grow so strong.
And I feared it might go hungry and I feared it might go wrong, Oh...
But you cannot close the acorn once the oak begins to grow.
And you cannot close your heart to what it fears and needs to know.
That the hardest part of love,
And the rarest part of love,
And the truest part of love...
Is the letting go...

Today, may you risk the gift of love—be vulnerable; let go; give—just as God does every day to and for us.

TUESDAY

Pursue righteousness, godliness, faith, love, endurance, gentleness ... take hold of the life that really is life
(I Timothy 6:12-19).

Pursue ... love ... gentleness ... Loving with gentleness can be a struggle in the world of today. "Natural Selection," a term associated with evolution, is a reality in our economic world.[3] Whether we like it or not, our free market economy inevitably creates winners and losers. Competition, the very premise of capitalism, recognizes that some will compete more readily, heartily, and vociferously than others; losers will be "naturally selected" and will be forced to drop out of competition. Small businesses and entrepreneurs contend with this daily.

Most understand this process of competition to be the very engine that fires new innovation and continues the need for a competitive edge in a global economy. And many agree (to varying degrees) that, since Adam Smith's *The Wealth of Nations*[4], the western world—and, increasingly, international markets—benefit from this same process of eliminating the weak at the behest of the strong.[5]

But, for the Christian, this economic reality creates issues. As disciples of Jesus, we are called to pause from our frantic pace of buying and our desperate need to compete—and remember. We are called to love, to be compassionate, to look out for one another, to lift up the downtrodden and bring in the outcast, to bind up the wounds of the afflicted, welcome the stranger, and maintain proper perspective on "life that is truly life" (I Timothy 6:19).

So, while our culture continues in competition unabated, engulfed by the necessary efforts of fending off the latest efforts from competitors or catching up with competition so as not to get passed over, Christians must attempt to reflect the light of Jesus. We are to be disenthralled from culture, uncoerced by marketing, at peace with who we are, content with what we have, thankful for God's blessings, open to God's love, and ready to be channels of that love to others. This is particularly true, and,

---

[3] Natural Selection is considered one of the basic mechanisms of evolution, along with mutation, migration, and genetic drift.

[4] Full title: *An Inquiry into the Nature and Causes of the Wealth of Nations*, by Adam Smith, 1776.

[5] Some call this "Social Darwinism" because it usually results in the "survival of the fittest." Exceptions might be in the auto or banking industry with the infamous term: "too big to fail."

sometimes, most difficult during the Christmas season. But do your best, today, to try to love as God hopes and expects.

WEDNESDAY

For God so loved the world that he gave his only son... (John 3:16).

Following yesterday's words on the difficulties of living in our world, I present my own poem on "natural selection":

NATURAL SELECTION AND JESUS

Natural Selection onward moves
Which forcibly, the weak, removes
And plies the stronger on, which proves
Our need for Jesus now.

The competition Darwin learned
Is evolution's main concern
But Jesus speaks to those who yearn
To learn more graceful ways.

Deeply aware of human needs,
He heals and teaches, sowing seeds
For Jesus' hopeful vision breeds
Compassion for God's world.

So let his vision speak anew
From competition moving through
A new, evolved, enlightened view:
Compassion's new success.

All tempered with God's love designed
To change a world before resigned
To selfishness but now assigned
Evolvement through our Lord.

So may it be with glad intent
To know again that Jesus sent
A new selection to present:
For God so loves the world.

Today, make your concern about others—because *God so loved the world...* Love, this sacred connection with and to something beyond ourselves, is expressed and expanded in accordance with our acceptance of God's love. See how much you can change the world that confronts you through the love that is in you.

> "All you need is love; love is all you need..." — The Beatles

THURSDAY

"This is my commandment, that you love one another as I have loved you" (John 15:12).

Venice is a city of bridges. With more than four hundred of every type and size, and used for every reason, one could do a study on each of their histories and never finish. When walking through this incredible city (as you *must* since there are no motor vehicles of any kind allowed), one cannot go very far before encountering a canal to cross. Venetians consider this an almost mystical reality—moving from one island to another, one part of the city to another across these canals. In some ways, it's like our passages through life, our movement from one stage to the next and one place to another. In every way, these bridges stand for a certain dividing line, represent a particular history, offer a unique perspective, connect a distinct neighborhood to another— and present new and good opportunities for unifying the disparate parts of what had been a vast swamp of muddy islands.[6] This is true for every bridge in Venice except one: *Ponte dei Sospiri* (which I'll save for tomorrow).

For today, recognize your connection to others and to God through those sacred bridges that bring together disparate parts of life into a glad and unifying whole. There remains a love among us that cannot be fully explained but is always available to be thoroughly enjoyed. This is especially true when we remember what God has done in Jesus, our eternal bridge between the now, then, and the unknown. So, live today with confidence and love.

> "Knowledge shall be done away with insofar as it is different from love; knowledge shall become eternal insofar as it is one with love."
> — Paul Tillich

FRIDAY

"By this everyone will know that you are my disciples, if you have love for one another" (John 13:35).

Also known as the "Bridge of Sighs," *Ponte dei Sospiri* is a short, enclosed bridge that connects the Doge's Palace with the *Prigioni*,

---
[6] See my February devotion on the making of Venice.

the prisons of the old Venetian Republic. Once convicted of crimes, the prisoners were led from their trial in the palace across this poignant bridge. With two small windows on either side of the enclosed walkway, the prisoner walked across the channel that separated the prisons and the palace. There, the prisoner had one final view of the outside world through these tiny portals. It was a suspended place of sadness and ultimate paradox—hanging between freedom and captivity, wealth and poverty, grandeur and filth—on one side, ultimate power, on the other, utter hopelessness.

Remembering God's love for us at Christmas represents a similar paradox, but in reverse. We are freed captives, like the Children of Israel crossing the Red Sea in the direction of the Promised Land. God leads us across a spiritual *bridge of sighs*—sighs of release and relief, sighs of gladness and thanksgiving, sighs of hope and love and new possibilities. From this bridge, we view the land we enter as children of hope and captivated by the wondrous love of God. Today, all you need to do is live the gift that has been given you.

SATURDAY

On this short day of frost and sun, to sleep before evening. We have an interval, and then our place knows us no more (Walter Pater).

As the days become shorter and nights longer, pay particular attention to the festive nature of lights—on houses, buildings, and shops. The above quote from Walter Pater echoing Psalm 103 reminds us of the shortness of daytime, and of life—and how quickly our legacies fall away. And yet, somehow the possibilities that come with love—and the connection to the broader love of God—allows us to remember the light of God continues, for the lights that illumine the darkness remind us: "the steadfast love of the Lord is from everlasting to everlasting" (Psalm 103:17). Relax today as you ruminate on this truth.

THE THIRD WEEK:
Joy

Rejoice in the Lord always, and again I say: rejoice! (Philippians 4:4).

Years ago, we attended a reunion of my wife's family that included aunts and uncles and cousins—dear people, many of whom I had never met. Fortunately, the gathering was at a home large enough to accommodate many. Metal chairs and tables borrowed from the church were set up in every conceivable place. People and food were everywhere.

What I remember most was the chaos, and I felt my children were creating most of it. All the excitement had revved my kids up so that it seemed, every time my wife or I turned around, something was spilling, the dog was being abused, food was being thrown, or a diaper had come loose. The kids were overly tired and excruciatingly hyper—like I said, chaos.

But, a few weeks later, we got a sweet Christmas card from Auntie, one of the matriarchs in Beth's family. She had written, "What a *joy* it was to be with you and your lovely family."

Was she joking? My first thought was: *Auntie needs to get out more.*

Then it struck me: part of experiencing the joy of God is noticing the small miracles and the hidden blessings of everyday life. For Auntie, she was calmly *aware*. Gracefully accepting of the children's excess energy, she gladly embraced the presence of family, kept in perspective the cramped nature of the surroundings, and felt—within and through the chaos—the brush of angel's wings and the presence of God. She experienced joy because she could put aside the distractions; she could treasure the positive moments as beauty, truth, and sacredness. She was aware. Such is the essence of Joy.[7]

---

[7] The more somber, reflective color of purple for the other three candles in the Advent Wreath usually gives way to a lighter shade, this less regal and more exuberant color of pink. This probably comes from the earlier tradition of popes handing a pink rose to someone in the crowd at St. Peter's in Rome. The color and the tradition evolved into Protestant circles adapting and modifying the tradition.

For the next few days, we shall explore this vital Christian quality, and this essential component of the Christmas season: awareness for the reality of Joy.

> Let us be open to joy this week, O God. Calm us in our actions and reactions; renew our spirits; invigorate our hope. Give us laughter that is free, easy, and filled with a sense of Christmas spirit in the truest sense. Let us be joyful, then, not in superficiality or silliness, but with solid, realistic, and glad understandings of the world and those in it—and what your being part of our lives means to us all. Amen.

REFLECTIONS FOR THE WEEK

MONDAY

May the God of hope fill you with all joy (Romans 15:13).

He had known poverty so understood the degrading, hopeless conditions many in Victorian England endured. He set about to do something, to make a difference, to draw attention to the deplorable conditions of the working poor.

In 1843, Charles Dickens considered writing a tract, a pamphlet that would educate the public and, he hoped, draw sympathy to their plight. But he became increasingly convinced that a fictional novella could be more powerful and reach more people. In six weeks, Dickens wrote *A Christmas Carol*. Some say his words did more to change the hearts and minds of nineteenth century England than any other influence. If nothing else, his vivid description of Christmas feasts, gift giving, and generosity unintentionally united with Queen Victoria's and Prince Albert's revival of English Christmas traditions. Decorations and feasting had been scorned by the Puritanical religious authorities prior to this time. Suddenly, almost overnight, the warmth, color, and joy of Christmas festivities returned enthusiastically.

Today, remember to enjoy the outward displays of Christmas cheer. Listen to the music, take a ride to look at the lights—celebrate Jesus' coming.

> "Joy in looking and comprehending is nature's most beautiful gift."
> — Albert Einstein

TUESDAY

There is rejoicing in the presence of the angels of God over one sinner who repents (Luke 15:10).

The embodiment of the selfish, industrial, capitalistic, and uncaring London elite of the time, Ebenezer Scrooge also represents winter—a cold, lifeless existence with no warmth and little light. But he changes. And his transformation comes like spring. A lifeless landscape gradually begins to color, and, slowly, the world returns to life. The life that Scrooge had forgotten, the love he once felt, and the warmth he once experienced all come flooding back in a dramatic change of heart and spirit that stands as one of the most endearing of all English literature. In a way, Scrooge is the Zacchaeus of London: a rich and contemptible abuser obsessed with money and power, oblivious to those in need, scornful, friendless, and, seemingly, soulless. This sordid character shows no sign of compassion—until vivid dreams and the stark confrontation of past, present, and future awaken him to both the joy of what could be and the horror of what will be if he continues as he is. Like Zacchaeus "called down" by Jesus, Scrooge is chastised then awakened to a better awareness.

Today, contemplate your own awareness. Are there things of the past that need to be repaired and forgiven? Things of the present that need to be enjoyed and embraced? Or things of the future that ought to be anticipated and changed? The joy of God that accompanies transformation surrounds us and fills us, even now, as the accompaniment of God's presence in us and among us. This is our Christmas message, "Emanuel!" (Hebrew for "God with us"). Your day will be different today as your awareness grows and as you allow God's presence to fill you and give you joy.

WEDNESDAY

Rejoice with me... (Luke 15:6).

Interestingly, Dickens' novella about Ebenezer Scrooge and the potential joy of Christmas is a strictly secular story. There is nothing said of Jesus' birth or the Christmas story. Yet, it is a story very much concerned about the plight of others. Dickens presents the selfishness and inward-looking Scrooge as a means for us to see into our own self-absorbed ways and the ease with which we all can become too engrossed in self-centeredness and overlook the world around us.

The real story, then, is not so much about Scrooge as about us. Like Luke's telling of Zacchaeus in Luke 19, there are aspects of these men in me and in you. Both authors expect us to feel a tang of guilt, a spark of compassion, a move to repentance, and a response to change. The surprise comes with the *joy* that ensues in a change of heart.

Today, prepare for Christmas by absolving yourself of any guilt or doubt. Forgive others in the same way, and respond to God's call to repent and be joyful.

> "Today, salvation has come to this house, for this man, too, is a son of Abraham."
> — Luke 19:9

THURSDAY

There is rejoicing in the presence of the angels of God over one sinner who repents (Luke 15:10).

The story of *A Christmas Carol* is also about being poor, living in conditions harsh and unfathomable yet too real and constant for many then and now. Dickens hoped to awaken a slumbering public to the everyday tragedies being played out before their unseeing eyes in lives of good but poor people like Bob Cratchit and Tiny Tim. This was his ultimate goal: to facilitate *awareness*, compassion, change—and, like with Scrooge's newly awakened heart, to finally access a sense of *joy*.

Long before Dickens, the Bible addressed such apathy and complacency—and the possibility for change, renewal, and transformation. Today, be sensitive to the needs around you— and to God's presence in the midst of those needs. For, surely, when awareness, compassion, and God's presence unite, the result is nothing less than joy.

> "Joy to the world, the Lord is come. Let earth receive her king."
> — Isaac Watts

FRIDAY

Be not afraid; for behold, I bring you good news of a great joy for all people (Luke 2:10).

The Gospel of Luke is my favorite of the four. There are many reasons for this, but perhaps the clearest is the way the Gospel story begins in Luke; the good news is presented to simple people, to the shepherds. These tend to be outcast people—smelly, uneducated, shunned, the bottom of the social ladder—yet it is to these shepherds the angel first proclaims Jesus' coming. They are not well-educated, influential, articulate spiritual leaders whose power would quickly elicit an audience. Shepherds. Nobodies. Why?

What kind of whacky marketing strategy is this that begins with beggars and outcasts and expects others to fall in line? Most of us would have chosen a different route to world evangelism. But this is the Gospel in Luke—this is about Jesus, who will offer good news to the poor, bind the wounds of those who need it most, find the lost, redeem the captive, embrace the marginalized. The angels sing and celebrate with joy when but one sinner responds to God's love.

The Gospel of Luke is about joy. It begins with singing—with Elizabeth as her barrenness gives way to fruitfulness, Mary in recognition of God's purposes fulfilled in her small life, Zachariah in awe of God's providence, angels proclaiming God's glory to the shepherds. Through the almost constant music in the first two chapters, there rises the joy of God that something new and good has come—the *advent* of Jesus birth, the *adven-ture* of the Christian life, and the grand opportunity for inexpressible joy in communion with God in this life and for always.

Today, strive to look past the bustle and "busy-ness" of this season to the deeper meaning of life and God's joyous gifts. Listen to your favorite Christmas hymn or, better yet, sing it!

"Joyful, joyful we adore thee, God of glory, Lord of Love."
— Henry van Dyke

SATURDAY

Rejoice in the Lord always, and again I say: rejoice! (Philippians 4:4).

If you must shop today, do so sparingly. Consider ways of sharing gifts this Christmas that might be less complicated but no less thoughtful. Be creative and loving. Allow the joy of God's love to warm your heart as you think of and give thanks for those in your life—and in the ways that God has woven your experiences into the lovely fabric of goodness and grace that is you.

> "I have told you this so that my joy may be in you and that your joy may be complete."
> — John 15:11

THE FOURTH WEEK:
Peace

May the peace of God, which passes all understanding, keep your hearts and minds in Christ Jesus (Philippians 4:7).

We remember Pearl Harbor Day on December 7. I recall some years ago wanting to make a point in a class I was teaching during Advent on this day. There were a number of older adults present who had been young women and men during World War II. My hope was to make the point that all the cooperation and teamwork following the bombing of Pearl Harbor, and throughout the war, had pulled people together to work unselfishly for a common cause. So, with a few leading questions, I expected to elicit the kinds of positive answers necessary to make my point.

"How did you feel, those of you left at home and working together?"

And their answers? "Afraid." "Lonely." "Depressed." "Angry."

These were not the emotions I expected. But I should have. I have studied a lot of WWII history. Years ago, when living in Europe, I even had spoken with numerous Europeans about their involvement on both sides of the war. What I had not studied, nor had I anticipated, were the feelings of those in the room that day on this side of the Atlantic. I was completely ignorant of what it had been like to live under fear, loneliness, and the threat of loss, even though the physical war was an entire ocean away. There was a *lack of conflict* on these shores in a literal sense. But there was *no peace*.

The Hebrew word for peace is *shalom*. It can be used as a greeting, farewell, blessing, or description. It holds within it a deep and substantive concern for a kind of vertical peace with God, a horizontal peace with those around us, and an inner peace with ourselves. When Jesus was asked the greatest commandment, he spoke in these terms: *to love God with all we are and have, and to love our neighbor as we love ourselves* (Matthew

22:37-38). Such perspective yields an inner peace, we can say, because two of the three imperatives focus outside of us.

It is difficult to love ourselves if we are not loving God and are unable to love those around us. And we can never be at peace if the feelings we have are solely self-centered and anxious. We can love ourselves most fully, we can be most deeply at peace, then, as we think and act beyond ourselves.

Peace can be an existence without conflict. But far more than *absence of conflict*, it is *presence with God*. It is having a life filled with relationships that are meaningful. It is a life that nourishes those relationships through spiritual depth and relishes a broader understanding of those around us through genuine compassion. This kind of godly peace doesn't just happen. It takes work. We will explore this more in the next couple of days.

> Give us peace this week, O God. Help us to discover the calming reassurance of your presence. Remind us that we have enough, in spite of the advertisements so inundating our lives. Remind us that we are enough, in spite of our insecurities; that your careful crafting of our substance and being offers all that we need; that your abiding spirit is sufficient for all that comes; that your broader wisdom encompasses whatever we face. Give us peace this week, O God. Amen.

REFLECTIONS FOR THE WEEK

MONDAY

Be doers of the word and not merely hearers who deceive themselves (James 1:22).

My high school basketball team in Tennessee played teams from all over the southeastern corner of that lovely state. On this particular afternoon, we were playing a school from the picturesque Sequatchie Valley called Whitwell (they pronounce it "Wutwel"). About halfway through the second quarter, one of their players, well-built and a good ball player, was limping noticeably down the court. The coach, already quite animated in his interactions with the players, held his arms up in a giant "V", and yelled loudly in the quiet gym: "What's the matter, Elroy?"

His voice echoed off the gym walls.

Elroy stopped, turned, and responded in a thick, deep, and authentically unrehearsed country accent while pointing dramatically and very seriously to his shoe: "It's my foot, Coach."

His coach got a disgusted look on his face, paused for a second or two, held up his arms in a giant "V" again, and—with a look of dismayed frustration—yelled back: "Well, do something about it, Elroy!"

We are called to do something—to bring about peace in our own lives and in those around us. Today, recognize the reality of God's peace and the need for it in your life each and every day.

> "All we are saying is: Give peace a chance." — John Lennon

TUESDAY

And the peace of God, which surpasses all understanding, will guard your hearts and your minds in Christ Jesus (Philippians 4:7).

Nicodemus could have philosophized with his friends, had stimulating conversations, continued to rise in the ranks of the elite of Jerusalem and maintain his lifestyle. Instead, he *did* something: he came to Jesus. The Woman at the Well did something: she told her town about Jesus. Lydia did something by offering her home as the first church in Europe. Zacchaeus did something when he gave back. Paul, Peter, Mary, Leah all responded to what God was doing in their lives by *doing*, by seeking to bring peace into the hearts and lives of others because peace had entered their own lives.

What about you, today? Do you have questions? Do you wonder why things aren't the way they should be? Are you frustrated by disillusionment? There is much God hopes for you. So, "Do something about it, Elroy!" Work for peace. Make a commitment to move in the direction of Jesus—*to be doers of the word and not merely hearers who deceive themselves.*

Peace doesn't just happen. It takes all of us "doing something about it!" Today, open yourself to God's peace and relax. Then touch a life, offer assistance, demonstrate kindness, be humble, show compassion. Make peace.

> "If we have no peace, it is because we have forgotten that we belong to each other."
> — Mother Teresa

WEDNESDAY

Peace I leave with you; my peace I give to you (John 14:27).

FROM DIANE:

In one of our family photo albums, there is a snapshot that is the very epitome of a peaceful scene. I am pictured with my two children sitting in a canoe on a still lake. The sun is sinking in the west, and the sky is ablaze with color. The children, then about eight and twelve, are paddling the canoe while I sit serenely in the middle. The photo shows us smiling, delighting in the sunset and quiet evening. Looking at that picture, one would say, "Oh, that's what peace looks like." What was really happening in that canoe was a family squabble.

Joy was saying to her older brother, "David, you're splashing me with your paddle!" And David was replying with, "No I'm not.

You're not paddling hard enough." Then louder, "Well, you're not steering right or I wouldn't have to paddle so hard. Quit splashing!" Then, even louder and stressed, "Children! Stop it! Both of you stop fussing! Just paddle and look at the sunset!"

Now, as I look at that photo, I laugh, realizing how little actual peace there was on that lovely lake as my husband recorded the moment. Real peace, the kind Jesus promised, is a matter of the heart and can be found even in the worst of times. No matter how lovely and "peaceful" (or not) the setting, if our hearts are not in tune with him, peace is elusive; but when we turn to him and ask for his peace, he gives it to us despite our outward circumstances. Jesus said, "These things I have spoken unto you that in me you might have peace. In the world you shall have tribulation, but be of good cheer; I have overcome the world" (John 16:33). I have found this promise to be true in my own life. Today, may God's real peace be yours as well.

> "When ignorance is our master, there is no possibility of real peace."
> — Dalai Lama

THURSDAY

I am the voice of one crying out in the wilderness, "Make straight the way of the Lord," as the prophet Isaiah said (John 1:23).

It is usually at the beginning of Advent that we hear John the Baptist preaching in the wilderness. He quotes Isaiah and utilizes the same imagery famous in the world of that ancient prophet. The imperial kings, Persia's, for example, would occasionally venture out to visit the provinces of the empire. In those days, the way needed to be prepared. The crooked needed to be made straight, the valleys lifted up, and the mountains brought low. In other words, a highway was made level and straight in the wilderness for the king to pass. John's usage of this image conveys the same idea for the role of God's messengers. So, this is not about John the Baptist but the one he is announcing and preparing the way for. John introduces the possibility of a peace that passes all understanding because he is introducing Jesus. And so it is for us. Our lives can be a grand preparation for a presence beyond ourselves—an offering of peace to those around us.

Today, prepare the way for Jesus in the lives and hearts of others—and yourself. Take a walk in the evening. Be aware of lights and colors. Breathe deeply in the evening air. Consider your blessings; think of good things. Look into the winter sky and stand in wonder.

> "Let there be peace on earth, and let it begin with me..."
> — Jill Jackson and Sy Miller

FRIDAY

And his name shall be called Wonderful Counselor, the mighty God, the everlasting Father, the Prince of Peace (Isaiah 9:6).

Shalom, this fascinating Hebrew word, remember, can be a greeting or a farewell. It can refer to inner or outer peace. It might refer to peace with God or peace with a neighbor—or peace with oneself. The breadth and depth of the word is virtually limitless—as is the very concept of biblical peace. Like a finely cut diamond turning in the light, this *Shalom*, this biblical peace, sparkles regardless of the facet we see. Each has its own value, its own place, its own necessity.

What God offers to us and asks from us is that we seek this kind of peace and live this kind of peace. Whether in greetings or goodbyes, we can wish for ourselves and those around us this invaluable gift—for our world so desperately needs it. Be aware of it in yourself today; be conscious of it in the lives of others. Seek to give it, to spread it, to cultivate it whenever and wherever you can.

Think of co-workers and acquaintances, neighbors and friends—and allow your mind to drift among all the faces and lives that come before you. What needs are you aware of in the group of people who come to mind? As you are calmed by your own sense of peace (with God's inspiration), pray for those your mind tells you are in need. Finally, follow your thoughts and prayer with an effort to reach out in some way through a card, e-mail, call, text, or visit: *I was thinking of you today... You were on my mind today... Your friendship means a lot to me... I know you are going through a difficult time right now...*

Your words, attention, and effort can make all the difference in the day and season of those God brings to your attention.

> "I heard the bells on Christmas day, their old familiar carols play, and wild and sweet the words repeat of peace on earth, good will..."
> — Henry W. Longfellow

SATURDAY

> "Peace cannot be kept by force; it can only be achieved by understanding."
> — Albert Einstein

Be at peace today. Do your best to refrain from shopping or returning items to stores overrun with holiday and post-holiday shoppers. Instead, take some quiet time to reflect on your holiday season. Then reflect more broadly: what have you learned over the course of this year? What do you believe God is doing in your life now as you prepare for a new year?

Give thanks for your family and friends and for all that has been a part of your year. Anticipate a good morning tomorrow in worship.

As we conclude this year and move into the new year, we wish you the most meaningful peace possible. May both the greeting and the farewell of this beautiful biblical word be our final blessing: Shalom!

We will now move into the new year with our final week's theme: Faith.

> Dona nobis pacem
> Give us peace.

The Fifth Week:
Faith

For the kingdom of heaven is like a landowner who went out early in the morning to hire laborers for his vineyard. After agreeing with the laborers for the usual daily wage, he sent them into his vineyard (Matthew 20:1-2).

"Having faith" is a phrase vastly overused, undervalued, and, too often, cliché. Thus, what follows, I hope, is a more comprehensive, even controversial, exploration of this foundational principle to people interested in becoming better interpreters of, participants in, and deeper thinkers on the concept of faith. Let us begin with what Jesus said.

Fair warning—this parable Jesus tells in Matthew makes faithful and fair-minded people mad. For those with good business sense and a high degree of responsibility, his story about what the kingdom of God is like creates all kinds of harsh responses. Interestingly, what follows, and the way Jesus describes the scene, is one repeated still today in cities and towns all over our country.

In Charlotte, not far from our church, there is a good example of this hiring procedure that Jesus depicts. Beginning around 5:30 in the morning, there are men, young and old, gathering in the parking lot of the old Kentucky Fried Chicken on Wendover. In Washington, D.C., not far from where I once lived, the same ritual occurred at the corner of New Hampshire Avenue and University Boulevard. The men in both instances were mostly Hispanic and ranged in ages from twenty to sixty. They wanted to be hired. Every day, they showed up and waited. And, as the sun rose, trucks and cars would pull into the parking area, a window would roll down, and a voice would say, "Anyone know how to lay brick?" or "I need someone with a strong back willing to work all day in the hot sun." or "Does anybody have carpentry experience?"

A crowd quickly formed around the vehicle, the workers attempting to sell their desire and talents. They were assessed, chosen, and driven off to the job site. This is exactly what happened in Jesus' story.

The landowner had a need for workers. The first were hired just at sunrise. The head man came for a second group, realizing he needed more hands. They were hired midmorning. The same occurred again at noon, at 3:00 p.m., and finally at 5:00 p.m. And to the last workers, the landowner asked, "Why are you standing here idle all day?"

And they said, "because no one has hired us" (Matthew 20:7). So, the master hired them.

Remember the introduction Jesus gave to this parable: "For the kingdom of heaven is like" ... this. And what follows is both odd and seemingly unfair but important for faithful people to understand. The nature of the Kingdom of Heaven becomes one of the foundational realities of our faith.

We will cover the controversial conclusion to this story tomorrow. For now, consider some of the surprising ways the perspectives of Jesus creep up on us. Read this parable for yourself and think about the ramifications of what Jesus might be saying. And see if what we share tomorrow reflects at all what you consider today.

> Help us to be people of faith this week, O God. Help us, as we seek to cultivate hope, love, joy, and peace, that faith be a growing and natural extension of lives that are more rich and full of Advent blessings. Amen

REFLECTIONS FOR THE WEEK

MONDAY

...they grumbled against the landowner, saying, "These last worked only one hour, and you have made them equal to us who have borne the burden of the day and the scorching heat" (Matthew 20:11-12).

The actions of this landowner elicits a response of "Socialism," or "Unfair," or "What a foolish way to run a business!" And, while running a business like Jesus' parable describes would indeed be problematic and unprofitable, this is not what the story is about. It's about the kingdom of God and how you and I fit, the perspectives we are to have, and what we are to believe in. In other words, our faith should reflect the social design Jesus describes. With this in mind, let's look at this very important and controversial story more closely.

When workers are being chosen in Charlotte or Washington, D.C., the employers are looking for strong, young, able-bodied people. There is no time for interviewing or checking references. The truck drives up and the individual is chosen. This is exactly what happens in the parable. The "best" and most "attractive" workers were chosen early on. Those still there later in the day were not lazy. They were still hoping to be hired. (remember, they were there probably before the sun rose), but "no one has hired us" (20:7).

Maybe they were old, injured, disabled. But these people had families to feed, mortgages to pay, debts to reduce, and the landowner knows this. Instead of taking a "survival of the fittest" stance, the landowner demonstrated a generosity that threw the community out of balance. Everyone got paid the same, even those not arriving until the end of the day: *these last worked only one hour, and you have made them equal?*

Yes, Jesus says, this is kingdom business. Pay scale is *irrelevant*. All created in the image of God *are relevant*. Dignity, compassion, generosity, and a vision for the broader, more holistic aspect of being human, catching and keeping Jesus' vision for who we are and what we are to be about—these are the vital aspects of faith. Having faith in God's wisdom, trusting God's perspective, relying on God's justice, and standing for those who cannot stand for themselves is unconditional.

It is insights like these that got Jesus in trouble. But it was to these standards he remained committed. In our faith, so must we. Today, explore more fully the potential and surprising elements to faith and compassion that Jesus declares and that God expects.

> "And the Pharisees and the scribes were grumbling and saying, 'This fellow welcomes sinners and eats with them'"
> — Luke 15:2

TUESDAY

Now faith is the assurance of things hoped for, the conviction of things not seen (Hebrews 11:1).

It was thrilling to see Gabby Douglas win the gold medal in the 2012 games as the Olympic women's gymnastics champion for the individual all-around event. And her story leading up to the Olympics is perhaps most instructive—and inspiring—when it comes to an example of faith.

Her mother, Natalie Hawkins, was a hard-working single mom and mother of four living in Virginia. The thought of the great expense and long hours of training in a sport so grueling and so incredibly competitive seemed overwhelming and unrealistic. Adding that an African-American had never won the gold in gymnastics, Natalie was firmly set against it. It took Gabby's sisters to convince their mother to have faith that this was the right path. And faith was exactly what was needed.

Missy and Travis Parton, in West Des Moines, Iowa, had just decided to open their home to top gymnasts coming to train with Liang Chow, the Chinese-American gymnastics coach for former gold medalist, Shawn Johnson. Their home was to be a place for those who couldn't afford housing with Chow. Gabby's mom was anxious about sending her daughter that far away from home, but, after talking to the Partons, she and they realized they shared a common faith, both in what they were doing for this potential young Olympian and, more importantly, in the God and spiritual foundation they believed in.

Missy Parton's mother had recently died. After much prayer and seeking a positive outlet for her grief and a redemptive gift for others, Missy and Travis welcomed Gabby into their lives. And Natalie Hawkins trusted the Partons with her daughter. The rest is history—literally. Gabby became the first African-American to claim the gold in gymnastics.

For Gabby, her mother, her sisters, and for the Partons, their common faith in the unseen, the abiding "assurance of things hoped for" inspires more than Olympic dreams. They all worked together in faithful service for a cause larger then themselves. They believed their efforts and their trust would offer a broader purpose.

Today, have faith that what lies ahead will be entwined with others, different, but on a similar path and with a similar faith. Together, your faith and your combined efforts will accomplish something of significance.

> "I have an advantage because I'm the underdog ... But I'm ready to shine."
> — Gabby Douglas

WEDNESDAY

Therefore, since we are surrounded by so great a cloud of witnesses, let us also lay aside every weight ... and let us run with perseverance the race that is set before us... (Hebrews 12:1).

Derek Redmond was a well-known and highly respected sprinter on the 1992 British Olympic team in Barcelona. He was expected to be the gold medalist in the two-hundred meters.

Approaching the Presence

But, in the semi-final, just as he was rounding the turn, he pulled up out of his sprint in agony. He fell to the track in pain with a severe hamstring injury. Out of sheer will, he got up and tried to continue. The other sprinters were already walking away, yet still Derek insisted on limping, slowly, painfully, toward the finish. His face showed the agony he was feeling, both from his leg and from his deep disappointment. As he hopped around the turn, Derek's father came running out of the stands and, taking his son by the arm, helped him to the finish line.

What struck me then, and still touches me every time the video of those moving moments are replayed, was not just the touching love of his father. It was the *reaction of the crowd.* As Derek and his father made their way around the track—slowly, hurting, and devastated by all that was lost—the crowd cheered them on. As father and son moved step by step, the cheers and encouragement became even more exuberant. The crowd became "a great cloud of witnesses."

Through courage, persistence, and acquired wisdom, many have endured heartache and loss, victory and defeat, joy and sadness. As the author of Hebrews portrays it, this "great cloud of witnesses," this gathered memory of those who have gone before us in faith, offers testimony, history, and encouragement for all of us as we go through our own trials and troubles.

Today, as you move through whatever obligations you have, imagine your endurance and courage being strengthened from the shouts and applause, smiles and encouragement of those who know what it is like to be brave and to have endured. Let your faith join with theirs and know that you can *run this race with perseverance*—for you are not alone!

> "Everything I had worked for was finished. I hated everybody. I hated the world. I hated hamstrings. I hated it all. I felt so bitter that I was injured again. I told myself I had to finish. I kept hopping round. Then, with one hundred meters to go, I felt a hand on my shoulder. It was my old man."
> — Derek Redmond

THURSDAY

I want you to know that our brother Timothy has been set free... (Hebrews 13:23).

What lies behind this simple declaratory sentence? Careful reading can determine a couple of clear issues. First, the whole series of exhortations in the sermon that is Hebrews[8] outlines clear strategies for maintaining faith in the midst of trials. The people in this early audience were under attack. Persecution, both physical and economic (loss of property or the boycotting of Christian businesses), created enormous pressure on these early Christians.

The natural tendency in all of us is to want to fit within the larger culture. No one enjoys being the outcast or the butt of cruel jokes. So, we can discern from this one sentence, "Timothy has been set free," that the threat of imprisonment and worse was very real. But, in spite of the dangers, this faith community was alive and well—and so was Timothy.

As a seminary student in the Spring of 1984, I had the opportunity to travel to Romania to lead a series of revival services. This was unusual in those days because of the "Cold War" and the ongoing tensions between the Soviet Union and the United States. Romania was communist and a solid part of the countries allied with the Soviet Union. It was a strange time, and one that, for millions, created true tests and trials of faith.

For the Christians of Romania, especially the Baptists with whom I was working, the dynamic to which Hebrews speaks was apparent. In Romania, it was to the advantage of all citizens to say and do what the Communist authorities expected. Those who didn't raised suspicions and created difficulties. Children of "subversives" were forced into lower-level schools and channeled into lower-paying jobs. So, the temptation to walk away from

---

[8] Hebrews tends to be different than the epistles of Paul—there is no greeting or salutation, just an immediate "Long ago God spoke to our ancestors..." (Hebrews 1:1). Only in the final three verses (13:22-25) is there a sense that the writer offers any personal connections, seen most vividly in the above verse about Timothy.

church attendance and loyal membership was significant. Yet, in the churches I visited[9], the sense of community, the power of fellowship, and the strength of faith were truly inspiring. Being together as a church was not simply to enjoy a good time. It was a matter of sharing meaningful life and dynamic faith together. It was being inspired to withstand another week of difficulties and being courageous in the face of hostile actions and intentional exclusion.

There are places in the world where these kinds of circumstances continue unabated. Romania still has its problems, but, thankfully, religious persecution is no longer one of them. As has happened so often in the past, the staying power of God's church and the devoted people of God's kingdom outlasted the empires that so vociferously fought to eliminate them.

Today, and as we prepare to conclude our time together, meditate on those who still struggle with the "powers and principalities" of this world. Pray for them. And let their faithfulness inspire in you a renewed sense of God's presence in all places and in every circumstance.

FRIDAY

...our brother Timothy... (Hebrews 12:23).

In this scripture, we see the ties that bound this early community of faith. The audience, along with the anonymous author, considered Timothy "our brother." There is something about faith, and something about a healthy, trusting faith community that facilitates the feeling of connectedness.

Instead of independence, there is *inter*dependence. People rely on one another, enjoy one another, grow in faith with one another. In such a place, we discover we not only *need* each other, but we can *enjoy* each other. Our lives can be enriched and spirits rejuvenated together in ways that are never possible when we are alone.

---

[9] Primarily in Sibiu and Orsava and to smaller churches around the Transylvania region.

Today, and as you continue this week, think about ways your life and faith could use some "interdependence." We can all benefit from expanding our relationships, even as we attempt to deepen our faith. Consider ways you could get to know some people in your life better and more conscientiously. Think about opportunities you have to engage in conversation about faith and be genuinely inquisitive about what others think and how they see the world. And if they are not already there, gladly invite them to your church.

Look for ways to make your community of faith closer, more trusting, and more broadly involved in healthy, interdependent relationships that give life and meaning to all involved.

> "Peace be to the whole community, and love with faith..."
> — Ephesians 6:23

SATURDAY

Therefore, my brothers and sisters, whom I love and long for, my joy and crown, stand firm in the Lord...
(Philippians 4:1).

I hope, from this year, your ability to "stand firm in the Lord" has been enhanced. I hope your study, experiences, and growing faith now result in new empathy, broader perspective, and deeper understanding. Psalm 139 remains the premier reminder of the faith we can claim:

Where can I go from your spirit? Or where can I flee from your presence? If I ascend to heaven, you are there; if I make my bed in Sheol, you are there. If I take to the wings of the morning and settle in the farthest limits of the sea, even there your hand shall lead me, and your right hand shall hold me fast... (Psalm 139:7-10).

As you move into the new year, you will inevitably be at various places on the spectrum of faith. Whether calm, despairing, or newly matured, may each step of the way be one of expectant anticipation. God is with you and guiding you. It will be good. May you have the patience and perspective necessary for whatever comes your way and wherever you go.

I hope and pray that you will continue on your journey of *Approaching the Presence*, moving ever in the direction of and always guided by God's grace. And may you do so with growing faith, fervent hope, expanding love, abundant joy, and an all-encompassing peace based upon and inspired by the *Prince of Peace*.

And thanks again for your participation, discipline, interest and endurance!

Sincerely and gratefully yours,
David Jordan and Diane Jordan

...to the only wise God, through Jesus Christ, to whom be the glory forever! Amen!
— Romans 16:27

BIBLIOGRAPHY

Astyk, Sharon and Aaron Newton. *A Nation of Farmers: Defeating the Food Crisis on American Soil.* Gabriola Island, Canada: New Society Publishers, 2009.

Bailey, Kenneth E. *Poet and Peasant.* Grand Rapids: Eerdmans, 1976.

Bailey, Kenneth E. *Through Peasant Eyes.* Grand Rapids: Eerdmans, 1980.

Barzini, Luigi. *The Italians: A Full-Length Portrait Featuring Their Manners and Morals.* New York: Simon and Schuster, 1964.

Bell, Brian. *Insight City Guide, Venice.* London: Insight Guides, 2005.

Bell, Rob. *Love Wins: A Book about Heaven, Hell, and the Fate of Every Person Who Ever Lived.* New York: HarperCollins, 2011.

Berger, Peter and Anton Zijderveld. *In Praise of Doubt: How to Have Convictions Without Becoming a Fanatic.* New York: HarperCollins, 2009.

Boring, M. Eugene. *Revelation.* Louisville: John Knox Press, 1989.

Brother Lawrence. *The Practice of the Presence of God.* Radford, VA: Wilder Publications, 2008.

Brueggemann, Walter. *Cadences of Home: Preaching Among Exiles.* Louisville: Westminster John Knox Press, 1997.

Brueggemann, Walter. *Genesis.* Atlanta: John Knox Press, 1982.

Burckhardt, Jacob. *The Civilization of the Renaissance in Italy.* New York: Barnes and Noble Books, 1999.

Cahill, Thomas. *The Gifts of the Jews: How a Tribe of Desert Nomads Changed the Way Everyone Thinks and Feels.* New York: Doubleday, 1998.

Card, Michael. *Scribbling in the Sand.* Westmont, IL: Inter-Varsity Press, 2002.

Craddock, Fred. *Luke.* Louisville: John Knox Press, 1990.

Craddock, Fred. *Philippians.* Louisville: John Knox Press, 1985.

De Waal, Esther. *Every Earthly Blessing: Rediscovering the Celtic Tradition.* Harrisburg: Morehouse Publishing, 1991.

Diamond, Jared. *Collapse: How Societies Choose to Fail or Succeed.* New York: Penguin Group, 2005.

Dickens, Charles. *Pictures from Italy.* New York: Penguin Books, 2006.

Edwards, Tilden. *Spiritual Friend.* New York: Paulist Press, 1951.

Efird, James M. *Revelation for Today.* Nashville: Abingdon, 1989.

Erasmus, Desiderius. *In Praise of Folly.* New York: Penguin, 1994.

Foster, Richard J. *Prayers from the Heart.* New York: HarperCollins, 1994.

Friedman, Thomas L. *The World Is Flat.* New York: Farrar, Straus and Giroux, 2005.

Greene, Robert. *The 48 Laws of Power.* New York: Penguin Books, 2000.

Harris, Robert. *Pompeii: A Novel.* New York: Random House, 2005.

Hunsinger, George. *How to Read Karl Barth: The Shape of His Theology.* New York: Oxford University Press, 1991.

Janson, Tore. *A Natural History of Latin: The Story of the World's Most Successful Language.* New York: Oxford University Press, 2004.

Job, Rueben. *Living Fully, Dying Well.* Nashville: Abingdon, 2005.

Job, Rueben. *Three Simple Questions.* Nashville: Abingdon, 2011.

Job, Rueben. *Three Simple Rules.* Nashville: Abingdon, 2007.

Jordan, David. *Subversive Words: Biblical Counterpoints to Conventional Wisdom.* Charlotte, NC: Pure Heart Press, 2011.

Jordan, Diane. Excerpts from her album, "It's a Good Life" recorded and produced in Chattanooga, TN, 1971.

Jordan-Lake, Joy. *Grit and Grace: Portraits of a Woman's Life.* Wheaton, IL: Harold Shaw Publishers, 1997.

Jung, C. G. *Modern Man in Search of a Soul.* San Diego: Harcourt Brace Jovanovich, 1933.

Kamkwamba, William. *The Boy Who Harnessed the Wind: Creating Currents of Electricity and Hope.* New York: HarperCollins, 2009.

Kidder, David S. and Noah D. Oppenheim. *The Intellectual Devotional: Revive Your Mind, Complete Your Education, and Roam Confidently with the Cultured Class.* New York: Rodal, 2006.

Kidder, David S. and Noah D. Oppenheim. *The Intellectual Devotional, American History: Revive Your Mind, Complete Your Education, and Converse Confidently about Our Nation's Past.* New York: Rodal, 2006.

King, Ross. *Michelangelo and the Pope's Ceiling.* New York: Penguin Books, 2003.

Kingsolver, Barbara. *Animal, Vegetable, Miracle: A Year of Food Life.* New York: HarperCollins, 2007.

Koenig, Dr. Harold. *Spirituality in Patient Care.* Second Edition, West Conshohochen, PA: Templeton Press, 2007.

Kullberg, Kelly and Lael Arrington. *A Faith and Culture Devotional.* Grand Rapids: Zondervan, 2008.

Legrand, Lucien. *The Bible on Culture.* New York: Maryknoll, Orbis, 2000.

Laubach, Frank. *Prayer, the Mightiest Force in the World.* Westwood, NJ: Fleming Revell Co., 1946.

Macur, Juliet. "The Price of Gold," *The Charlotte Observer*, Friday, August 3, 2012, pp. 1A, 6A.

Marshall, Catherine. *Adventures in Prayer.* Ada, MI: Chosen Books, 1975.

Marx, Karl and Friedrich Engels. *The Communist Manifesto.* Arlington Heights, IL: Harlan Davidson, 1955.

McCormack, Bruce L. *Karl Barth's Critically Realistic Dialectical Theology: It's Genesis and Development 1909–1936.* New York: Oxford University Press, 1995.

McLaren, Brian D. *A New Kind of Christianity: Ten Questions That Are Transforming the Faith.* New York: HarperCollins, 2010.

Micklethwait, John and Adrian Woolridge. *God Is Back: How the Global Revival of Faith Is Changing the World.* New York: The Penguin Press, 2009.

Moliere. Tartuffe: *The Hypocrite.* Woodbury, NY: Barron's Educational Series, Inc., 1959.

Morris, Danny. *Yearning to Know God's Will.* Grand Rapids: Zondervan, 1991.

Mother Teresa. *No Greater Love.* New York: MJF Books, 1995.

The New Oxford Annotated Bible, New Revised Standard Version (with Apocrypha). Nashville: Abingdon, 1993.

The New Interpreter's Study Bible, New Revised Standard Version (with Apocrypha). Nashville: Abingdon, 2003.

Newell, J. Philip. *Listening for the Heartbeat of God: A Celtic Spirituality.* New York: Paulist Press, 1997.

Nouwen, Henri. *With Open Hands.* Notre Dame, IN: Ave Maria Press, 1972.

O'Brien, Randall. *Set Free By Forgiveness.* Grand Rapids, MI: Baker Books, 2005.

Peterson, Eugene. *Earth and Altar.* Downers Grove, IL: Inter-Varsity Press, 1985.

Phillips, J.B. *Is God At Home?* Nashville: Abingdon, 1958.

Plato. *The Republic.* New York: Oxford University Press, 1998.

Potkay, Prof. Monica Brzezinski. *The Eternal Chalice: The Grail in Literature and Legend.* Lecture Series at the College of William and Mary.

Richardson, Peter. *Herod: King of the Jews and Friend of the Romans.* Columbia, SC: University of South Carolina Press, 1996.

Rieger, Joerg. *Liberating the Future: God, Mammon and Theology.* Minneapolis: Fortress Press, 1998.

Rieger, Joerg. *No Rising Tide: Theology, Economics, and the Future.* Minneapolis: Fortress Press, 2009.

Schwartz, Stephen. *Children of Eden.* Two-act musical, first performed in 1991, based on a book by John Caird.

Shanks, Hershel, ed. "Past Perfect: The Day the Earth Shook." *Archeology Odyssey*, May/June, 2001, p. 37.

Steinbeck, John. *The Grapes of Wrath.* New York: Viking Press, 1939.

Tillich, Paul. *The New Being.* New York: Charles Scribner's Sons, 1955.

Tolstoy, Leo. *Anna Karenina.* New York: Simon and Shuster, 2010.

Weatherhead, Leslie. *A Private House of Prayer.* Nashville: Abingdon, 1958.

West, Cornell. *Keeping Faith: Philosophy and Race in America.* New York: Routledge, 1993.

Willimon, William H. *Acts.* Atlanta: John Knox Press, 1988.

Young, Sarah. *Jesus Calling: Enjoying Peace in His Presence.* Nashville: Thomas Nelson, 2004.